PARRAGON

Pocket Encyclopedia of the World

CONTENTS

oads

Motorway/Highway

Other Main Road

– at scales smaller than 1:3 million

Principal Road: Motorway/Highway

Other Main Road

Main Railway

Towns & Cities – Population

□ > 5,000,000

□ 1-5,000,000

○ 500,000 -1,000,000

○ < 500,000

Paris National Capital

Airport

International Boundary

International Boundary – not defined or in dispute

Internal Boundary

River

Canal

Marsh or Swamp

Relief

Note – The 0-100 contour layer appears only at scales larger than 1:3 million

▲ 1510 Peak (in metres)

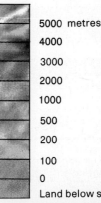

5000 metres

4000

3000

2000

1000

500

200

100

0

Land below sea level

THE WORLD

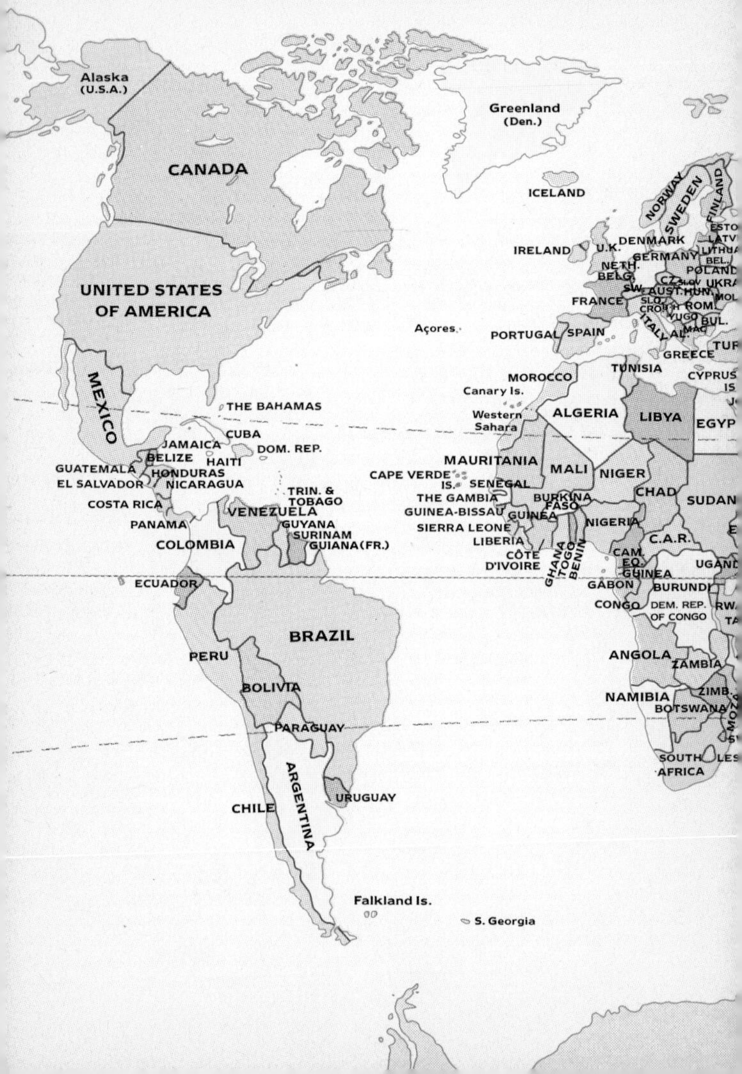
Alaska
(U.S.A.)
Greenland
(Den.)
CANADA
ICELAND
NORWAY
SWEDEN
FINLAND
IRELAND
U.K.
DENMARK
GERMANY
NETH.
BELG.
POLAND
UNITED STATES
OF AMERICA
CZ.
SLOV.
SW.
AUST.
HUN.
FRANCE
SLO.
CRO.
B-H
ROM.
YUGO.
BUL.
ITALY
MAC.
AL.
Açores
PORTUGAL
SPAIN
GREECE
TUNISIA
CYPRUS
MOROCCO
Canary Is.
MEXICO
THE BAHAMAS
Western
Sahara
ALGERIA
LIBYA
CUBA
JAMAICA
BELIZE
HAITI
DOM. REP.
GUATEMALA
HONDURAS
EL SALVADOR
NICARAGUA
MAURITANIA
MALI
NIGER
CAPE VERDE
IS.
SENEGAL
CHAD
TRIN. &
TOBAGO
THE GAMBIA
BURKINA
FASO
COSTA RICA
VENEZUELA
GUINEA-BISSAU
GUINEA
SUDAN
PANAMA
GUYANA
SIERRA LEONE
NIGERIA
SURINAM
COLOMBIA
GUIANA (FR.)
LIBERIA
C.A.R.
CÔTE
D'IVOIRE
GHANA
TOGO
BENIN
CAM.
EQ.
GUINEA
ECUADOR
GABON
BURUNDI
CONGO
DEM. REP.
OF CONGO
BRAZIL
PERU
ANGOLA
ZAMBIA
BOLIVIA
ZIMB.
NAMIBIA
BOTSWANA
PARAGUAY
SOUTH
AFRICA
ARGENTINA
URUGUAY
CHILE
Falkland Is.
S. Georgia

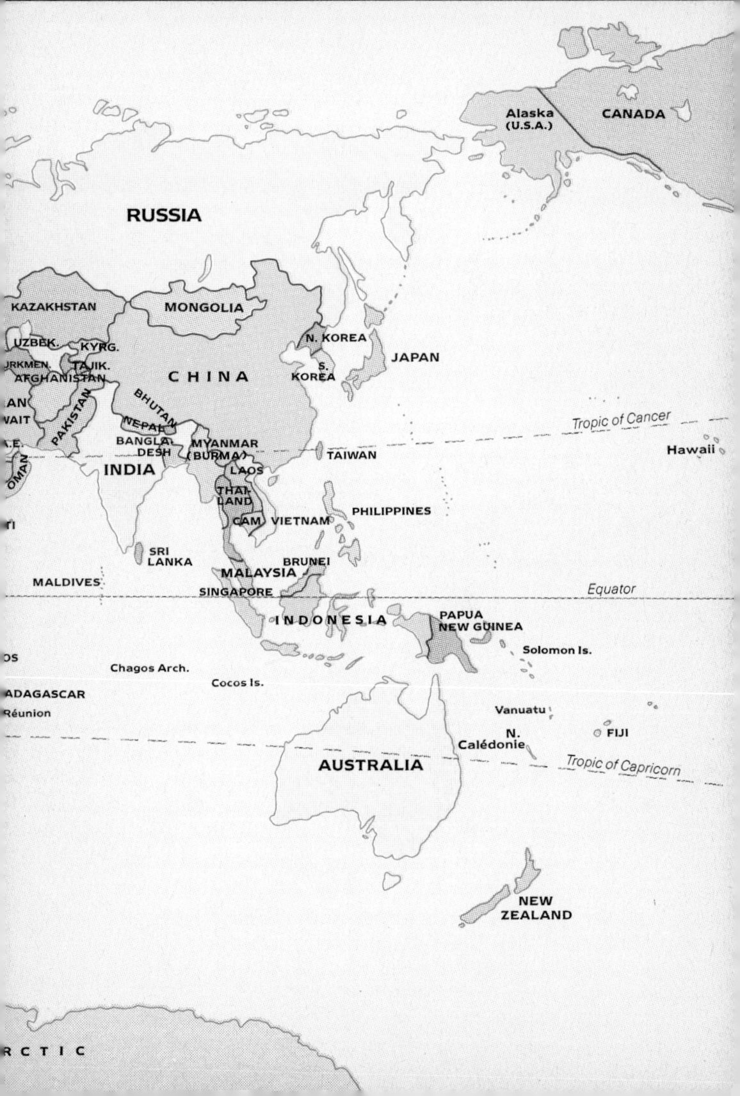
Alaska
(U.S.A.)
CANADA
RUSSIA
KAZAKHSTAN
MONGOLIA
UZBEK.
KYRG.
RKMEN.
TAJIK.
AFGHANISTAN
CHINA
N. KOREA
JAPAN
S. KOREA
AN
VAIT
PAKISTAN
BHUTAN
NEPAL
.E.
BANGLA-
DESH
MYANMAR
(BURMA)
TAIWAN
Tropic of Cancer
Hawaii
OMAN
INDIA
LAOS
THAI-
LAND
PHILIPPINES
CAM
VIETNAM
SRI
LANKA
BRUNEI
MALAYSIA
MALDIVES
SINGAPORE
Equator
INDONESIA
PAPUA
NEW GUINEA
Solomon Is.
OS
Chagos Arch.
Cocos Is.
ADAGASCAR
Réunion
Vanuatu
N.
Calédonie
FIJI
AUSTRALIA
Tropic of Capricorn
NEW
ZEALAND
RCTIC

NORTH & CENTRAL AMERICA

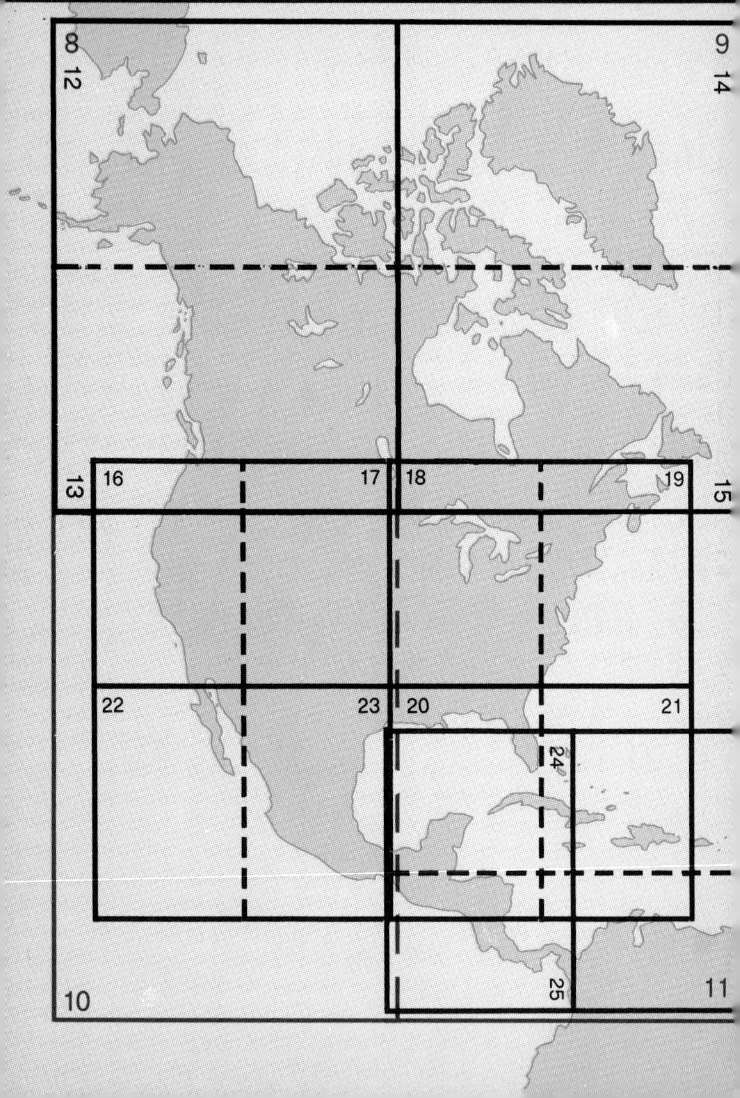

NORTH AMERICA POLITICAL (N)

OCEAN
Ellesmere I.
GREENLAND
(Denmark)
ICELAND
Reykjavik
Arctic Circle
Baffin Bay
Baffin Island
Davis Strait
Godthåb
ITORIES
LABRADOR SEA
Hudson Strait
Hudson Bay
A
D
A
A
NEWFOUNDLAND & LABRADOR
St. John's
QUÉBEC
ONTARIO
St. Lawrence
NEW BRUNSWICK
PR. EDWARD I.
NOVA SCOTIA
Halifax
Québec
ipeg
0°
10°
20°
30°
40°
50°
60°
70°
80°

NORTH AMERICA POLITICAL (S)

Montreal
Ottawa
VER.
MAINE
N.H.
WISCONSIN
Toronto
Boston
Buffalo
MASS.
MICHIGAN
N.Y.
CONN.
R.I.
Detroit
New York
Milwaukee
PENN.
Pittsburgh
Cleveland
N.J.
Philadelphia
Chicago
OHIO
INDIANA
Baltimore
M.
DEL.
Washington D.C.
Indianapolis
ILLINOIS
Cincinnati
W. VIRGINIA
VIRGINIA
KENTUCKY
Raleigh
AMERICA
NORTH CAROLINA
Bermuda (U.K.)
TENNESSEE
ARKANSAS
Memphis
S. CAROLINA
Atlanta
Charleston
MISSISSIPPI
Birmingham
ALABAMA
Jackson
GEORGIA
Jacksonville
ATLANTIC OCEAN
LOUISIANA
New Orleans
FLORIDA
Tampa
THE BAHAMAS
Tropic of Cancer
Miami
Nassau
GULF OF MEXICO
La Habana (Havana)
CUBA
HAITI
Santo Domingo
Puerto Rico (U.S.A.)
San Juan
Port au Prince
DOMINICAN REPUBLIC
Mérida
JAMAICA
Kingston
BELIZE
Belmopan
CARIBBEAN SEA
GUATEMALA
HONDURAS
Tegucigalpa
San Salvador
EL SALVADOR
NICARAGUA
Managua
San José
COSTA RICA
Panamá
PANAMA
VENEZUELA
COLOMBIA
Bogatá
40°
60°
30°
20°
10°
90°
80°
70°

ARCTIC OCEAN
Queen Elizabeth Islands
Sverdrup Island
Bathurst I.
Melville I.
Prince of Wales
McClure Strait
Banks I.
Victoria Island
NORTHWEST TERRITORIES
Great Bear Lake
Mackenzie
Fort Simpson
C. Bathurst
Inuvik
BEAUFORT SEA
Mackenzie Mts
Prudhoe Bay
Brooks Range
Porcupine
Fort Yukon
Pt. Barrow
Barrow
Fairbanks
YUKON TERRITORY
Whitehorse
Mt. Logan 6050
Mt. St. Elias 5489
Juneau
ALASKA (U.S.A.)
Alaska Range
Yukon
Anchorage
Mt. McKinley 6194
Gulf of Alaska
Seward Peninsula
Arctic Circle
Bering Strait
RUSSIA
Alaska Pen.
Kodiak I.
St. Lawrence I.
BERING SEA
Nunivak I.

CANADA
MANITOBA
SASKATCHEWAN
ALBERTA
BRITISH COLUMBIA
NORTH DAKOTA
SOUTH DAKOTA
NEBRASKA
MONTANA
WYOMING
IDAHO
UTAH
NEVADA
OREGON
WASHINGTON
CALIFORNIA
UNITED STATES OF AMERICA
Great Plains
Rocky Mountains
Coast Mountains
Cascade Range
Coast Ranges
Selkirk Mts.
Hay River
Peace
Athabasca
L. Athabasca
Reindeer Lake
Saskatchewan
N. Saskatchewan
S. Saskatchewan
Missouri
N. Platte
Finlay
Fraser
Columbia
Great Salt Lake
Winnipeg
Saskatoon
Regina
Medicine Hat
Calgary
Edmonton
Billings
Butte
Dawson Creek
Mt Robson 3954
Prince George
Kamloops
Vancouver
Seattle
Portland
Sacramento
San Francisco
Prince Rupert
Mt Waddington 4047
Queen Charlotte Islands
Vancouver I.
C. Flattery
PACIFIC OCEAN
100°
110°
120°
130°
140°
40°
50°
5
6
E
F
G
H

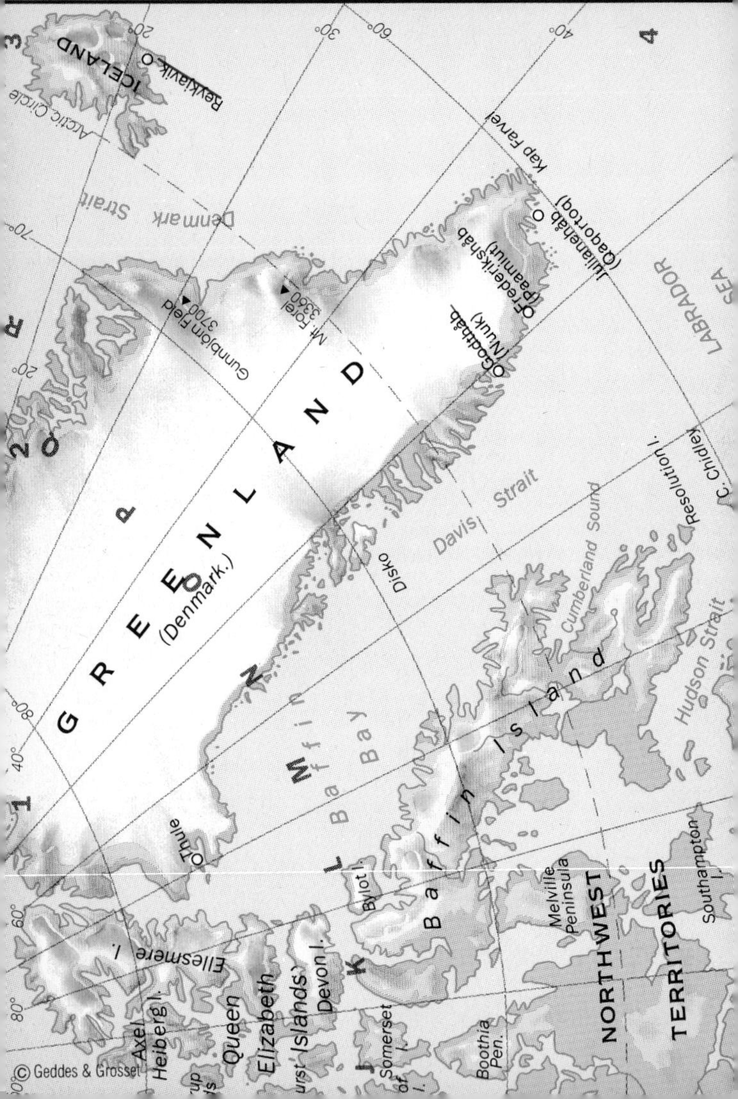
ICELAND
Reykjavik
Arctic Circle
Denmark Strait
Kap Farvel
Julianehåb (Qaqortoq)
Frederikshåb (Paamiut)
Godthåb (Nuuk)
Gunnbjørn Fjeld 3700
Mt Forel 3360
GREENLAND (Denmark.)
LABRADOR SEA
Davis Strait
Disko
Resolution I.
C. Chidley
Cumberland Sound
Hudson Strait
Baffin Bay
Baffin Island
Thule
Bylot I.
Melville Peninsula
Southampton I.
NORTHWEST TERRITORIES
Ellesmere I.
Axel Heiberg I.
Queen Elizabeth Islands
Devon I.
Somerset I.
Boothia Pen.
© Geddes & Grosset

CANADA
NEWFOUNDLAND & LABRADOR
Island of Newfoundland
St. John's
C. Race
Channel-Port-aux-Basques
Cape Breton I.
Anticosti I.
Gulf of St. Lawrence
St. Lawrence
QUEBEC
Laurentian plateau
Nain
Peninsula
Arvida
Québec
Montréal
NEW BRUNSWICK
Charlottetown
P.E.I.
NOVA SCOTIA
Halifax
C. Sable
Saint John
P.E.I. PRINCE EDWARD ISLAND
CONN. CONNECTICUT
MASS. MASSACHUSETTS
R.I. RHODE ISLAND
ATLANTIC OCEAN
MAINE
NEW HAMPSHIRE
VERMONT
MASS.
CONN.
R.I.
Boston
C. Cod
New York
NEW JERSEY
Philadelphia
PENNSYLVANIA
NEW YORK
Buffalo
Niagara
Lake Ontario
Toronto
Hamilton
Lake Erie
Cleveland
OHIO
Detroit
Ottawa
North Bay
Sudbury
Lake Huron
MICHIGAN
Lake Michigan
Milwaukee
Chicago
INDIANA
Sault Ste Marie
Lake Superior
Thunder Bay
ONTARIO
James Bay
Eastmain
Belcher Is.
Hudson Bay
Churchill
Nelson
Lake Winnipeg
Kenora
MINNESOTA
Fargo
Minneapolis
St. Paul
WISCONSIN
Mississippi
IOWA
UNITED STATES OF AMERICA
5
6
M
J

1
2
130°
120°
40°
30°
C. Flattery
Vancouver
BRITISH COL
WASHINGTON
Seattle
Olympia
Spokane
4392
Portland
Columbia
Salem
CASCADE RANGE
COAST RANGES
OREGON
Great Sandy Desert
Snake
Bois
Winnemucca
Sacramento
San Francisco
San Jose
Reno
Carson City
Stockton
NEVADA
Great Basin
Sierra Nevada
3997
CALIFORNIA
Fresno
Death Valley
Las Vegas
L. Mead
Colorado
PACIFIC
OCEAN
Los Angeles
Pasadena
Channel Islands
San Diego
Tijuana
Mexicali
Sonora Desert

110°
100°
B
C
D
ALBERTA
SASKATCHEWAN
MANITOBA
CANADA
Calgary
Medicine Hat
Regina
Winnipeg
ROCKY MOUNTAINS
Great Plains
Missouri
MONTANA
NORTH DAKOTA
Helena
Butte
Yellowstone
Billings
Bismarck
Fargo
MINNESOTA
Range
IDAHO
4202
Buffalo
SOUTH DAKOTA
Rapid City
Pierre
WYOMING
UNITED STATES OF AMERICA
Casper
Missouri
Sioux Falls
Ogden
City
4114
NEBRASKA
Omaha
Cheyenne
Platte
Lincoln
UTAH
Denver
4399
Richfield
COLORADO
San Juan Mts.
Sangre de Cristo Mts
Colorado Springs
Powell
KANSAS
Topeka
Arkansas
Wichita
4011
Flagstaff
SantaFe
Tulsa
OKLAHOMA
Albuquerque
Amarillo
Oklahoma City
3532
NEW MEXICO
Phoenix
Red
Lubbock

D
E
F
90°
80°
CANADA
ONTARIO
QUÉ
Kenora
Thunder Bay
Lake Superior
Sault Ste. Marie
Sudbury
North Bay
Ottawa
Ottawa
Mo
MINNESOTA
Duluth
MICHIGAN
Lake Huron
Minneapolis
St. Paul
WISCONSIN
Rochester
Lake Michigan
Toronto
L. Ontario
Hamilton
Niagara Falls
Buffalo
NEW
Grand Rapids
Madison
Milwaukee
Lansing
Detroit
Lake Erie
Cleveland
PENNSYLV
IOWA
Rockford
Chicago
Toledo
Pittsburgh
Des Moines
Ft. Wayne
Akron
OHIO
Harrisbu
INDIANA
ILLINOIS
Columbus
Indianapolis
Dayton
Springfield
Cincinnati
WEST VIRGINIA
Kansas City
UNITED STATES OF AMERICA
Frankfort
Charleston
Jefferson City
St. Louis
Louisville
Richm
MISSOURI
Evansville
KENTUCKY
Ozark Plateau
Springfield
Greensboro
Raleigh
Knoxville
Nashville
TENNESSEE
NORTH CAR
APPALACHIAN
Blue
Charlott
Chattanooga
ARKANSAS
Memphis
SOUTH CAROLINA
Huntsville
Columbia
Little Rock
Atlanta
Augusta
Birmingham

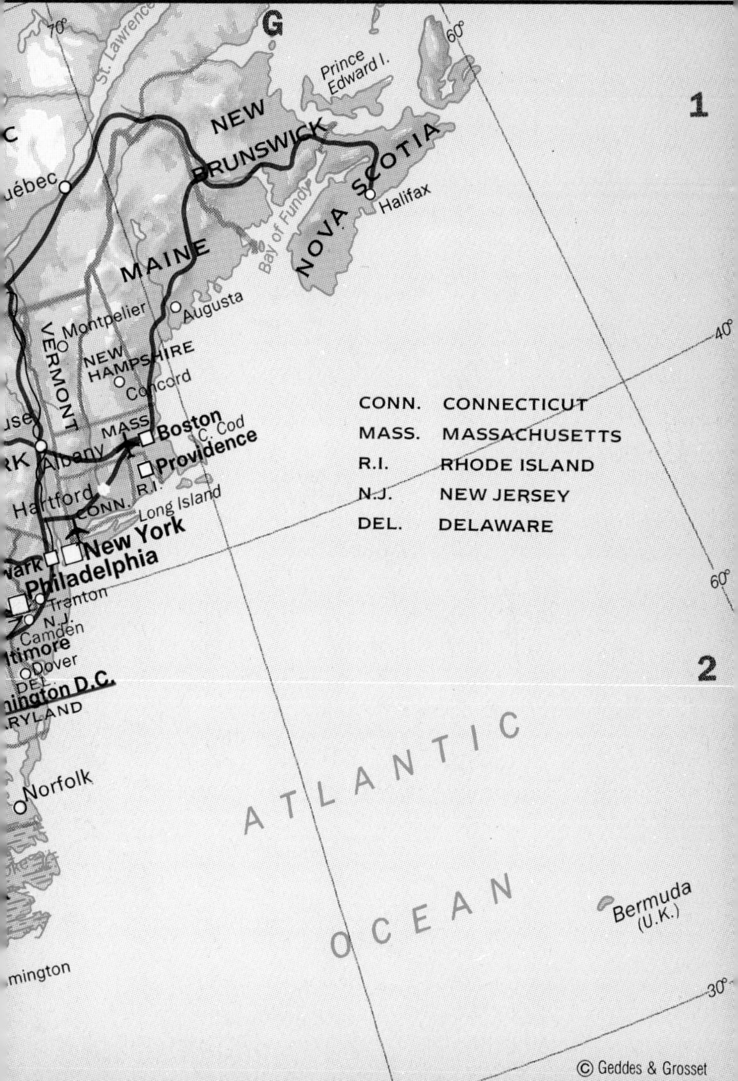
G
1
2
70°
60°
40°
30°
St. Lawrence
Prince Edward I.
NEW BRUNSWICK
NOVA SCOTIA
Halifax
Bay of Fundy
uébec
MAINE
Augusta
Montpelier
VERMONT
NEW HAMPSHIRE
Concord
MASS.
Boston
C. Cod
Providence
R.I.
Albany
Hartford
CONN.
Long Island
New York
Philadelphia
Trenton
N.J.
Camden
Dover
DEL.
ington D.C.
RYLAND
Norfolk
mington
ATLANTIC
OCEAN
Bermuda
(U.K.)
CONN. CONNECTICUT
MASS. MASSACHUSETTS
R.I. RHODE ISLAND
N.J. NEW JERSEY
DEL. DELAWARE

U.S.A. (S.E.) & WESTERN CARIBBEAN

3
Grand Bahama I.
Great Abaco I.
Lauderdale
Tropic of Cancer
Eleuthera I.
THE BAHAMAS
ami
Nassau
Cat I.
Andros I.
Long I.
Acklins I.
DOMINICAN REPUBLIC
Camaguey
Great Inagua I.
CUBA
Guantánamo
HAITI
Santo Domingo
Santiago de Cuba
Port au Prince
Cayman Is. (U.K.)
4
Kingston
JAMAICA
SEA
CARIBBEAN
Aruba (Neth.)
F
COLOMBIA
VENEZUELA
80°

U.S.A. (S.W.), MEXICO, ALASKA & HAWAIIAN IS.

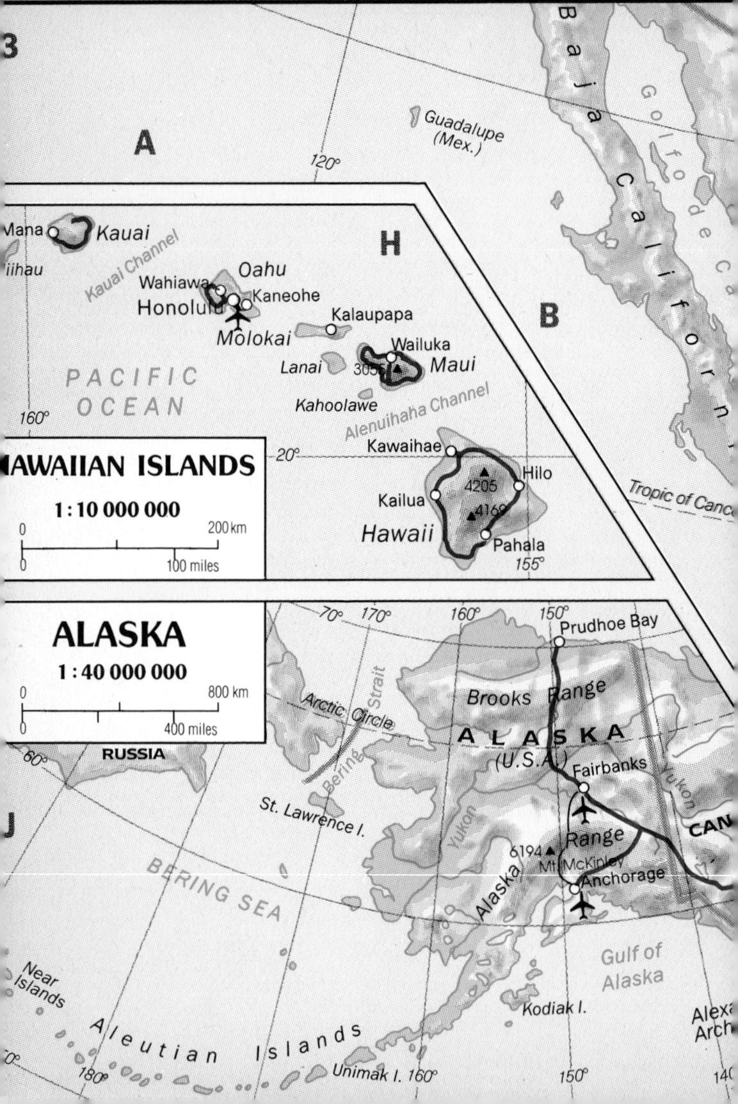

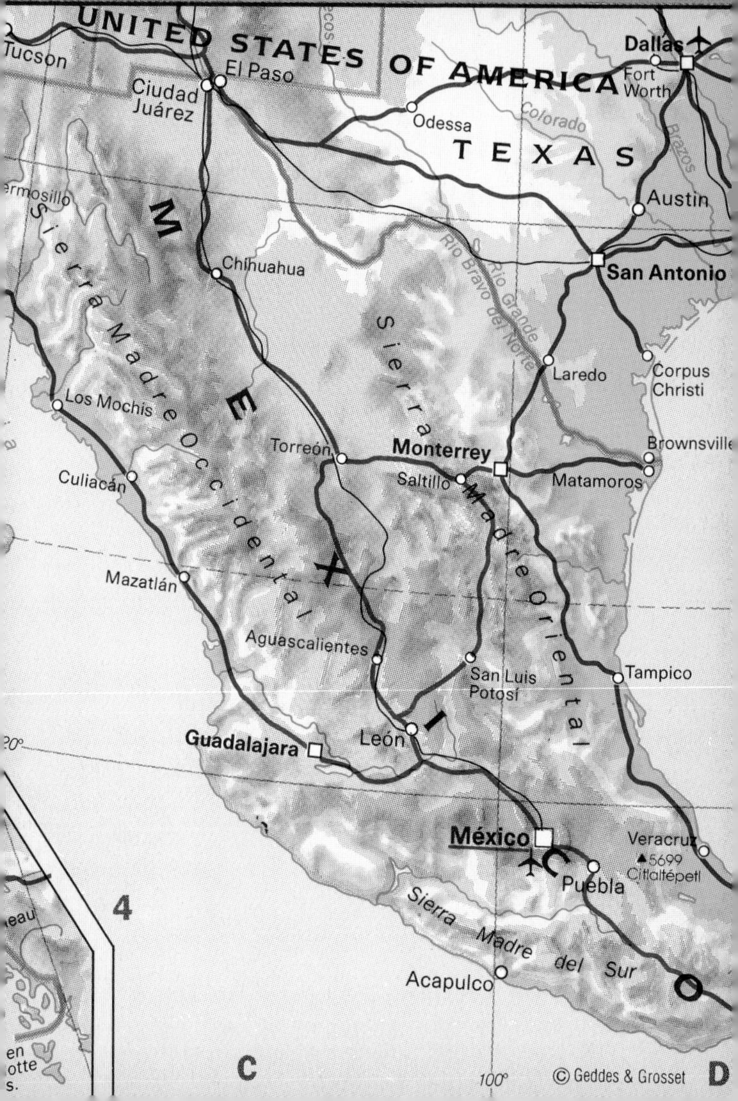
UNITED STATES OF AMERICA
Tucson
El Paso
Ciudad Juárez
Dallas
Fort Worth
Odessa
Colorado
TEXAS
Brazos
Austin
San Antonio
Rio Bravo del Norte
Rio Grande
Chihuahua
MEXICO
Sierra Madre Occidental
Sierra Madre Oriental
Laredo
Corpus Christi
Los Mochis
Torreón
Monterrey
Brownsville
Saltillo
Matamoros
Culiacán
Mazatlán
Aguascalientes
San Luis Potosí
Tampico
Guadalajara
León
México
Veracruz
5699
Citlaltépetl
Puebla
Sierra Madre del Sur
Acapulco
4
C
D
100°
20°
© Geddes & Grosset

A
B
C
D
1
2
3
25°
20°
80°
85°
90°
GULF OF MEXICO
Tropic of Cancer
Bahía de Campeche
Yucatán Channel
Straits of Florida
GREATER ANTILLES
U.S.A.
FLORIDA
CUBA
JAMAICA
MEXICO
St. Petersburg
Tampa
Orlando
West Palm Beach
Fort Lauderdale
Miami
Cape Sable
Key West
Grand Bahama I.
Great Abaco I.
Eleuthera I.
Nassau
Andros I.
Great Exuma I.
La Habana (Havana)
Matanzas
Santa Clara
Cienfuegos
Sancti Spíritus
Camagüey
Holguín
Santiago de Cuba
Manzanillo
Jardines de la Reina
I. de la Juventud
Pinar del Río
Cayman Islands (U.K.)
Montego Bay
Kingston
Swan Is. (Hond.)
Puerto Juárez
I. de Cozumel
Valladolid
Progreso
Mérida
Campeche
Cuidad del Carmen
Yucatán
Chetumal
Belize
Belmopan
Turneffe Is.

CARIBBEAN SEA
PACIFIC OCEAN
HONDURAS
NICARAGUA
COSTA RICA
PANAMA
EL SALVADOR
Guatemala
San Salvador
Tegucigalpa
Managua
San José
Panamá
Quezaltenango
Cobán
Santa Ana
San Miguel
San Pedro Sula
La Ceiba
Puerto Cabo Gracias à Dios
Puerto Cabezas
Matagalpa
León
Corinto
Granada
Masaya
Bluefields
San Juan del Norte
San Juan del Sur
L. de Nicaragua
L. de Managua
Río Grande
Segovia
Patuca
Coco
San Juan
Puntarenas
Alajuela
Cartago
Limón
Bocas del Toro
David
Puerto Armuelles
I. Coiba
Santiago
Colón
I. del Rey
Golfo de Panamá
Cartagena
Montería
Medellín
15°
10°
5°
90°
85°
80°
A
B
C
D
4
5
6
© Geddes & Grosset

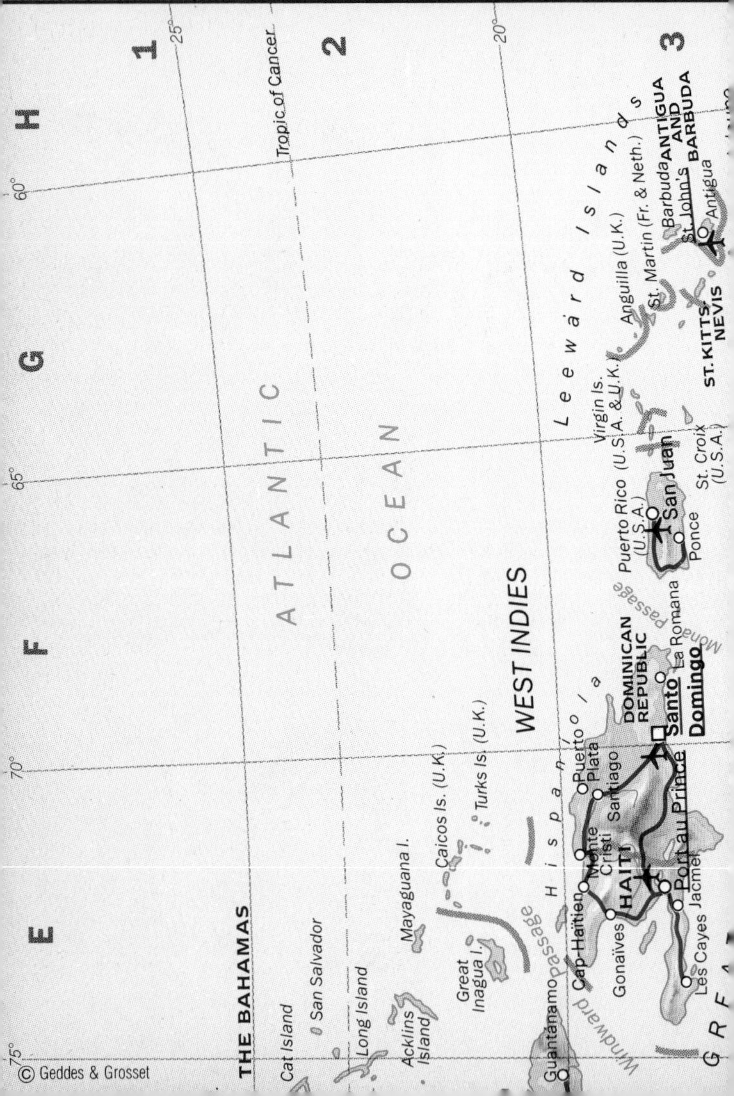
E
F
G
H
1
2
3
25°
20°
60°
65°
70°
75°
THE BAHAMAS
Cat Island
San Salvador
Long Island
Acklins Island
Mayaguana I.
Great Inagua I.
Caicos Is. (U.K.)
Turks Is. (U.K.)
Tropic of Cancer
ATLANTIC
OCEAN
WEST INDIES
Guantánamo
Windward Passage
Hispaniola
Cap-Haïtien
Gonaïves
Monte Cristi
HAITI
Port au Prince
Jacmel
Les Cayes
Santiago
Puerto Plata
DOMINICAN REPUBLIC
Santo Domingo
La Romana
Mona Passage
Puerto Rico (U.S.A.)
San Juan
Ponce
St. Croix (U.S.A.)
Virgin Is. (U.S.A. & U.K.)
Leeward Islands
Anguilla (U.K.)
St. Martin (Fr. & Neth.)
ST. KITTS-NEVIS
Barbuda
ANTIGUA AND BARBUDA
St. John's
Antigua

CARIBBEAN SEA
LESSER ANTILLES
Windwards Islands
Roseau
Martinique (Fr.)
Fort-de-France
ST. LUCIA
Castries
BARBADOS
Bridgetown
ST. VINCENT & THE GRENADINES
Georgetown
GRENADA
St. George's
Tobago
TRINIDAD AND TOBAGO
Port of Spain
Trinidad
I. Blanquilla
I. Margarita
Carupano
Güiria
Barcelona
Maturín
Ciudad Guayana
Ciudad Bolívar
Orinoco
La Tortuga
Caracas
Is. Los Rogues
Maracay
Valencia
Bonaire
Netherlands Antilles
Curaçao
Aruba
Coro
Barquisimeto
Cabimas
Pta. Gallinas
Maracaibo
Lago de Maracaibo
San Cristóbal
Cúcuta
Bucaramanga
Barranquilla
Santa Marta
Valledupar
Magdalena
Meta
Bello
Manizales
Bogotá
VENEZUELA
COLOMBIA
GUYANA
BRAZIL
2810
4
5
E
F
G
10°
5°
60°
65°
70°
75°
15°

SOUTH AMERICA

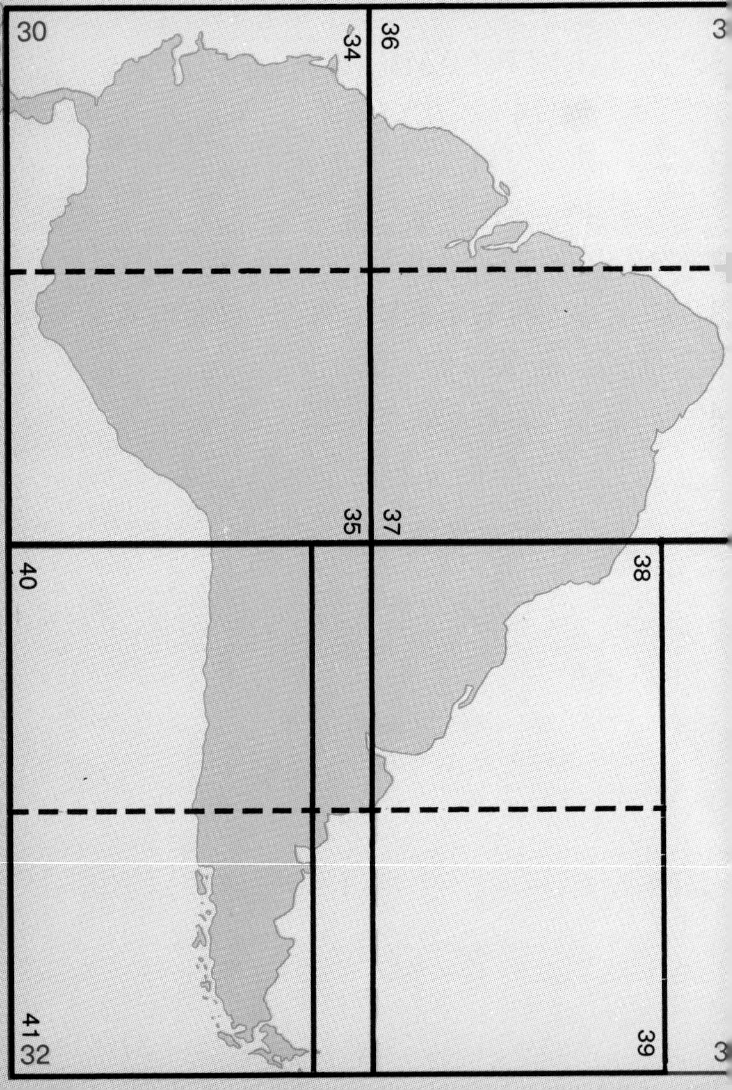

SOUTH AMERICA POLITICAL (N)

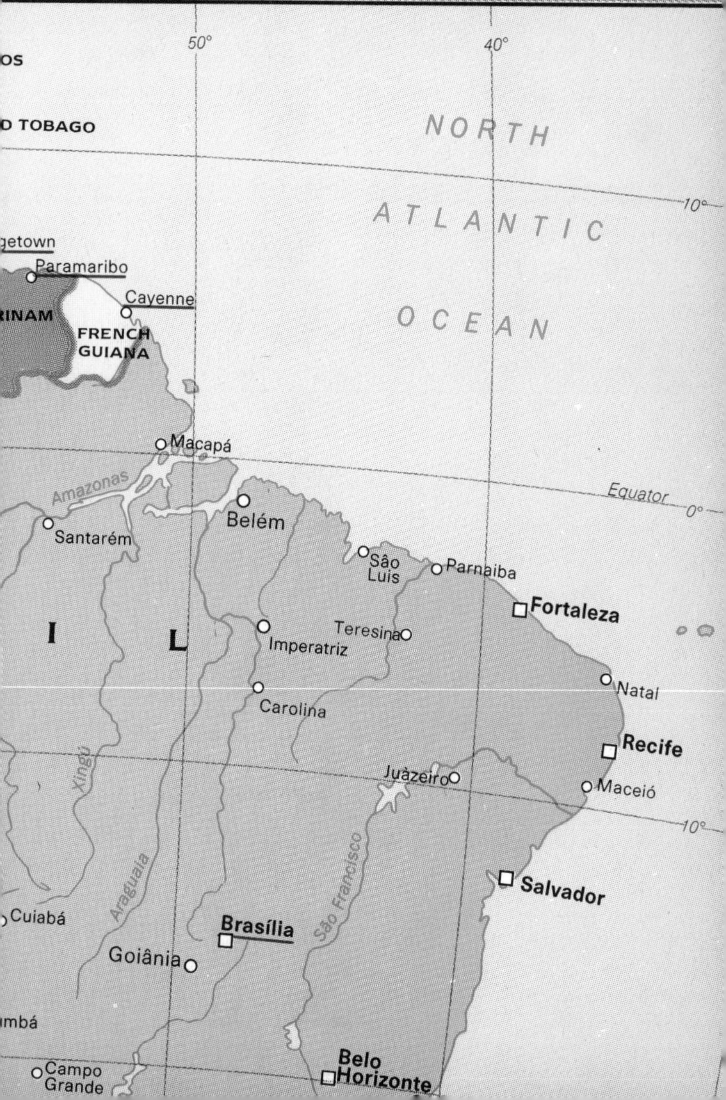
50°
40°
OS
D TOBAGO
NORTH
ATLANTIC
OCEAN
10°
getown
Paramaribo
Cayenne
RINAM
FRENCH
GUIANA
Macapá
Amazonas
Equator
0°
Belém
Santarém
São
Luis
Parnaiba
Fortaleza
I
L
Teresina
Imperatriz
Natal
Carolina
Recife
Xingu
Juàzeiro
Maceió
10°
Araguaia
São Francisco
Salvador
Cuiabá
Brasília
Goiânia
mbá
Belo
Horizonte
Campo
Grande

SOUTH AMERICA POLITICAL (S)

20°
Tropic of Capricorn
Antofagasta
Salta
San Miguel de Tucumán
CHILE
PACIFIC OCEAN
30°
San Juan
Córdoba
Santa Fé
Viña del Mar
Santiago
Mendoza
Rosario
ARGENTIN
Concepción
Bahía
Neuquén
NEUQUÉN
90°
Puerto Montt
40°
Comodoro Rivadavia
Río Gallegos
Est. de Magallanes
Tierra del Fuego
Punta Arenas
50°
90°
80°
70°
60

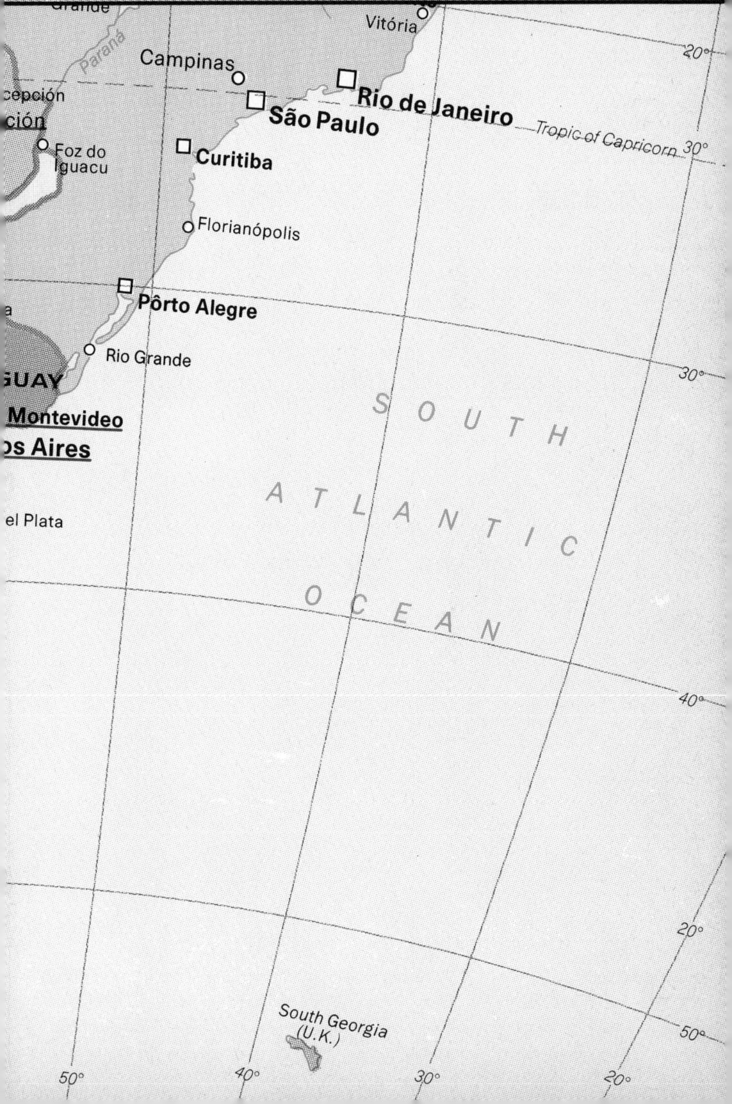
Grande
Vitória
Paraná
Campinas
Rio de Janeiro
São Paulo
cepción
ción
Tropic of Capricorn
Foz do Iguacu
Curitiba
Florianópolis
Pôrto Alegre
Rio Grande
GUAY
Montevideo
os Aires
el Plata
SOUTH ATLANTIC OCEAN
South Georgia (U.K.)
20°
30°
40°
50°
20°
30°
40°
50°

SOUTH AMERICA (N.W.)

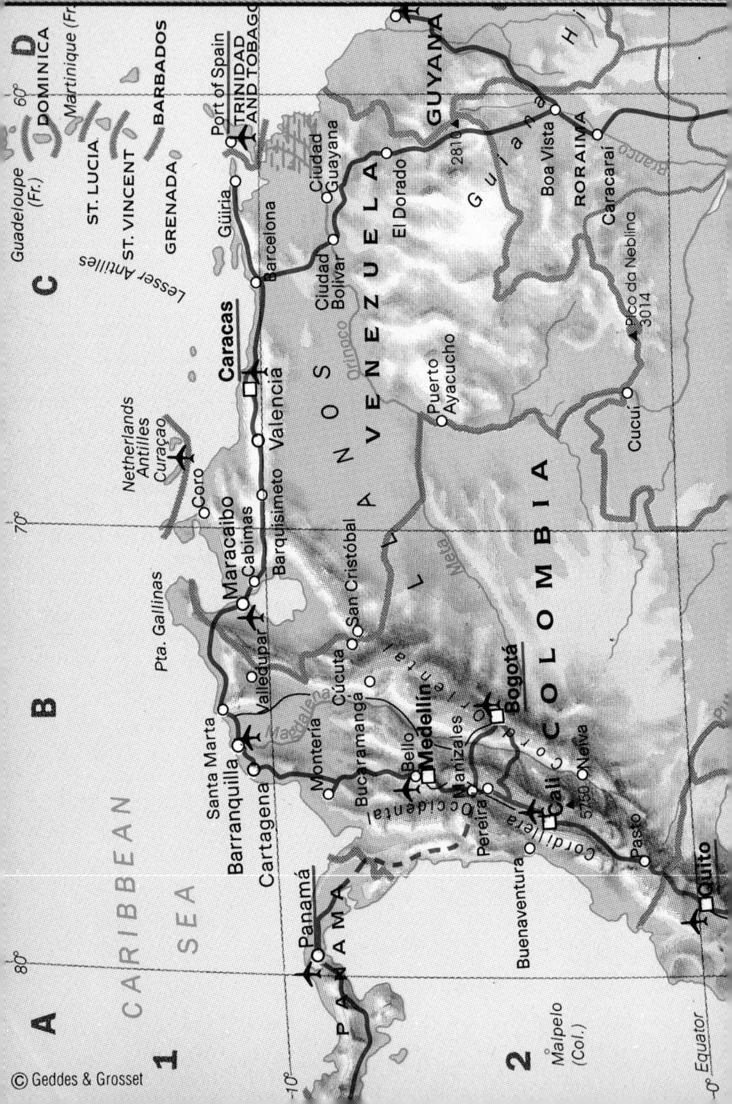

A M A Z O N A S
S E L V A S
BRAZIL
ACRE
RONDÔNIA
Serra dos Parecis
PERU
BOLIVIA
CORDILLERA DE LOS ANDES
PACIFIC OCEAN
Madeira
Purus
Ucayali
Iquitos
Humaitá
Pôrto Velho
Lábrea
Rio Branco
Cruzeiro do Sul
Pucallpa
Huascarán 6768
Piura
Chiclayo
Trujillo
Chimbote
Loja
Callao
Lima
Huancayo
Ica
Cuzco
Arequipa
Mollendo
Arica
Iquique
La Paz
Ancohuma 6388
6542
Oruro
Altiplano
Cochabamba
Santa Cruz
Sucre
Potosí
3
4
10°

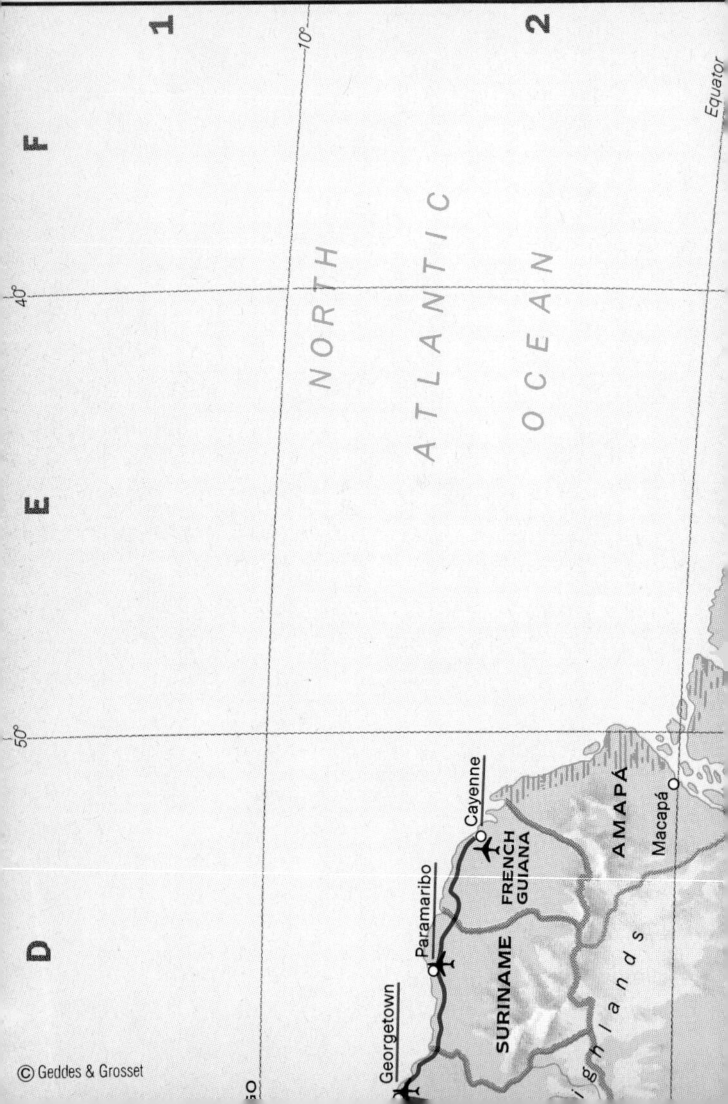
D
E
F
1
2
10°
40°
50°
Equator
NORTH
ATLANTIC
OCEAN
Georgetown
Paramaribo
Cayenne
SURINAME
FRENCH
GUIANA
AMAPÁ
Macapá

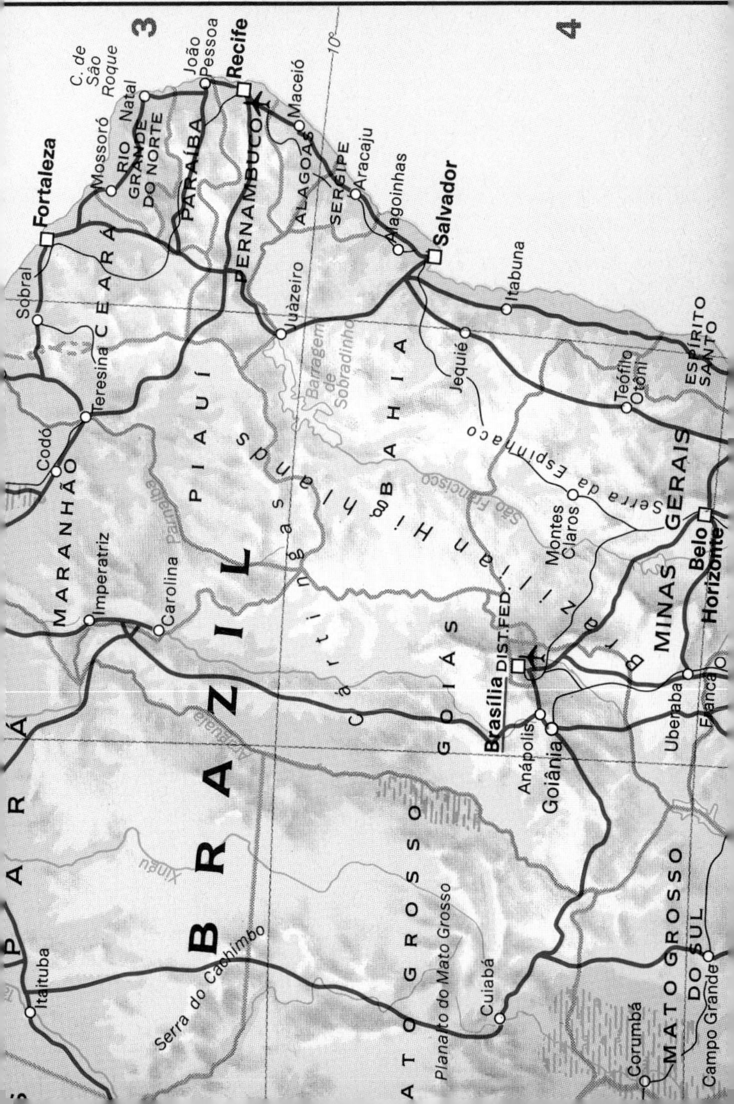
3
4
10°
C. de São Roque
Natal
João Pessoa
Recife
Maceió
Aracaju
Alagoinhas
Salvador
Itabuna
Fortaleza
Mossoró
RIO GRANDE DO NORTE
PARAÍBA
PERNAMBUCO
ALAGOAS
SERGIPE
CEARÁ
Sobral
Teresina
Juàzeiro
Barragem de Sobradinho
BAHIA
Jequié
Teófilo Otôni
ESPÍRITO SANTO
Codó
MARANHÃO
PIAUÍ
Chapada das Mangabeiras
Espinhaço
Serra da Espinhaço
São Francisco
Montes Claros
MINAS GERAIS
Belo Horizonte
Parnaíba
Imperatriz
Carolina
BRAZIL
DIST.FED.
Brasília
GOIÁS
Anápolis
Goiânia
Uberaba
Franca
Araguaia
PARÁ
Xingu
Itaituba
Serra do Cachimbo
MATO GROSSO
Planalto do Mato Grosso
Cuiabá
Corumbá
MATO GROSSO DO SUL
Campo Grande

5
6
Vitória
Campos
RIO DE JANEIRO
Rio de Janeiro
São Carlos
São Paulo
Campinas
Sorocaba
SÃO PAULO
Marília
Dourados
Curitiba
Florianópolis
PARANA
Foz do Iguacu
SANTA CATARINA
Lajes
Passo Fundo
Pôrto Alegre
Rio Grande
RIO GRANDE DO SUL
Bagé
Montevideo
Melo
URUGUAY
Salto
Concordia
MISIONES
Encarnación
Asunción
Concepción
PARAGUAY
Paraguay
CORRIENTES
Corrientes
Resistencia
FORMOSA
CHACO
ENTRE RIOS
Paraná
Rosario
Santa Fé
SANTA FÉ
Buenos Aires
La Plata
Río de la Plata
BUENOS AIRES
Pilcomayo
© Geddes & Grosset

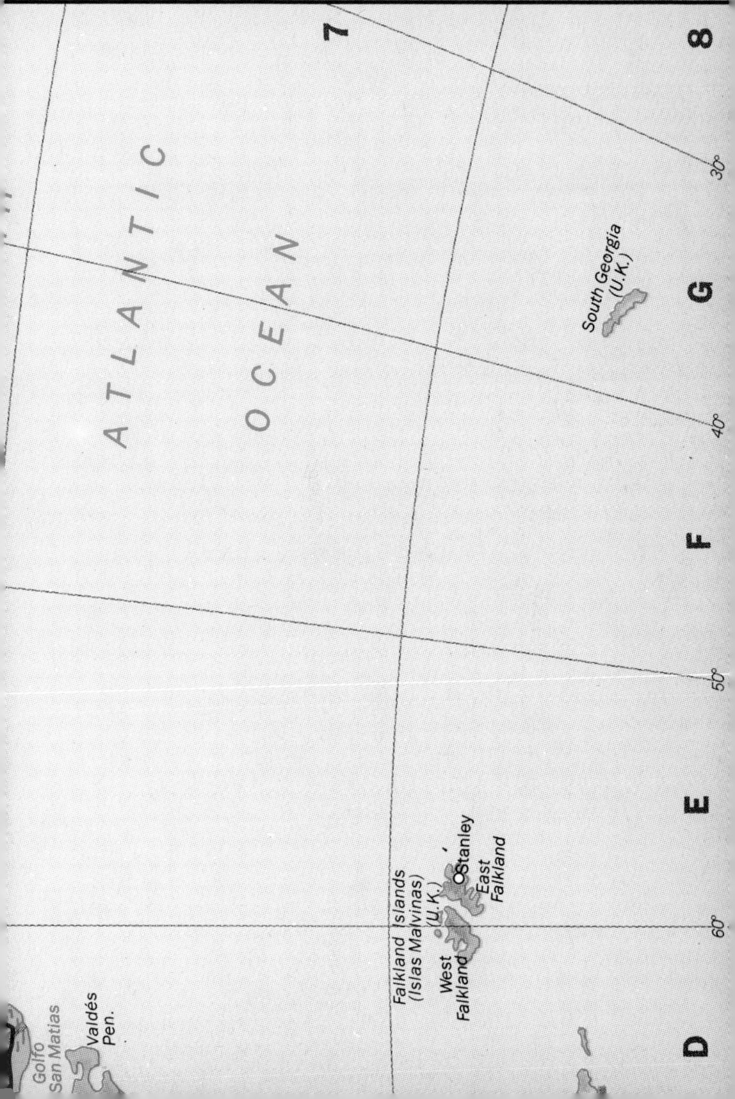
7
8
ATLANTIC
OCEAN
South Georgia
(U.K.)
30°
40°
50°
60°
D
E
F
G
Falkland Islands
(Islas Malvinas)
(U.K.)
Stanley
East
Falkland
West
Falkland
Golfo
San Matías
Valdés
Pen.

PARAGUAY
FORMOSA
Pilcomayo
GRAN CHACO
CHACO
Resistencia
Corrientes
CORRIENTES
SANTA FÉ
Concordia
ENTRE RÍOS
Paraná
Rosario
Santa Fé
Buenos Aires
La Plata
BUENOS AIRES
ARGENTINA
SANTIAGO DEL ESTERO
CÓRDOBA
Córdoba
Mercedes
SAN LUIS
Santa Rosa
LA PAMPA
Salado
JUJUY
SALTA
Salta
TUCUMÁN
San Miguel de Tucumán
CATAMARCA
LA RIOJA
SAN JUAN
San Juan
Mendoza
MENDOZA
Santiago
Aconcagua 6960
6908
Calama
Desierto de Atacama
ANDES
CHILE
Antofagasta
Chañaral
La Serena
Viña del Mar
Valparaíso
Rancagua
Talca
Talcahuano
Concepción
Islas Juan Fernández (Chile)
Islas de Los Desventurados (Chile)
Tropic of Capricorn
20°
30°
5
6

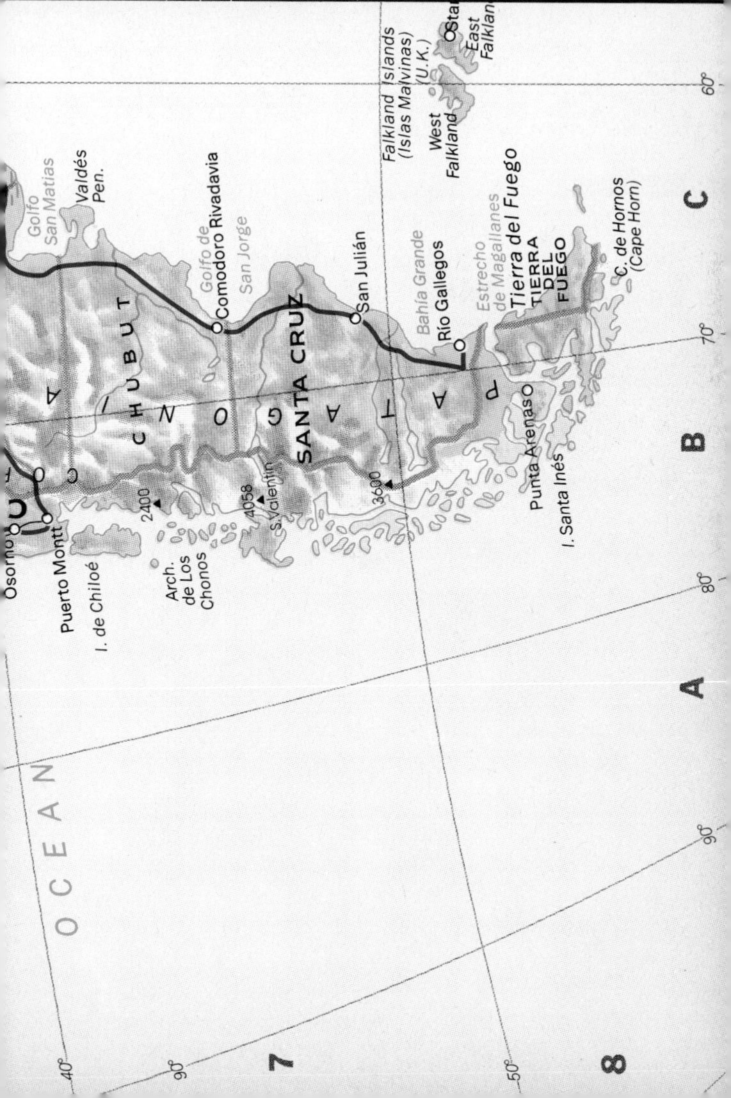
Falkland Islands
(Islas Malvinas)
(U.K.)
West Falkland
East Falklan
Stal
60°
Golfo San Matias
Valdés Pen.
Golfo de San Jorge
Comodoro Rivadavia
CHUBUT
SANTA CRUZ
San Julián
Bahía Grande
Río Gallegos
Estrecho de Magallanes
Tierra del Fuego
TIERRA DEL FUEGO
C. de Hornos
(Cape Horn)
70°
Punta Arenas
I. Santa Inés
3600
4058
S. Valentin
2400
Osorno
Puerto Montt
I. de Chiloé
Arch. de Los Chonos
80°
90°
OCEAN
40°
50°
A
B
C
7
8

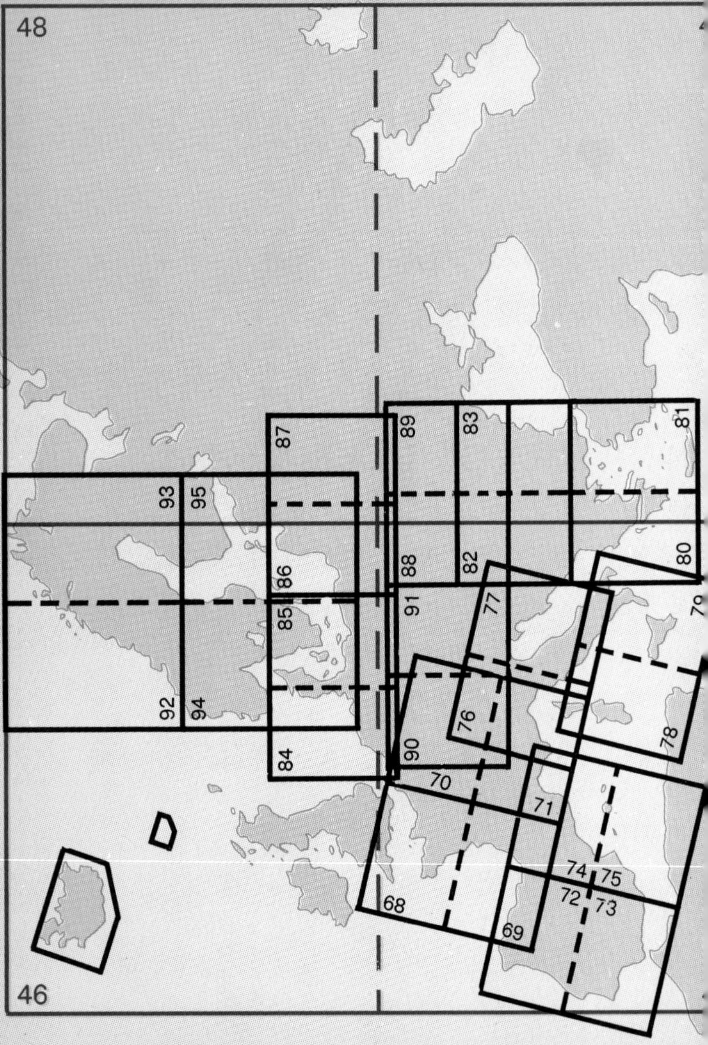
48
46
87
89
83
81
93
95
86
88
82
80
85
91
77
92
94
76
78
84
90
70
71
74
75
72
73
68
69

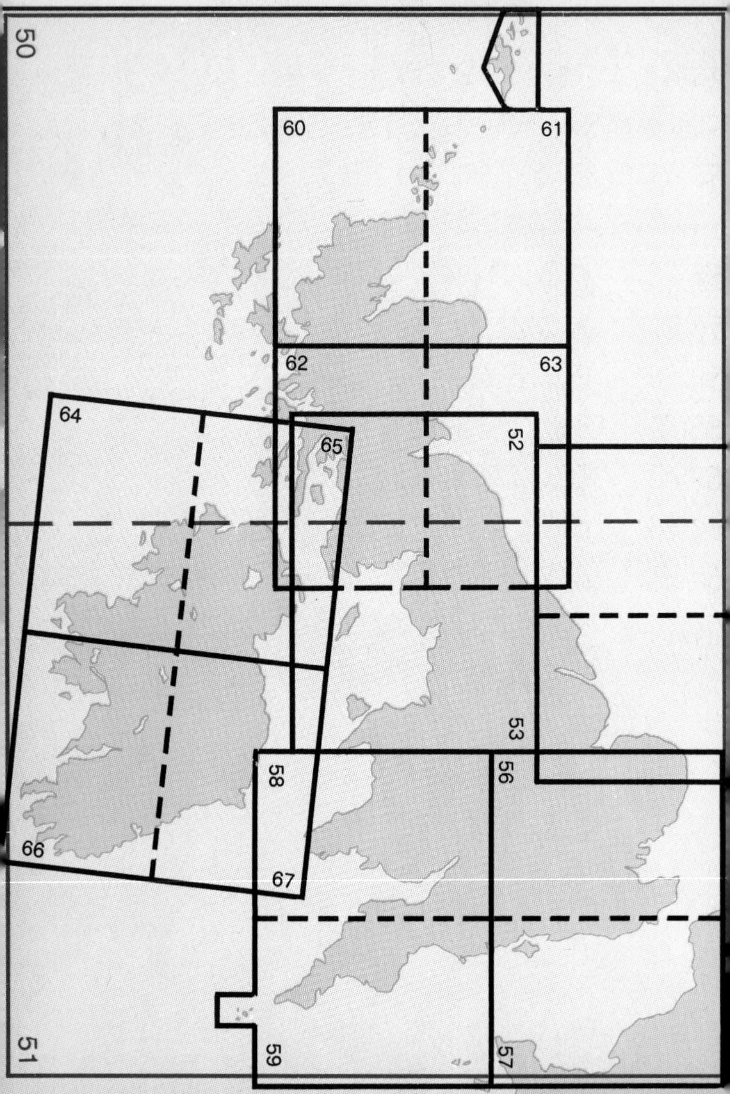
50
60
61
62
63
64
65
52
53
56
58
66
67
59
57
51

EUROPE POLITICAL (W)

NORWAY
SWEDEN
Gulf of Bothnia
BALTIC SEA
LATVIA
LITHUANIA
R.
Stockholm
Vättern
Vänern
Göteborg
Malmö
Trondheim
Oslo
Bergen
DENMARK
København
NORWEGIAN SEA
NORTH SEA
NETHER
Shetland Is.
Orkney Is.
Føroyar (Den.)
Hebrides
Edinburgh
Glasgow
UNITED KINGDOM
Leeds
Liverpool
Manchester
Belfast
Dublin
IRELAND
ICELAND
Reykjavik
BOS. – HERZ. BOSNIA – HERZEGOVINA
L. LIECHTENSTEIN
LUX. LUXEMBOURG
MAC. MACEDONIA
R. RUSSIA
SER. SERBIA
S.M. SAN MARINO
SWITZ. SWITZERLAND
70°
65°
60°
55°
50°
30°
25°
20°
15°
10°
5°
0°

MEDITERRANEAN SEA
IONIAN SEA
TYRRHENIAN SEA
ADRIATIC SEA
Bay of Biscay
Channel Is.
GREECE
ALBANIA
Tiranë
MAC.
Skopje
YUGOSLAVIA
Beograd
Timişoara
HUNGARY
Budapest
Miskolc
SLOVAKIA
Bratislava
Kraków
Wrocław
Lodz
CZECH REPUBLIC
Praha
Dresden
Odra
Elbe
Leipzig
GERMANY
Frankfurt
Stuttgart
München
Danube
Essen
Köln
Bonn
Rhein
AUSTRIA
Wien
Graz
SLOVENIA
Ljubljana
CROATIA
Zagreb
BOS.-HERZ.
Sarajevo
CRO.
SWITZ.
Zürich
Bern
L.
Milano
Torino
Genova
Venezia
Bologna
Firenze
Po
S.M.
ITALY
Roma
Napoli
Bari
Sicilia
Palermo
MALTA
Corse
Sardegna
MONACO
Nice
Marseille
FRANCE
Lyon
Rhône
Loire
Paris
Nantes
Bordeaux
Toulouse
Lille
BELGIUM
LUX.
Luxembourg
ANDORRA
Barcelona
Islas Baleares
SPAIN
Madrid
Zaragoza
Ebro
Bilbao
Valencia
Duero
Tajo
Sevilla
Malaga
Gibraltar (U.K.)
PORTUGAL
Porto
Lisboa
TUNISIA
Tunis
ALGERIA
Alger
Oran
MOROCCO
Rabat
Casablanca
45°
40°
35°
20°
10°
5°
0°
5°

RUSSIA
KHSTAN
Chelyabinsk
Yekaterinburg
Ufa
Samara
Perm
Kazan
Nizhniy Novgorod
Moskva
Sankt Peterburg
Archangel
Murmansk
BARENTS SEA
Arctic Circle
Irtysh
Tobol
Ob
Oka
Sev. Dvina
Ozero Onezhskoye
Ladozhskoye Ozero
FINLAND
Tampere
Helsingfors
Tallinn
ESTONIA
Riga
LATVIA
LITHUANIA
Vilnius
30°
35°
40°
45°
50°
55°
60°
65°
70°
75°
© Geddes & Grosset

CASPIAN
SEA
BLACK
SEA
AEGEAN SEA
UKRAINE
MOLDOVA
ROMANIA
BULGARIA
TURKEY
GEORGIA
ARMENIA
AZERBAIJAN
AZER.
IRAN
IRAQ
SYRIA
LEBANON
CYPRUS
Kiyev
Khar'kov
Dnepropetrovsk
Donetsk
Volgograd
Rostov-na-Donu
Astrakhan
Odessa
Chişinău
Lvov
Cluj-Napoca
Bucureşti
Constanţa
Sofiya
Plovdiv
Thessaloníki
Athínai
Istanbul
Bursa
Izmir
Ankara
Samsun
Kayseri
Adana
Nicosia
Dimashq
Tbilisi
Baku
Yerevan
Erzurum
Tabríz
Tehrān
Al Mawşil
Baghdād
Tigris
Euphrates
Don
Dnepr
Danube
Ródhos
Kríti
45°
40°
35°
30°
25°
50°

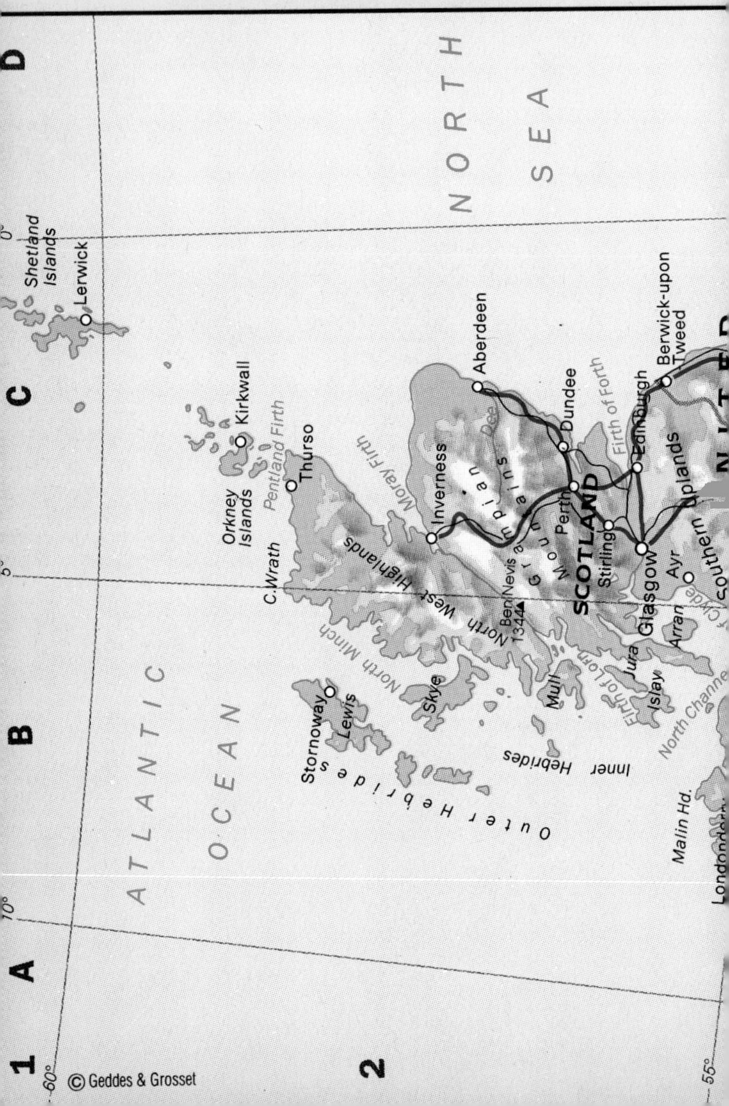
A
B
C
D
1
2
ATLANTIC
OCEAN
NORTH
SEA
Shetland Islands
Lerwick
Orkney Islands
Kirkwall
Pentland Firth
Thurso
C.Wrath
North West Highlands
Moray Firth
Inverness
Aberdeen
Dee
Grampian Mountains
Dundee
Perth
Firth of Forth
Edinburgh
Berwick-upon Tweed
Ben Nevis 1344
SCOTLAND
Stirling
Glasgow
Southern Uplands
Ayr
Firth of Clyde
Arran
Jura
Islay
Firth of Lorn
Mull
Skye
North Minch
Lewis
Stornoway
Outer Hebrides
Inner Hebrides
North Channel
Malin Hd.
Londonderry
0°
5°
10°
55°
60°

KINGDOM
ENGLAND
WALES
IRELAND
IRISH SEA
CELTIC SEA
English Channel
London
Birmingham
Dublin
Middlesbrough
York
Leeds
Bradford
Huddersfield
Manchester
Bolton
Stockport
Blackpool
Liverpool
Chester
Derby
Nottingham
Sheffield
Kingston-upon-Hull
Grimsby
The Wash
Leicester
Coventry
Cambridge
Norwich
Ipswich
Harwich
Luton
Oxford
Reading
Cheltenham
Dover
Strait of Dover
Calais
Brighton
Southampton
Isle of Wight
Bristol
Newport
Cardiff
Swansea
Fishguard
Cambrian Mts.
Cardigan Bay
Bristol Channel
Exeter
Plymouth
Penzance
Lands End
Isles of Scilly
Isle of Man
Anglesey
Holyhead
1085
Dun Laoghaire
Dundalk
852
Wexford
Waterford
St. George's Channel
Sligo
Athlone
Galway
Galway Bay
Limerick
Cork
Mizen Hd.
1041
Shannon
Cherbourg
Le Havre
Caen
Rouen
Channel Is.
50°
10°
3

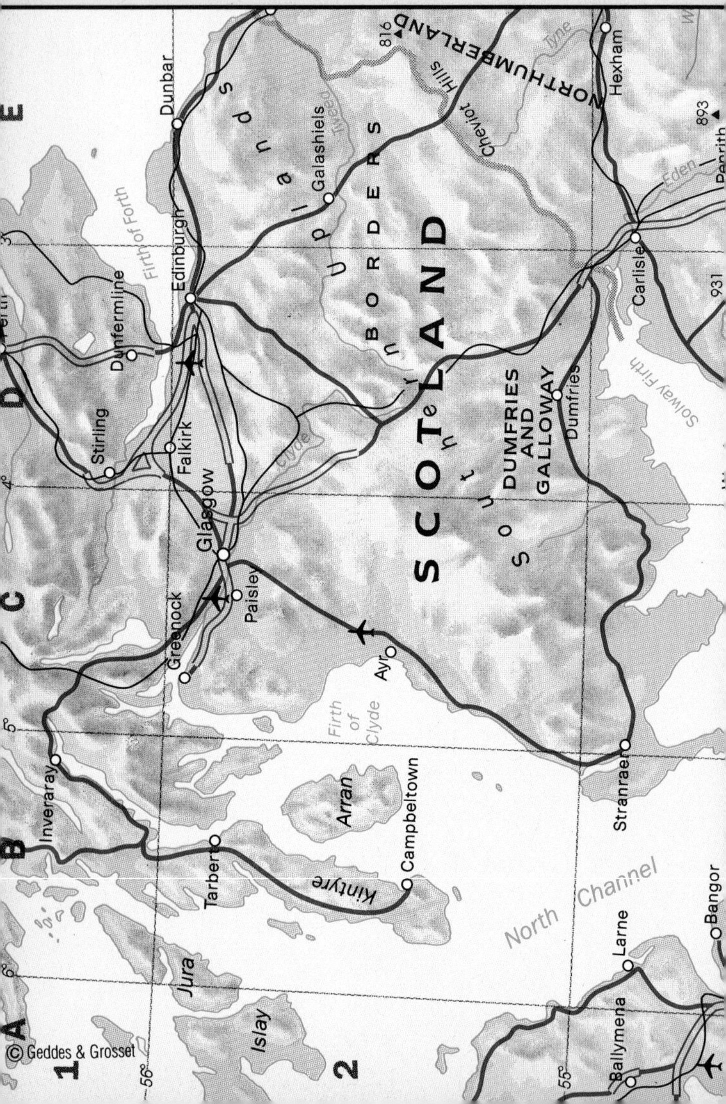
SCOTLAND
BORDERS
Southern Uplands
DUMFRIES AND GALLOWAY
NORTHUMBERLAND
Cheviot Hills
Dunbar
Edinburgh
Firth of Forth
Dunfermline
Stirling
Falkirk
Glasgow
Paisley
Greenock
Ayr
Firth of Clyde
Clyde
Galashiels
Tweed
Tyne
Hexham
Carlisle
Eden
Solway Firth
Dumfries
Stranraer
Inveraray
Tarbert
Kintyre
Campbeltown
Arran
Jura
Islay
North Channel
Larne
Bangor
Ballymena
816
893
931
A
B
C
D
E
1
2
56°
55°
6°
5°
4°
3°

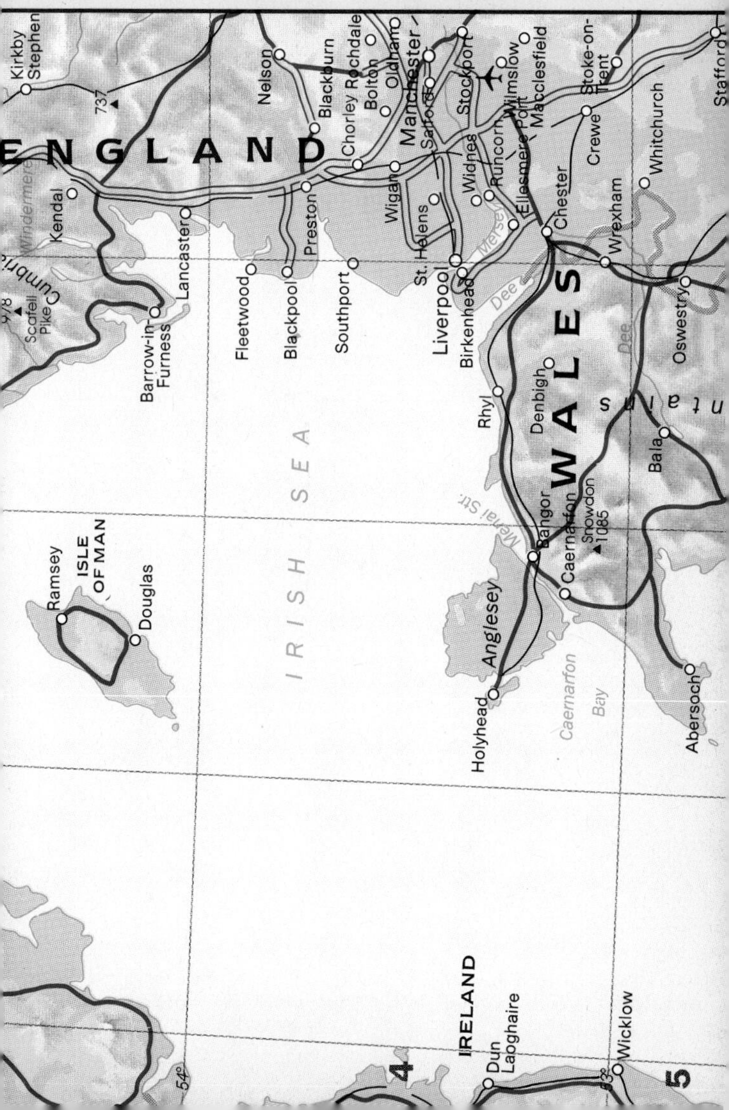
ENGLAND
WALES
IRELAND
ISLE OF MAN
IRISH SEA
Kirkby Stephen
737
Nelson
Blackburn
Chorley
Rochdale
Bolton
Oldham
Manchester
Salford
Stockport
Wilmslow
Macclesfield
Stoke-on-Trent
Stafford
Whitchurch
Crewe
Runcorn
Ellesmere Port
Widnes
Wigan
St. Helens
Liverpool
Birkenhead
Mersey
Dee
Chester
Wrexham
Oswestry
Windermere
Kendal
Lancaster
Preston
Fleetwood
Blackpool
Southport
Cumbria
Scafell Pike
Barrow-in-Furness
Rhyl
Denbigh
Bala
Menai Str.
Bangor
Caernarfon
Snowdon
1085
Anglesey
Holyhead
Caernarfon Bay
Abersoch
Ramsey
Douglas
Dun Laoghaire
Wicklow
54°
53
4
5

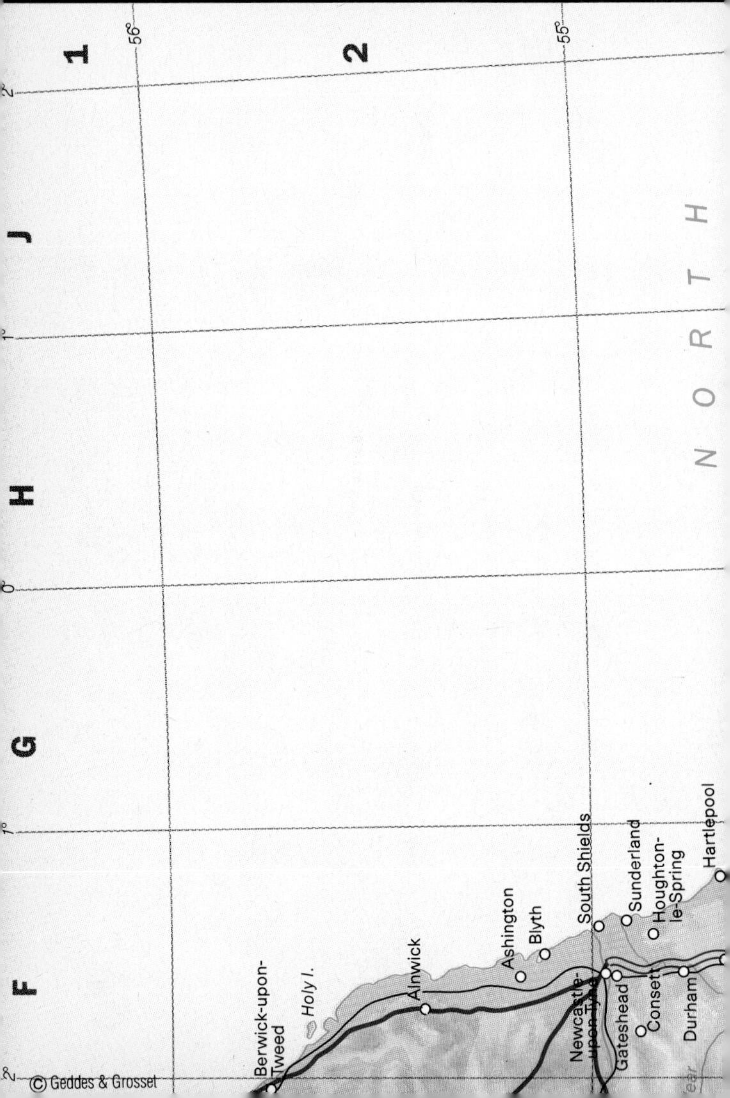
56°
55°
1
2
J
H
G
F
2°
1°
0°
1°
2°
NORTH
Berwick-upon-Tweed
Holy I.
Alnwick
Ashington
Blyth
South Shields
Newcastle-upon-Tyne
Gateshead
Sunderland
Houghton-le-Spring
Consett
Durham
Hartlepool

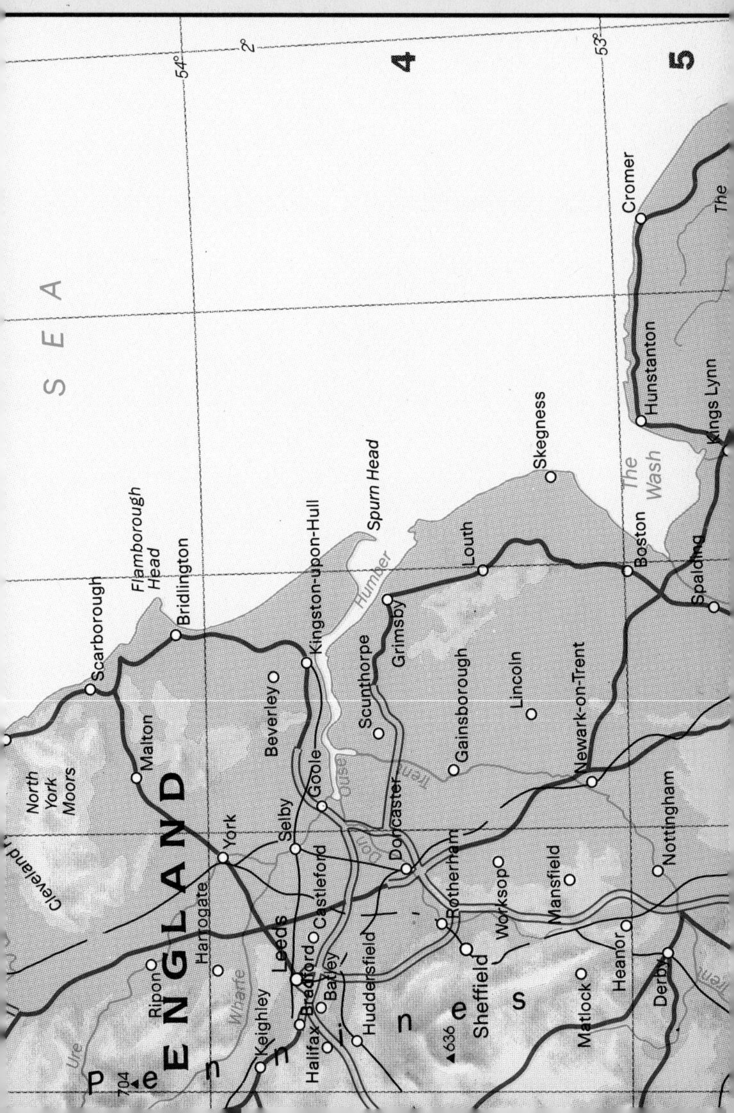
S E A
54°
2°
53°
4
5
ENGLAND
North York Moors
Cleveland
Scarborough
Flamborough Head
Bridlington
Malton
York
Harrogate
Ripon
Leeds
Bradford
Halifax
Keighley
Batley
Huddersfield
Castleford
Selby
Goole
Beverley
Kingston-upon-Hull
Spurn Head
Humber
Ouse
Scunthorpe
Grimsby
Doncaster
Don
Rotherham
Sheffield
Gainsborough
Trent
Lincoln
Louth
Skegness
Worksop
Mansfield
Newark-on-Trent
Nottingham
Heanor
Matlock
Derby
Boston
Spalding
The Wash
Hunstanton
Kings Lynn
Cromer
The
Wharfe
Ure
636
704

5
6
52°
51°
Great Yarmouth
Broads
Norwich
Waveney
Saxmundham
Felixstowe
Harwich
Clacton-on-Sea
Ipswich
Bury St. Edmunds
Thetford
Stour
Colchester
Chelmsford
Basildon
Southend-on-Sea
Thames
Margate
Canterbury
Dover
Channel Tunnel
Hythe
Rochester
Maidstone
Ashford
Royal Tunbridge Wells
North Downs
Tonbridge
London
Gt Ouse
Ely
Cambridge
Harlow
Peterborough
The Fens
St Albans
Watford
Horsham
Crawley
Bedford
Chesham
Luton
Milton Keynes
Aylesbury
Corby
Northampton
Welland
Windsor
Guildford
Aldershot
Chiltern Hills
Leicester
Hinckley
Rugby
Banbury
Buckingham
Reading
Thames
Winchester
Basingstoke
Oxford
Didcot
Warwick
Coventry
Stratford-on-Avon
Birmingham
West Bromwich
Walsall
Warley
Cheltenham
Swindon
Kennet
Salisbury
Avon

Eastbourne
Worthing
Bognor Regis
Portsmouth
Cowes
Newport
The Solent
ISLE OF WIGHT
Bournemouth
Poole
English Channel
Dieppe
Rouen
Seine
Le Havre
Baie de la Seine
Caen
Cherbourg
FRANCE
7
8
West from Greenwich 0° East from Greenwich
© Geddes & Grosset

WALES
Telford
Wolverhampton
Dudley
Warle
Severn
Worcester
Hereford
Gloucester
Cotswold Hills
Stroud
Kingswood
Chippenham
Bath
Trowbridge
Warminster
Church Stretton
Shrewsbury
Welshpool
Llandrindod Wells
Builth Wells
Wye
Abergavenny
Cwmbran
Newport
Bristol
Weston-super-Mare
Cardiff
Barry
Bridgwater
Mon
Cambrian
Dolgellau
892
Aberystwyth
Cardigan Bay
Cardigan
Fishguard
St. Davids
Milford Haven
Pembroke
Carmarthen
Carmarthen Bay
Tywi
886
Breacon Beacons
Merthyr Tydfil
Port Talbot
Swansea
Bristol Channel
Exmoor
Barnstaple
Ilfracombe
Bideford
Lundy
St. George's Channel
52°
5
6

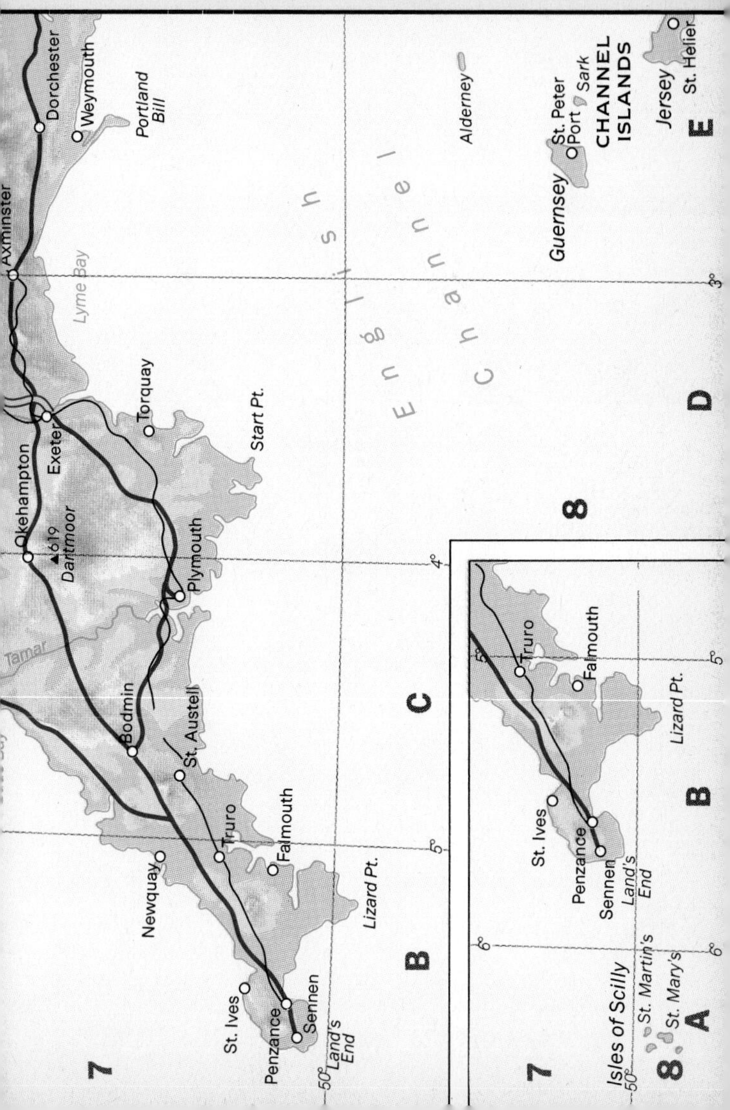
Dorchester
Weymouth
Portland Bill
Axminster
Lyme Bay
Exeter
Okehampton
Torquay
Start Pt.
619
Dartmoor
Plymouth
Tamar
Bodmin
St. Austell
Truro
Falmouth
Newquay
St. Ives
Penzance
Sennen
Land's End
Lizard Pt.
English Channel
Alderney
Guernsey
St. Peter Port
Sark
CHANNEL ISLANDS
Jersey
St. Helier
Isles of Scilly
St. Martin's
St. Mary's
50°
5°
4°
3°
6°
A
B
C
D
E
7
8

A
B
C
D
1
2
3
7°
6°
5°
59°
58°
57°
ATLANTIC
OCEAN
C. Wrath
Durnes
Butt of Lewis
Outer Hebrides
927
Scourie
Stornoway
Lewis
North Minch
Lochinver
998
799
L. Broom
Oyke
Tarbert
L. Ewe
Ullapool
Sd. of Harris
Harris
1081
Gairloch
L. Maree
L. Torridon
L. Snizort
Lochmaddy
North Uist
1046
Little Minch
Uig
Torridon
Garve
Benbecula
Inner Sound
Raasay
Beau
Skye
South Uist
Kyle of Lochalsh
Dornie
North West Highlands
S
C
Lochboisdale
1009
Cuillin Sd.
Great Glen
Fort Augus
Eriskay
Mallaig
Barra
© Geddes & Grosset

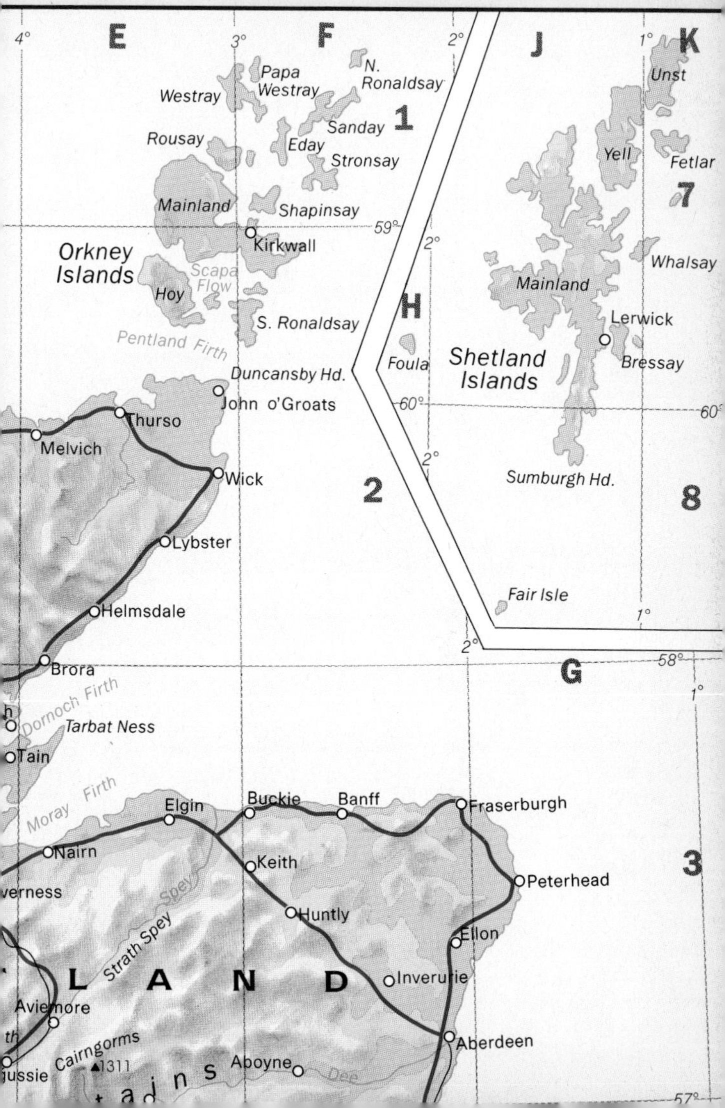
4°
E
3°
F
2°
J
1°
K
Papa Westray
N. Ronaldsay
Westray
Unst
1
Sanday
Rousay
Eday
Yell
Stronsay
Fetlar
7
Mainland
Shapinsay
59°
Kirkwall
2°
Orkney Islands
Whalsay
Scapa Flow
Mainland
Hoy
H
S. Ronaldsay
Lerwick
Pentland Firth
Shetland Islands
Foula
Bressay
Duncansby Hd.
John o'Groats
60°
60°
Thurso
Melvich
2°
Wick
2
Sumburgh Hd.
8
Lybster
Fair Isle
Helmsdale
1°
2°
Brora
G
58°
1°
Dornoch Firth
Tarbat Ness
Tain
Moray Firth
Elgin
Buckie
Banff
Fraserburgh
Nairn
Keith
3
Peterhead
Spey
Huntly
Strath Spey
Ellon
L A N D
Inverurie
Aviemore
Cairngorms
1311
Aberdeen
Aboyne
Dee
57°

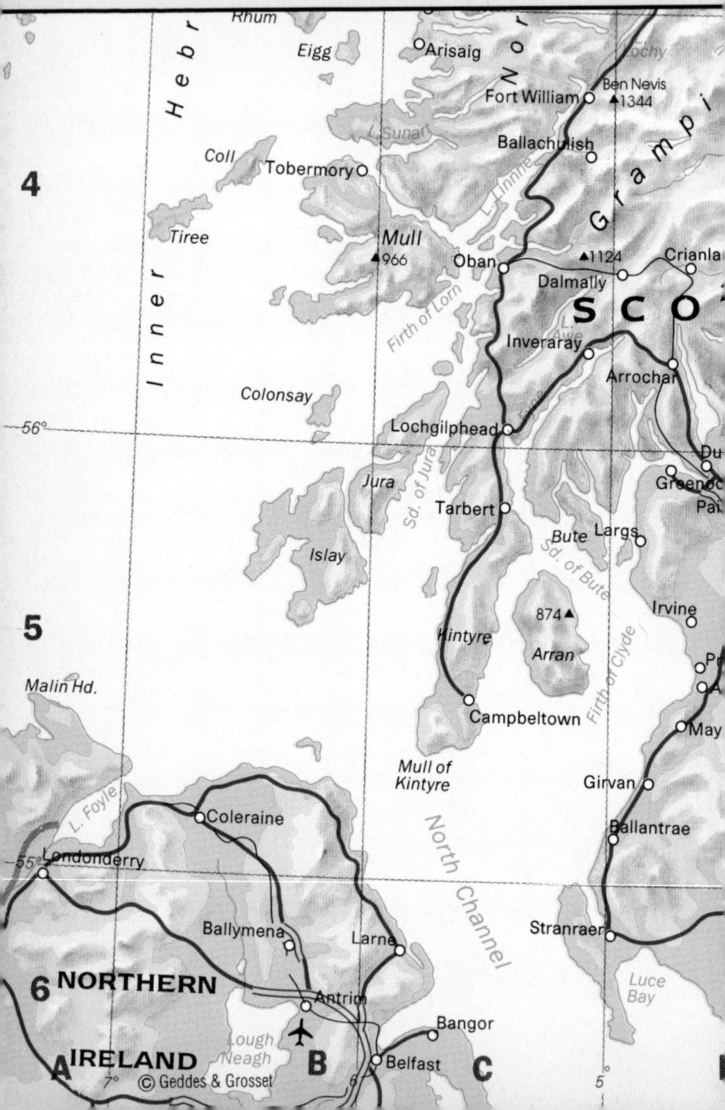
Rhum
Eigg
Arisaig
Inner Hebr
Nor
Fort William
Ben Nevis
1344
Grampi
Ballachulish
L. Sunart
L. Linnhe
Coll
Tobermory
Tiree
Mull
966
Oban
1124
Dalmally
Crianla
SCO
Firth of Lorn
Inveraray
Arrochar
Colonsay
56°
Lochgilphead
Jura
Sd. of Jura
Greenoc
Tarbert
Bute
Largs
Sd. of Bute
Islay
874
Irvine
Kintyre
Arran
Firth of Clyde
Malin Hd.
Campbeltown
May
Mull of Kintyre
Girvan
L. Foyle
Coleraine
North Channel
Ballantrae
55°
Londonderry
Ballymena
Larne
Stranraer
Luce Bay
NORTHERN
Antrim
Bangor
Lough Neagh
IRELAND
Belfast
A
B
C
4
5
6
7°
6°
5°
© Geddes & Grosset

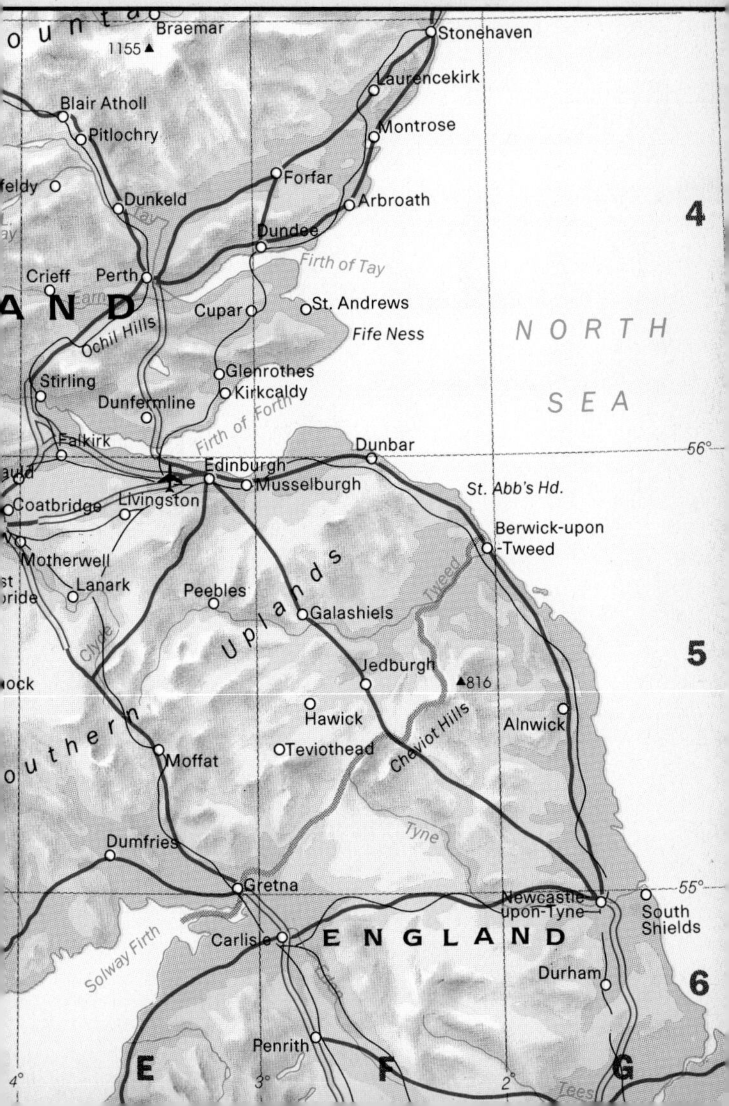
Braemar
1155
Stonehaven
Laurencekirk
Blair Atholl
Pitlochry
Montrose
Forfar
Dunkeld
Arbroath
4
Dundee
Firth of Tay
Crieff
Perth
A N D
Cupar
St. Andrews
Ochil Hills
Fife Ness
N O R T H
Glenrothes
Stirling
Kirkcaldy
S E A
Dunfermline
Firth of Forth
Falkirk
Dunbar
56°
Edinburgh
Musselburgh
St. Abb's Hd.
Coatbridge
Livingston
Berwick-upon-Tweed
Motherwell
Lanark
Peebles
Tweed
Galashiels
Uplands
Clyde
5
Jedburgh
816
Hawick
Alnwick
Cheviot Hills
Teviothead
Southern
Moffat
Tyne
Dumfries
Gretna
55°
Newcastle upon-Tyne
South Shields
Carlisle
E N G L A N D
Solway Firth
Durham
6
Penrith
E
F
G
4°
3°
2°
Tees

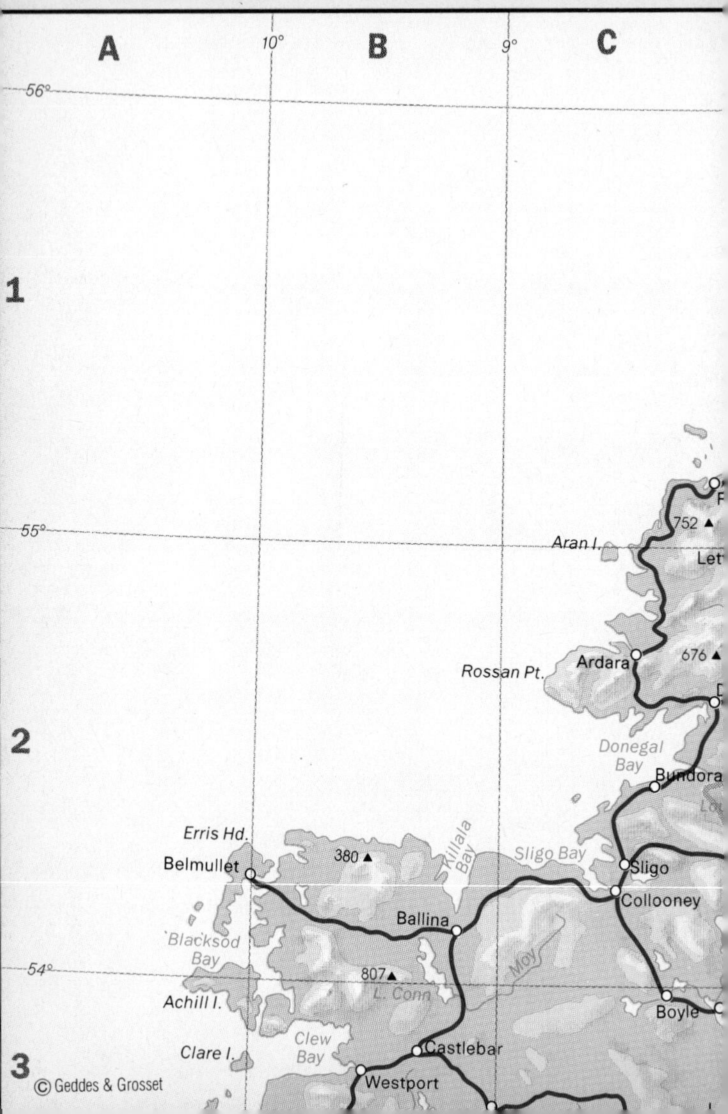
A
10°
B
9°
C
56°
1
55°
Aran I.
752
Let
Ardara
676
Rossan Pt.
2
Donegal Bay
Bundora
Erris Hd.
Belmullet
380
Killala Bay
Sligo Bay
Sligo
Collooney
Ballina
Blacksod Bay
54°
807
L. Conn
Moy
Achill I.
Boyle
Clew Bay
Clare I.
Castlebar
3
Westport

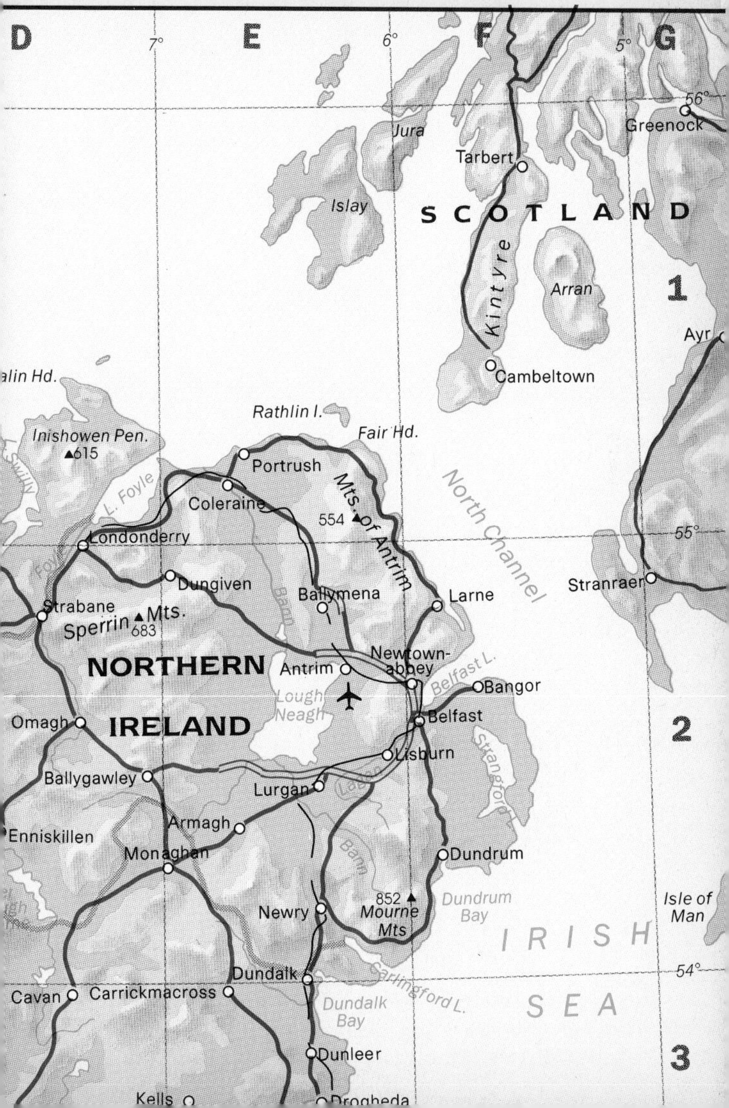
D
E
F
G
7°
6°
5°
56°
55°
54°
1
2
3
Jura
Greenock
Tarbert
Islay
SCOTLAND
Kintyre
Arran
Ayr
alin Hd.
Cambeltown
Rathlin I.
Fair Hd.
Inishowen Pen.
615
L. Swilly
Portrush
L. Foyle
Coleraine
Mts. of Antrim
554
North Channel
Londonderry
Foyle
Dungiven
Bann
Ballymena
Larne
Stranraer
Strabane
Sperrin Mts.
683
Newtown-abbey
NORTHERN
Antrim
Belfast L.
Bangor
Lough Neagh
Omagh
IRELAND
Belfast
Strangford
Lisburn
Ballygawley
Lurgan
Armagh
Enniskillen
Monaghan
Bann
Dundrum
852
Mourne Mts
Dundrum Bay
Isle of Man
Newry
IRISH
SEA
Dundalk
Carlingford L.
Cavan
Carrickmacross
Dundalk Bay
Dunleer
Kells
Drogheda

Killary Harbour
Claremorris
Roscommon
L. Mask
3
Clifden
Slyne Hd.
L. Corrib
Suck
Athlon
Ballinasloe
Galway
Athenry
Kilkieran Bay
Galway Bay
Kinvarra
Shannon
Aran Is.
Gort
53°
I R E
Derg
Hags Hd.
Ennistymon
Ennis
Nena
▲695
Kilrush
Limerick
Golden Va
4
Loop Hd.
Tarbert
Shannon Estuary
Tipperary
Tralee Bay
Feale
Ráth Luirc
Tralee
Kno
Sybil Pt.
▲953
Dingle
Mallow
Blackwater
Fermo
Dingle Bay
Carrauntoohil ▲1041
Killarney
52°
774 ▲
Kenmare
Cork
Cobh
Bandon
Cork Harbo
Bantry
5
Dursey Hd.
Bantry Bay
Old Head of Kinsale
Mizen Hd.
A
B
C
10°
9°

Kells
Drogheda
Edgeworthstown
An Uaimh (Navan)
Boyne
Balbriggan
3
Mullingar
Kinnegad
Howth Hd.
Dublin Bay
IRISH
Liffey
Dublin
Tullamore
Bog of Allen
Dun Laoghaire
Bray
Naas
Kildare
850
Mts
Port Laoise
SEA
A N D
Wicklow
Wicklow Hd.
53°
926
Wicklow
Barrow
Durrow
Carlow
Arklow
Kilkenny
Slaney
4
Enniscorthy
722
Wexford Bay
New Ross
Suir
Wexford
Rosslare
Waterford
Carnsore Pt.
Dungarvan
Waterford Harbour
St. George's Channel
52°
Fishguard
WALES
5
D
E
F
7°
6°
5°

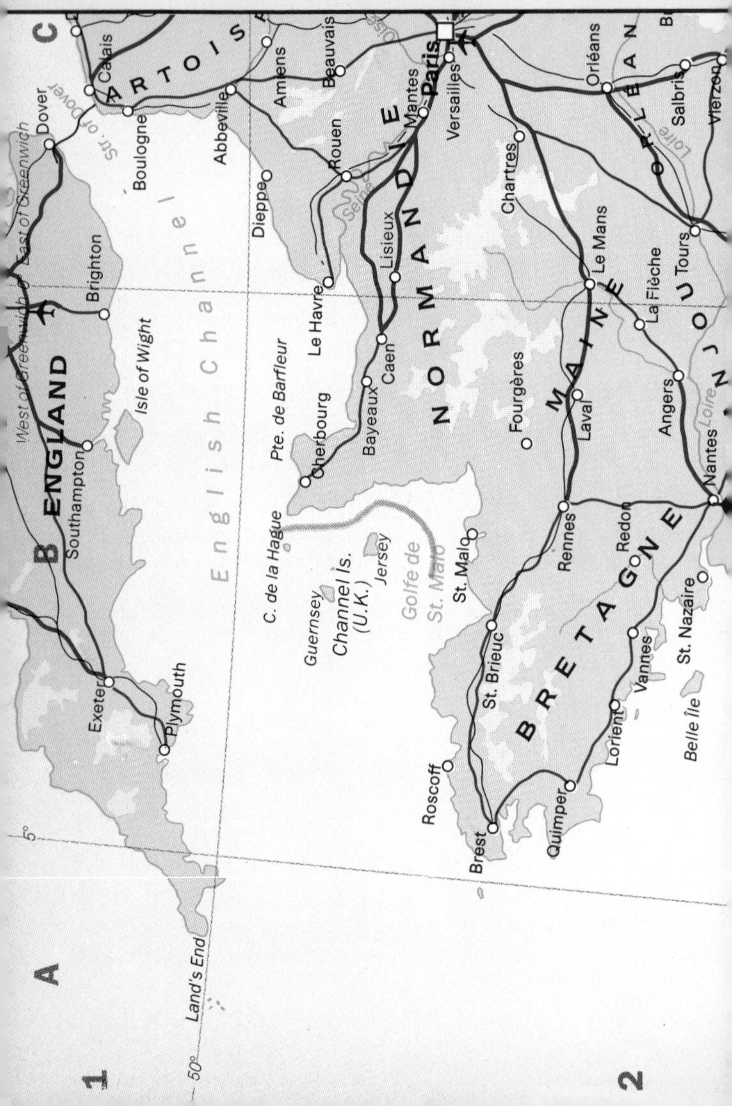
ENGLAND
ARTOIS
NORMANDIE
MAINE
BRETAGNE
ORLÉAN
ANJOU
English Channel
Str. of Dover
Channel Is. (U.K.)
Golfe de St. Malo
West of Greenwich
East of Greenwich
Dover
Calais
Boulogne
Abbeville
Amiens
Beauvais
Paris
Versailles
Mantes
Rouen
Dieppe
Le Havre
Lisieux
Caen
Bayeux
Cherbourg
Pte. de Barfleur
C. de la Hague
Guernsey
Jersey
St. Malo
Rennes
St. Brieuc
Roscoff
Brest
Quimper
Lorient
Vannes
Belle Île
St. Nazaire
Redon
Nantes
Angers
Laval
Fougères
Le Mans
La Flèche
Tours
Chartres
Orléans
Salbris
Vierzon
Loire
Seine
Oise
Brighton
Isle of Wight
Southampton
Exeter
Plymouth
Land's End
50°
5°
A
B
C
1
2

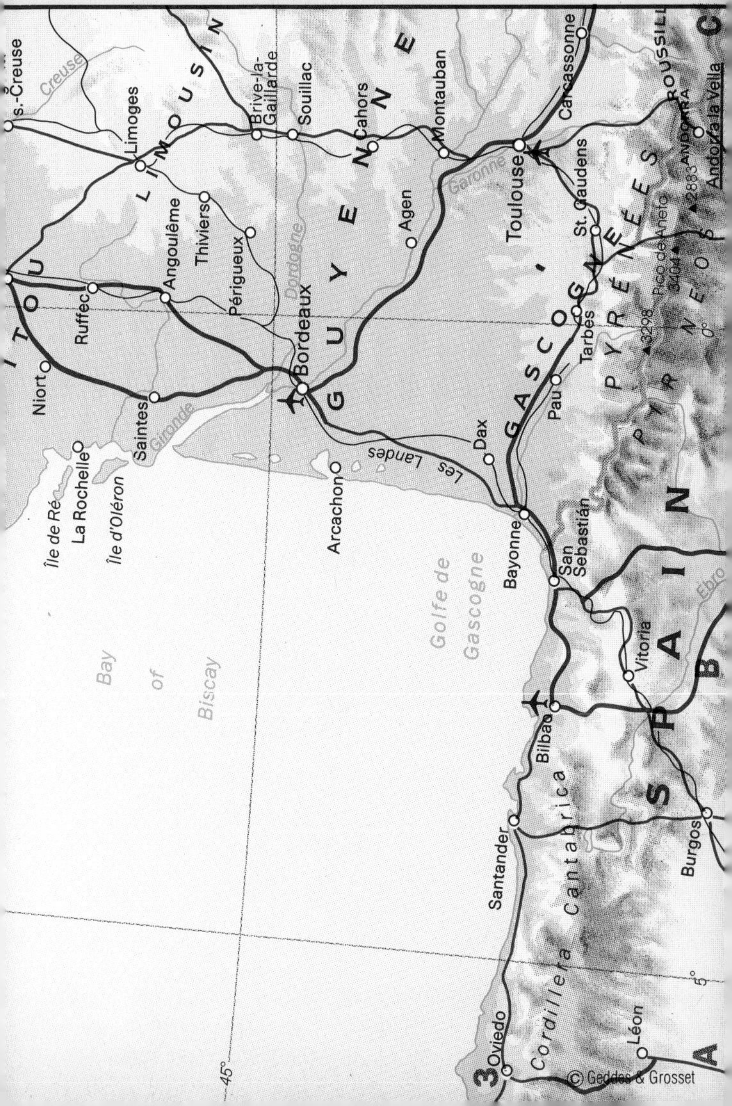

Creuse
Limoges
LIMOUSIN
Brive-la-Gaillarde
Souillac
Cahors
Montauban
Carcassonne
Toulouse
Garonne
GUYENNE
Angoulême
Thiviers
Périgueux
Ruffec
Niort
Agen
Dordogne
Bordeaux
Saintes
Gironde
La Rochelle
Île de Ré
Île d'Oléron
Arcachon
Les Landes
Dax
Pau
Tarbes
St. Gaudens
GASCOGNE
PYRÉNÉES
Pico de Aneto
3404
3298
2883
ANDORRA
Andorra la Vella
ROUSSILLON
Bayonne
San Sebastián
Golfe de Gascogne
Bay of Biscay
Ebro
Vitoria
Bilbao
Santander
Burgos
Cordillera Cantabrica
Oviedo
Léon
SPAIN
45°
5°
0°
3
© Geddes & Grosset

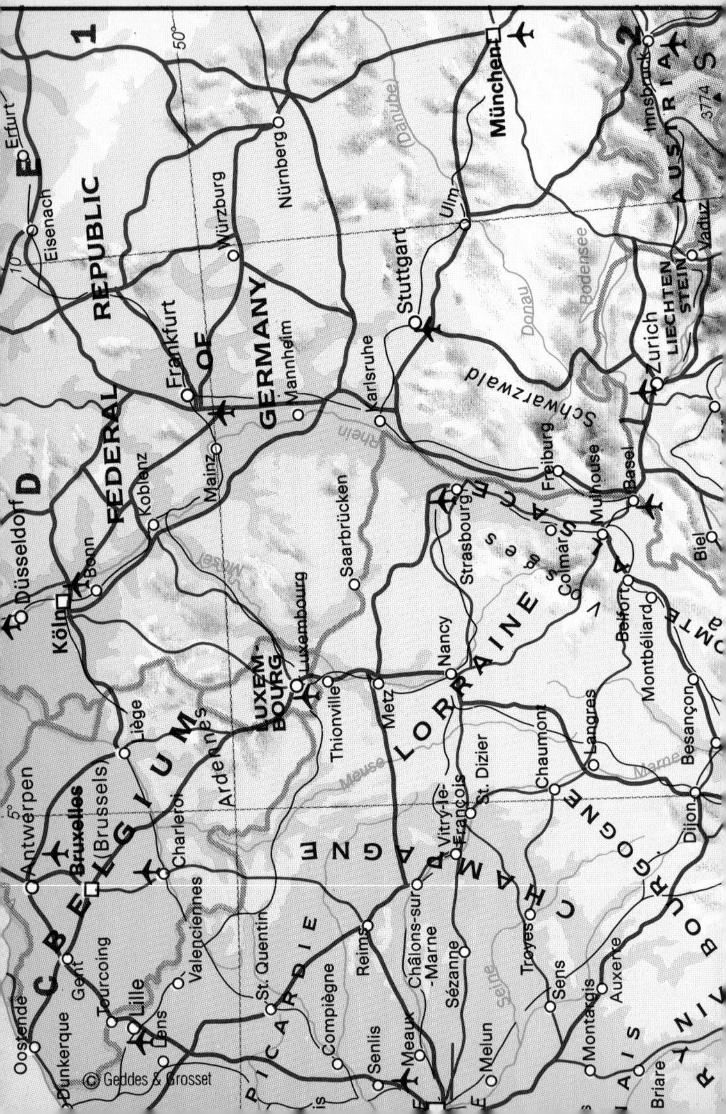

FEDERAL REPUBLIC OF GERMANY
D
BELGIUM
LUXEMBOURG
LORRAINE
AUSTRIA
LIECHTENSTEIN
Erfurt
Eisenach
Nürnberg
Würzburg
München
Ulm
Stuttgart
Frankfurt
Mannheim
Karlsruhe
Mainz
Koblenz
Bonn
Köln
Düsseldorf
Saarbrücken
Luxembourg
Innsbruck
Vaduz
Zurich
Basel
Freiburg
Mulhouse
Strasbourg
Colmar
Belfort
Montbéliard
Biel
Besançon
Dijon
Nancy
Metz
Thionville
Liège
Antwerpen
Bruxelles
(Brussels)
Charleroi
Ardennes
Oostende
Dunkerque
Gent
Tourcoing
Lille
Lens
Valenciennes
St. Quentin
Compiègne
Senlis
Reims
Meaux
Châlons-sur-Marne
Sézanne
Melun
Vitry-le-François
St. Dizier
Chaumont
Langres
Troyes
Sens
Montargis
Auxerre
Briare
Schwarzwald
Bodensee
Donau
(Danube)
Rhein
Mosel
Meuse
Marne
Seine
Vosges
PICARDIE
CHAMPAGNE
BOURGOGNE
3774
50°
10°
5°
© Geddes & Grosset

ITALY
Trento
Verona
L. di Garda
Brescia
Milano
Piacenza
Modena
Genova
Pisa
Livorno
Elba
Bastia
Cap Corse
Mte. Cinto 2710
LIGURIAN SEA
G. di Genova
Corse (Fr.)
San Remo
MONACO
Monaco
Côte d'Azur
Nice
Cannes
St. Tropez
Îles d'Hyères
MEDITERRANEAN SEA
Toulon
Marseille
Arles
Avignon
Orange
PROVENCE
Montpellier
Nîmes
Golfe du Lion
Béziers
Narbonne
Perpignan
Millau
LANGUEDOC
Mende
Valence
Rhône
Lyon
St. Étienne
Loire
Roanne
Mâcon
Moulins
Montluçon
Clermont Ferrand
1886
AUVERGNE
Massif Central
Bourg-en-Bresse
Saône
Annecy
Genève
Chambéry
SAVOIE
Grenoble
Briançon
DAUPHINÉ
Durance
3053
3841
Torino
Po
4061
Aosta
Mt. Blanc 4807
Matterhorn 4477
Novara
45°
10°
5°
3
C
D
E

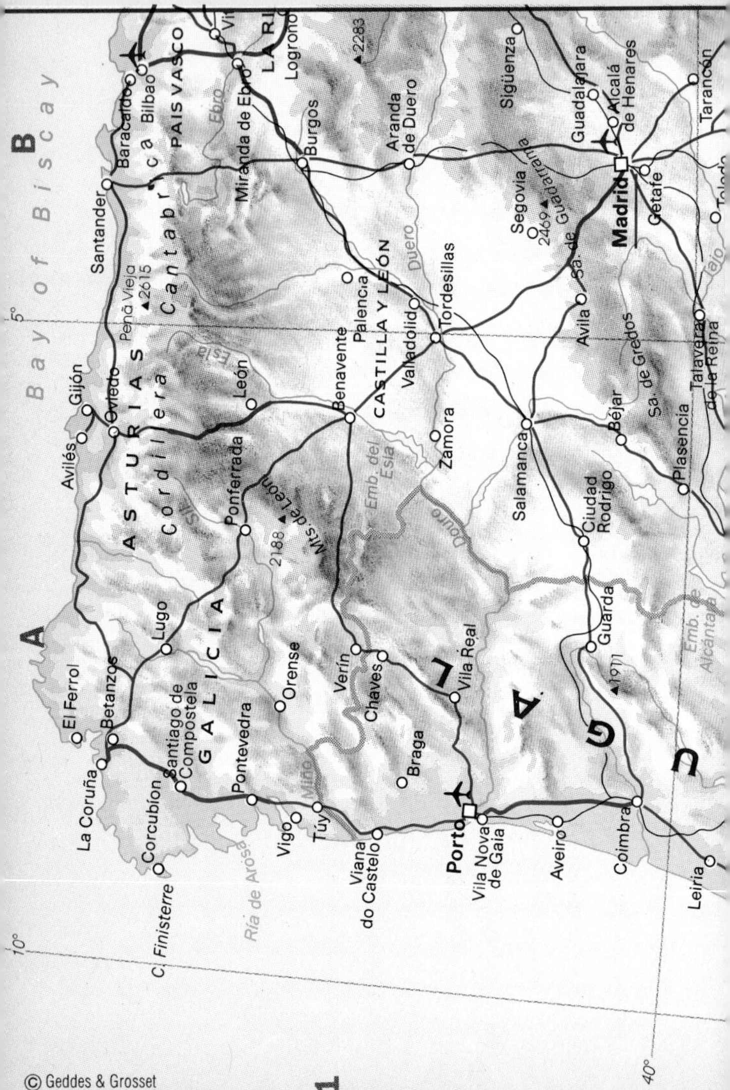
A
B
1
Bay of Biscay
La Coruña
El Ferrol
Betanzos
Corcubion
C. Finisterre
Santiago de Compostela
GALICIA
Lugo
Pontevedra
Ría de Arosa
Vigo
Túy
Miño
Orense
Avilés
Gijón
Oviedo
ASTURIAS
Cordillera Cantabrica
Peña Vieja 2615
Santander
Baracaldo
Bilbao
PAIS VASCO
Vitoria
Ebro
Miranda de Ebro
LA RIOJA
Logroño
2283
Burgos
Aranda de Duero
Sigüenza
Guadalajara
Alcalá de Henares
Madrid
Getafe
Toledo
Tarancón
Tajo
Segovia
2469
Guadarrama
Sa. de
Avila
Sa. de Gredos
Talavera de la Reina
Plasencia
Béjar
Salamanca
Ciudad Rodrigo
Palencia
Valladolid
Tordesillas
Duero
CASTILLA Y LEÓN
León
Esla
Benavente
Zamora
Emb. del Esla
Ponferrada
Mts. de León
2188
Douro
Guarda
1991
Emb. de Alcántara
Verín
Chaves
Vila Real
Braga
Porto
Vila Nova de Gaia
Viana do Castelo
Aveiro
Coimbra
Leiria
PORTUGAL
5°
10°
40°

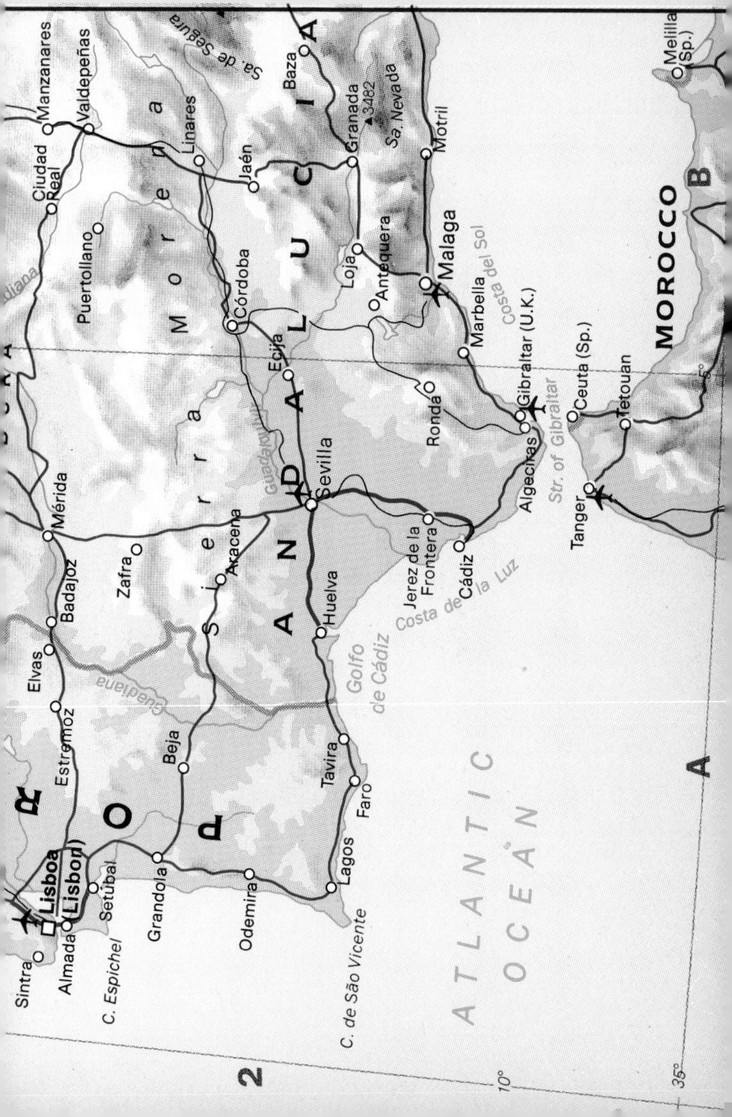
Manzanares
Valdepeñas
Ciudad Real
Puertollano
Linares
Sa. de Segura
Baza
Granada
3482
Sa. Nevada
Motril
Jaén
Córdoba
Loja
Antequera
Malaga
Marbella
Costa del Sol
Gibraltar (U.K.)
Ceuta (Sp.)
Melilla (Sp.)
MOROCCO
Tetouan
Tanger
Str. of Gibraltar
Algeciras
Ronda
Ecija
Guadalquivir
Sevilla
Mérida
Badajoz
Zafra
Aracena
Huelva
Jerez de la Frontera
Cádiz
Costa de la Luz
Golfo de Cádiz
Elvas
Guadiana
Estremoz
Beja
Tavira
Faro
Lagos
Lisboa (Lisbon)
Setúbal
Almada
Sintra
C. Espichel
Grandola
Odemira
C. de São Vicente
ATLANTIC OCEAN
Sierra Morena
ANDALUCIA
2
10°
5°
35°

Marseille
Montpellier
Golfe du Lion
Perpignan
Narbonne
Toulouse
FRANCE
GASCOGNE
ROUSSILLON
ANDORRA
Andorra la Vella
PYRÉNÉES
PIRINEOS
Pico de Aneto 3404
2883
3298
Viella
C. Creus
Figueras
Gerona
Costa Brava
Barcelona
Badalona
Sabadell
Tarrasa
CATALUÑA
Lérida
Valls
Tarragona
Costa Dorada
C. de Tortosa
Tortosa
Amposta
Ebro
Benicarló
Castellón de la Plana
Fraga
Cinca
Caspe
Alcañiz
ARAGÓN
2019
Sarrion
Teruel
Monreal del Campo
Daroca
Calatayud
Zaragoza
Tudela
Calahorra
Pamplona
NAVARRA
San Sebastián
Bayonne
RIOJA
Tajo
Serranía de Cuenca
Cuenca
SPAIN
Menorca (Minorca)
Mahón
Mallorca (Majorca)
B
C
D
1
0°
5°
40°
© Geddes & Grosset

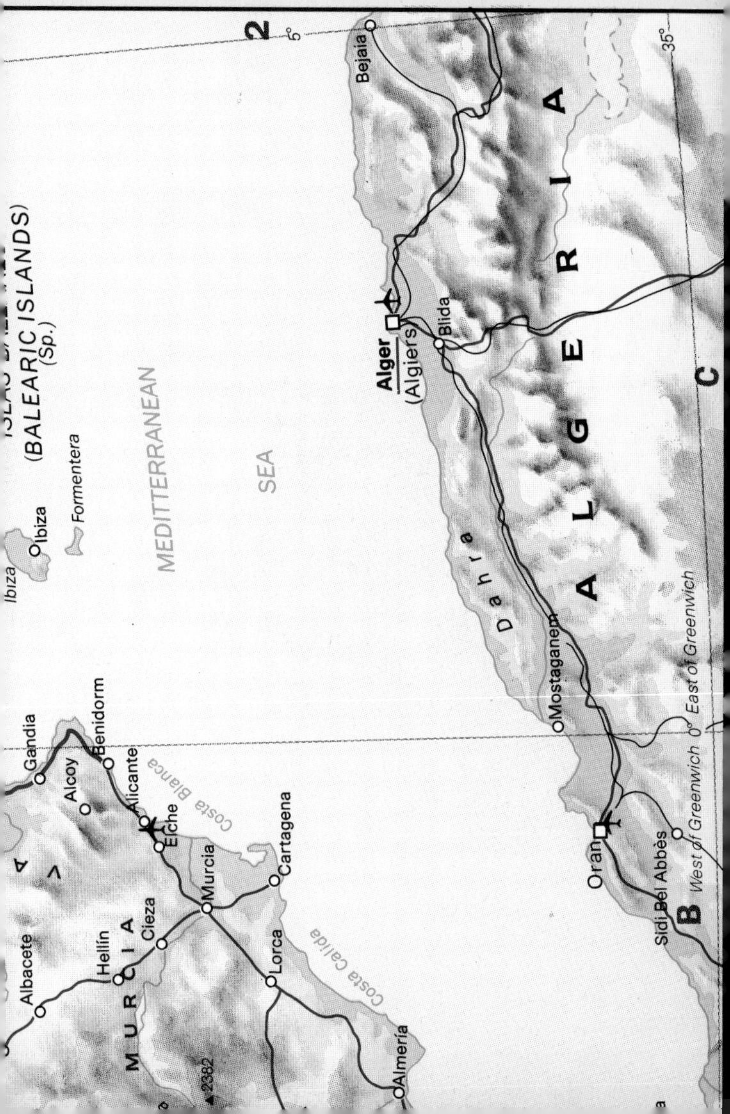
(BALEARIC ISLANDS)
(Sp.)
Ibiza
Ibiza
Formentera
MEDITTERRANEAN
SEA
Gandia
Alcoy
Benidorm
Alicante
Costa Blanca
Elche
Cartagena
Murcia
Cieza
Hellín
Albacete
MURCIA
Lorca
Costa Calida
Almería
2382
Bejaia
Alger
(Algiers)
Blida
ALGERIA
Dahra
Mostaganem
Oran
Sidi Bel Abbès
West of Greenwich
East of Greenwich
5°
35°
0°
2
B
C

A
B
1
2
Dijon
Biel
Zurich
Luzern
LIECHTEN-STEIN
Vaduz
Bern
FRANCHE-COMTE
Jura
SWITZERLAND
Rhein
Mâcon
Saône
Lausanne
L. Leman
Genève
Rhône
SAVOIE
Mt. Blanc 4807
4477
Matterhorn
Domodossola
L. Maggiore
L. di Como
Lyon
Aosta
Como
Monza
Bergamo
4061
Novara
Milano
Brescia
FRANCE
45°
Grenoble
DAUPHINE
Valence
Torino
Po
Piacenza
Alessandria
Rhône
Mondovi
Cuneo
Genova
Savona
Avignon
Durance
G. di Genova
La Spezia
PROVENCE
Nice
San Remo
Monaco
MONACO
LIGURIAN SEA
Massa
Marseille
Cannes
Pisa
Toulon
St. Tropez
Cecina
C. Corse
Piombino
Bastia
Elba
Calvi
Mt. Cinto 2710
Ajaccio
Cateraggio
CORSE (Fr.)
Porto Vecchio
Bonifacio

Salzburg
15°
Bruck an der Mur
AUSTRIA
Brenner P.
3798
Grossglockner
Graz
Raba
Villach
Tarvisio
Klagenfurt
3342
Maribor
Nagykanizsa
Varazdin
Kranj
Adige
Dolomiti
Udine
Ljubljana
Sava
Rovereto
Monfalcone
SLOVENIA
Zagreb
Treviso
Vicenza
Trieste
Karlovac
Sisak
Padova
Venezia
Vrbovsko
Rijeka
CROATIA
G. di Venezia
Rovigo
Istra
Krk
Seni
Ferrara
Pula
Cres
Rab.
Banja Luka
BOSNIA - HERZEGOVINA
Reno
Bologna
Lošinj
Gospić
Ravenna
Karlobag
ADRIATIC SEA
Pag
Jajce
Forli
Rimini
SAN MARINO
San Marino
Prato
Zadar
Dugi
DALMATIA
Fano
Firenze
Kornat
Livno
Šibenik
Ancona
Citta di Castello
Arezzo
Split
Siena
Civitanova Marche
Brač
Makarska
Perugia
ITALY
San Benedetto del Tronto
Vis
Hvar
1738
Foligno
Korčula
Grosseto
Terni
Lastovo
Viterbo
2912
Pescara
L'Aquila
Vasto
Termoli
Avezzano
Roma (Rome)
Ostia
Frosinone
S. Severo
Manfredonia
Cassino

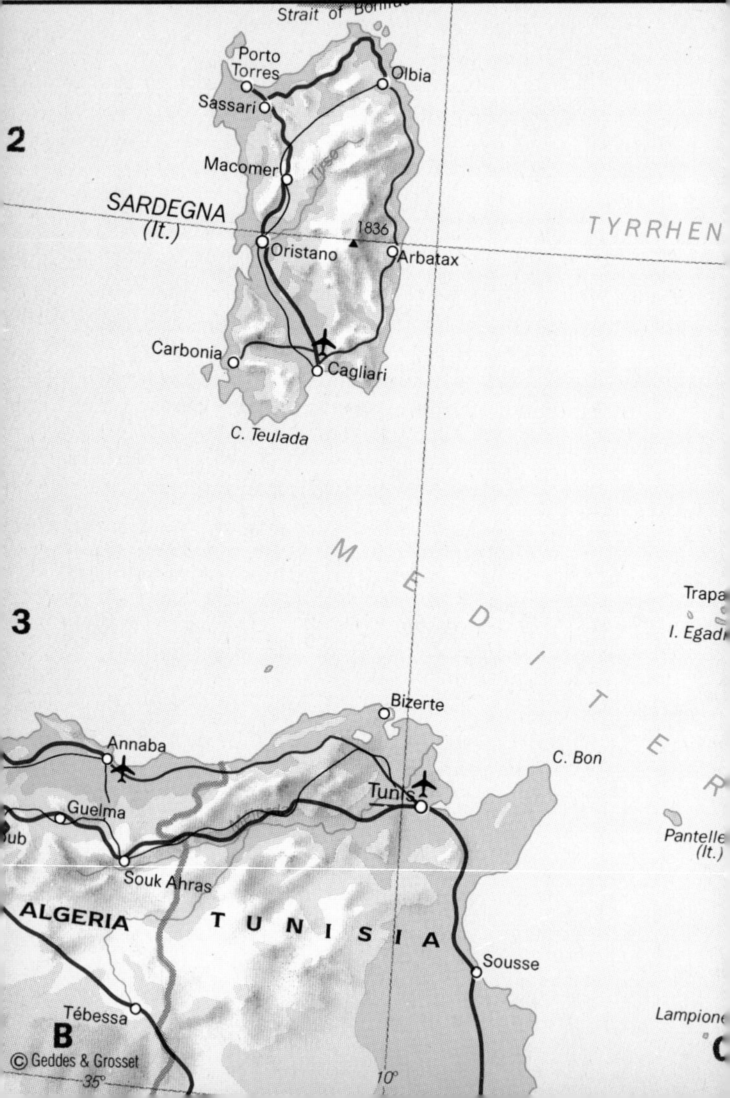

Strait of Bonifacio
Porto Torres
Olbia
Sassari
2
Macomer
Tirso
SARDEGNA (It.)
1836
TYRRHEN
Oristano
Arbatax
Carbonia
Cagliari
C. Teulada
M E D I T E R
3
Trapa
I. Egad
Bizerte
Annaba
C. Bon
Tunis
Guelma
Pantelle (It.)
Souk Ahras
ALGERIA
TUNISIA
Sousse
Tébessa
Lampione
B
35°
10°

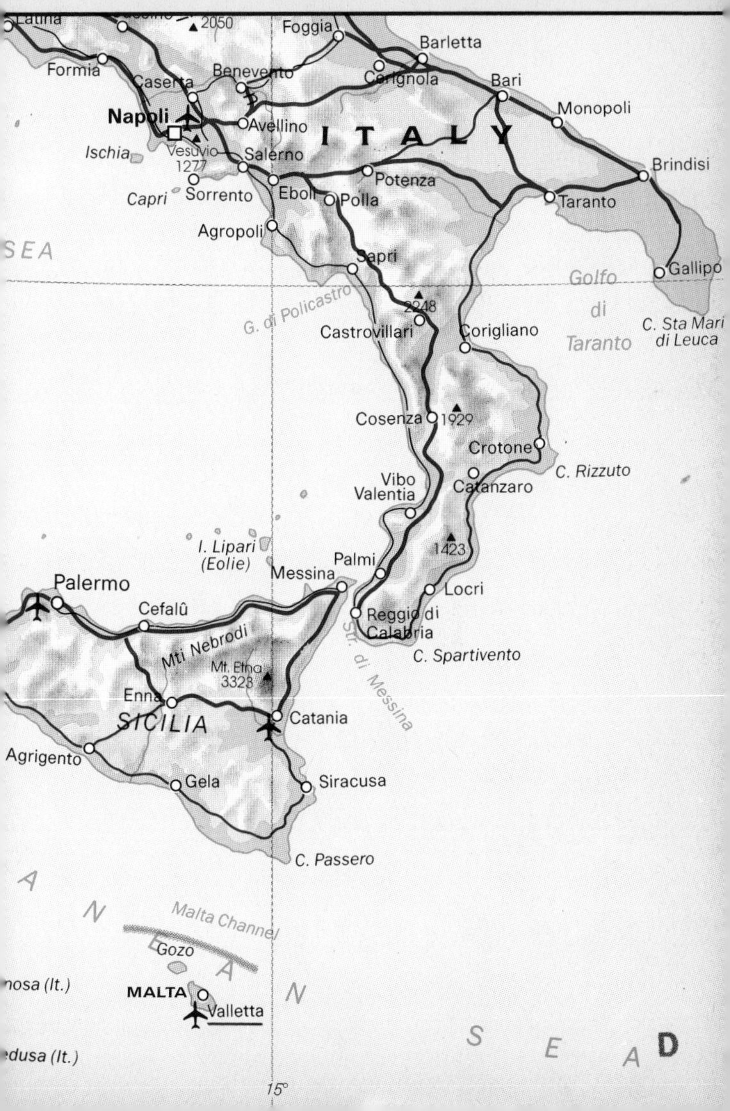
Formia
Caserta
Benevento
Foggia
Barletta
Cerignola
Bari
Monopoli
Napoli
Avellino
ITALY
Ischia
Vesuvio
1277
Salerno
Capri
Sorrento
Eboli
Polla
Potenza
Brindisi
Taranto
Agropoli
SEA
Sapri
Gallipo
Golfo
di
Taranto
G. di Policastro
2248
Castrovillari
Corigliano
C. Sta Mari
di Leuca
Cosenza
1929
Crotone
C. Rizzuto
Vibo
Valentia
Catanzaro
I. Lipari
(Eolie)
1423
Palmi
Messina
Palermo
Locri
Cefalû
Reggio di
Calabria
C. Spartivento
Str. di Messina
Mti Nebrodi
Mt. Etna
3328
Enna
SICILIA
Catania
Agrigento
Gela
Siracusa
C. Passero
Malta Channel
Gozo
MALTA
Valletta
D
15°

MACEDONIA
Gevgelija
Durrës
Tiranë
Ohrid
Bitola
Ohridsko ezero
Prespansko ezero
Monopoli
Berat
2480
Kastoria
Brindisi
Korcë
Vlorë
Katerini
Taranto
ALBANIA
2503
Aliakmon
Olimbos
2917
Strait of Otranto
Gallipoli
Golfo di Taranto
Kalabáka
Ioannina
Lárisa
C. Sta Maria di Leuca
Kérkira
Kérkira (Corfu)
GREECE
Piniós
Igoumenítsa
Árta
1726
Lamía
IÓNIOI NÍSOI
Pindhos
C. Rizzuto
Amfilokhia
Levkás
Mesolóngian
Pátrai
Kefallinía
Kórinth
Pelopónnisos
IONIAN SEA
Pírgos
Zákinthos
Tripolis
Kalámai
Pílos
Messiniakós Kólpos
D
20°

Sea of Marmara
Marmara
Kavála
Alexandroúpolis
Thásos
Bandirma
Bursa
Gelibolu
K. Strimonikós
Samothráki
Eceabat
Çanakkale
Gökçeada
2033
K. Singitikós
Límnos
Balikesir
Simav
Edremit
Ayvalik
Áyios Evstrátios
Akhisar
Iliodhrómia
Lésvos
TURKEY
Skópelos
Skiros
Manisa
Évvoia
AEGEAN SEA
Izmir
Khalkis
Khíos
Selçuk
Athínai (Athens)
Ándros
Sámos
Ikaría
Kéa
Tinos
Mikonos
Muğla
Síros
DHODHEKÁNISOS
Léros
Bodrum
Kíthnos
KIKLÁDHES
Kálimnos
Ídhra
Sérifos
Páros
Náxos
Marmaris
Kós
Mirtoan Sea
Sífnos
Amorgós
Ródhos
Síkinos
Íos
Mílos
Astipálaia
Tílos
Ródhos (Rhodes)
Thíra
Anáfi
Kárpathos
Sea of Crete
Kríti (Crete)
Khaniá
Iráklion
Kásos
Akr. Sídheros
2456
Timbákion
35°
25°
40°
2
3
F

D
E
Győr
Budapest
20°
Tisza
Debrecen
Karcag
Szekesfehèrvar
Szolnok
Oradea
Cluj-
Kecskemet
Salonta
HUNGARY
Kiskunfelegyháza
1836
Balaton
Duna
Turda
1849
Szekszárd
Szeged
Makó
Arad
Seb
Pécs
Subotica
Mureş
Deva
Timişoara
ROM
Osijek
Caransebeş
CROATIA
Tisza
Bosanski Brod
Dunav
Novi Sad
Vršac
Ruma
Beograd (Belgrade)
Dobreta-Turnu-Severin
Šabac
Sava
Bosna
Tuzla
Loznica
Craio
BOSNIA-HERZEGOVINA
Morava
YUGOSLAVIA
Drina
Svetozarevo
Kragujevac
Vidin
Zenica
Sarajevo
Paraćin
Čačak
Lo
SERBIA
Konjic
Kruševac
2169
2032
Niš
Pirot
Mostar
Novi Pazar
2522
Leskovac
Blace
Kosovska-Mitrovica
Ivangrad
Priština
Sofiya (Sofia)
Mljet
CRO.
MONTENEGRO
Peć
Vranje
Dubrovnik
Podgorica
Uroševac
Kotor
2692
2252
Skadarsko Jez
Shkodër
2702
Kumanovo
Skopje
ALBANIA
Drin
Titov Veles
MACEDONIA

F
G
1
2
25°
30°
45°
Carpathian Mts.
Meridionali
2543
Mureş
Tîrgu Mureş
Iaşi
Chisinau
Odessa
Roman
MOLDOVA
Bacău
Siret
Prut
UKRAINE
Bîrlad
Tecuci
Focşani
Braşov
Galati
Izmail
Brăila
Buzău
Cîmpina
Ploieşti
Urziceni
Hîrşova
Bucureşti
(Bucharest)
Medgidia
Constanţa
Dunărea
Slatina
Videle
Caracal
Mangalia
Giurgiu
Ruse
Ludogorie
Tolbukhin
Olt
Razgrad
Byala
Šumen
Varna
Pleven
BLACK
SEA
Veliko Turnovo
Sliven
Planina
Kazanlŭk
Burgas
BULGARIA
Stara Zagora
Michurin
Dimitrovgrad
Plovdiv
Edirne
Babaeski
Rodopi Planina
TURKEY
Çorlu
Istanbul
Üsküdar
Néstos
Dráma
Xánthi
Komotiní

A
B
1
2
5°
55°
NORTH SEA
Esbjerg
Flensb
Cuxhaven
Wilhelmshaven
Leeuwarden
Groningen
Den Helder
Oldenburg
Bremerhaven
Bremen
IJsselmeer
Zaandam
Haarlem
Amsterdam
NETHERLANDS
's-Gravenhage
Utrecht
Apeldoorn
Enschede
Osnabrück
Rotterdam
Arnhem
Hanno
Nijmegen
Münster
Rhein
Tilburg
Wesel
Breda
Hamm
Paderborn
Eindhoven
Oostende
Duisburg
Dortmund
BELGIUM
Antwerpen
Essen
Gent
Krefeld
Hagen

C
D
10°
15°
Göteborg
Jönköping
Frederikshavn
Ålborg
SWEDEN
Kattegat
Växjö
Halmstad
Kalmar
Randers
Öland
Århus
Helsingør
Helsingborg
Kristianstad
Karlskrona
NMARK
København
(Copenhagen)
Lund
Odense
Malmö
Ystad
Fyn
Sjaelland
Rønne
Bornholm
Lolland
Rødbyhavn
Falster
BALTIC SEA
Puttgarden
Sassnitz
Kiel
Stralsund
Rügen
übeck
Rostock
Koszalin
Schwerin
Szczecinek
Hamburg
Neubrandenburg
Chojnice
Szczecin
Elbe
Oder
DERAL REPUBLIC OF GERMANY
Piła
POLAND
Wolfsburg
Gorzów Wielkopolski
Potsdam
Berlin
Braunschweig
Poznań
Gniezn
Salzgitter-Bad
Magdeburg
Spree
Dessau
Zielona Gora
Cottbus
Halle
en
Bor

D
E
20°
25°
Visby
Gotland
Gulf of Riga
Ventspils
Riga
LA
Dvina
Jelgava
Liepāja
BALTIC
SEA
Šiauliai
Panevežys
Klaipeda
LITHUANIA
Šilute
Ukme
Kaunas
Vilni
Gulf of Danzig
Kaliningrad
Gusev
Gdynia
RUSSIA
Gdańsk
Elblag
Augustow
Olsztyn
Grodno
Tucholskie
Wista
Nema
Grudziadz
Bydgoszcz
Mława
Białystok
Toruń
POLAND
Włocławek
Bug
Warszawa
(Warsaw)
Siedlce
Brest
Kobri
Konin
Kalisz
Łódź
Radom

F
G
30°
Ostrov
RUSSIA
Rzhev
1
A
Velikiye-Luki
Rezekne
Polotsk
Novopolotsk
Dvina
Vitebsk
55
Smolensk
Lepel'
Orsha
Borisov
Molodechno
Mogilev
Minsk
BELARUS
Bobruysk
2
Baranovichi
Dneprovskaya
Soligorsk
Gomel
Rechitsa
Dnepr
Mozyr
Pinsk
Pripyat
Nizmennost'
Chernigov
Nezhin
Sarny
UKRAINE

Lublin
Kovel'
Bug
Kepno
Kielce
Częstochowa
Opole
POLAND
Wisla
Bytom
Sosnowiec
Gliwice
Katowice
Rybnik
Kraków
Rzeszów
Tarnów
Przemys'l
Ostrava
CZECH REPUBLIC
Beskidy Zachodnie
Stryy
Žilina
2655
SLOVAKIA
Košice
Uzhgorod
Nitra
Miskolc
Nyíregyháza
Satu Mare
HUNGARY
Baia M
Győr
Budapest
Tisza
Debrecen
Karcag
Székesfehérvár
Szolnok
Oradea
Balaton
Kecskemét
Cluj-N
Salonta
1836
Duna
Kiskunfélegyháza
Turda
1849
anizsa
Szekszárd
Szeged
Makó
Arad
Mures
Pécs
Deva
Timişoara
YUGOSLAVIA
CROATIA
R
O
M
Caransebeş
Osijek
E
© Geddes & Grosset
Novi Sad
20°

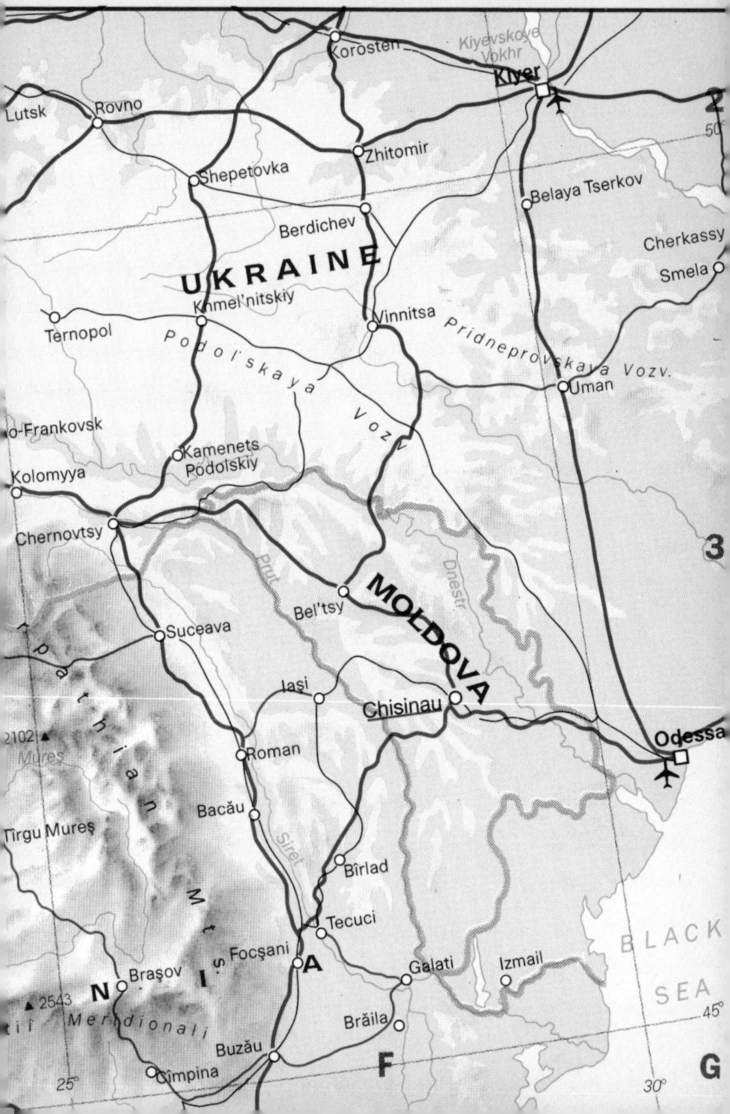
Korosten
Kiyevskoye Vdkhr
Kiyev
Lutsk
Rovno
Zhitomir
Shepetovka
Belaya Tserkov
Berdichev
Cherkassy
Smela
UKRAINE
Khmel'nitskiy
Ternopol
Vinnitsa
Podol'skaya Vozv.
Pridneprovskaya Vozv.
Uman
o-Frankovsk
Kamenets Podolskiy
Kolomyya
Chernovtsy
Prut
Dnestr
MOLDOVA
Bel'tsy
Suceava
Iaşi
Chisinau
Odessa
2102
Mureş
Roman
Bacău
Tîrgu Mureş
Siret
Bîrlad
Tecuci
Focşani
Galati
Izmail
BLACK SEA
Braşov
2543
Meridionali
Brăila
Buzău
Cîmpina
25°
30°
45°
50°
2
3
F
G

Maastricht
Kassel
Lille
Bruxelles
(Brussels)
Aachen
Köln
Siegen
Bonn
Charleroi
Liège
Marburg
Valenciennes
BELGIUM
50°
Ardennes
Koblenz
St-Quentin
Frankfurt
Offenbach
LUXEMBOURG
Mosel
Mainz
Darmstadt
Luxembourg
Meuse
FEDERAL
Reims
Thionville
Marne
Mannheim
Heidelberg
Châlons-sur-Marne
Metz
Saarbrücken
Vitry-le-François
Rhein
Sézanne
Karlsruhe
Nancy
Stuttgart
Troyes
St. Dizier
Sens
Strasbourg
FRANCE
CHAMPAGNE
LORRAINE
Seine
Vosges
Chaumont
Colmar
Ulm
Schwarzwald
Freiburg
ALSACE
Langres
BOURGOGNE
3
Mulhouse
Belfort
Montbéliard
Dijon
Basel
Bodensee
Besançon
Zürich
Biel
LIECHTENSTEIN
FRANCHE-COMTÉ
Jura
Luzern
Bern
Vaduz
Saône
Rhein
Mâcon
SWITZERLAND
Lausanne
Léman
Genève
Rhône
Lyon
SAVOIE
ALPS
Domodossola
Sondrio
Mt. Blanc
4807
Matterhorn
4477
Aosta
Como
IT
Bergamo
4061
Rhône
45°
Novara
Milano
Grenoble
Valence
Torino
Piacenza
A
B
5°
10°

Leipzig
Jena
Erfurt
Gera
Dresden
Chemnitz
Zwickau
POLAND
Wroclaw
Jelenia Góra
Liberec
Usti
Erzgebirge
Kladno
Hradec-Králové
1490
Jeseniky
Praha
(Prague)
Bamberg
Bayreuth
BLIC
Plzeň
CZECH REPUBLIC
Erlangen
Nürnberg
Olomouc
Böhmerwald
Jihlava
Regensburg
1452
(Danube)
České Budějovice
Brno
Znojmo
Augsburg
Donau
Linz
Wien
(Vienna)
München
Bratislava
Salzburg
Enns
AUSTRIA
Bruck an der Mur
Brenner P.
3798
Grossglockner
Rába
Graz
Villach
Klagenfurt
Bolzano
3342
Dolomiti
Drava
Maribor
Tarvisio
Kranj
Nagyk
Trento
Varazdin
Udine
Ljubljana
Monfalcone
Sava
SLOVENIA
Zagreb
Treviso
Trieste
Venezia
CROATIA
Padova
C
Rijeka
D
© Geddes & Grosset

SCANDINAVIA & THE BALTIC (N)

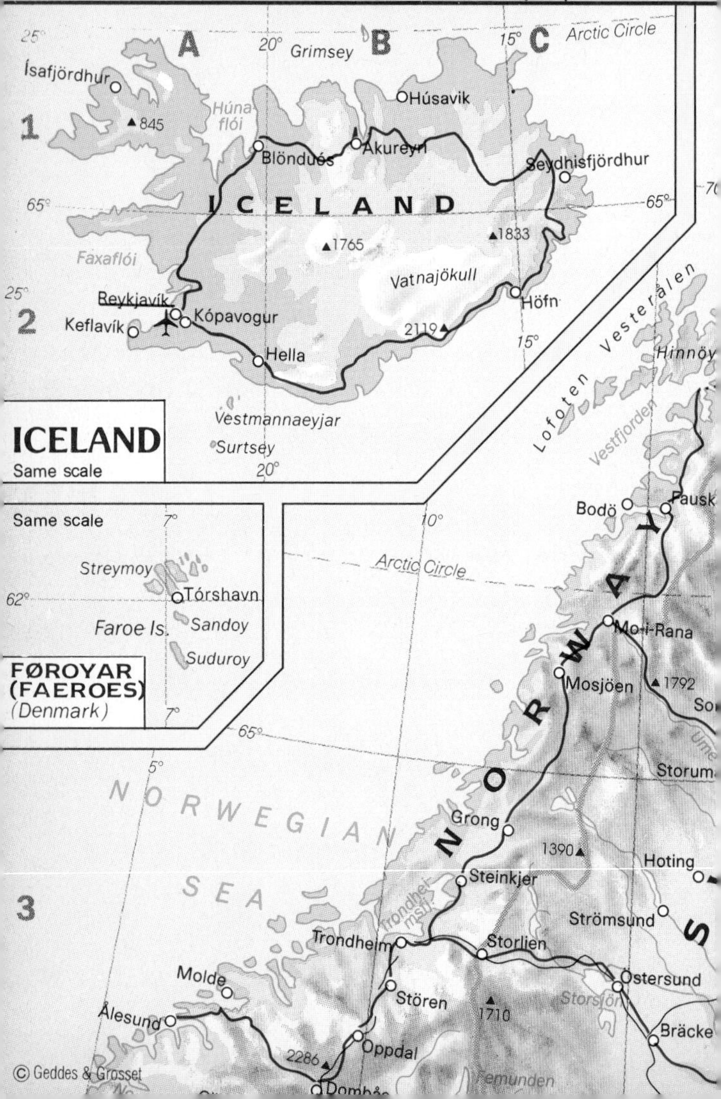

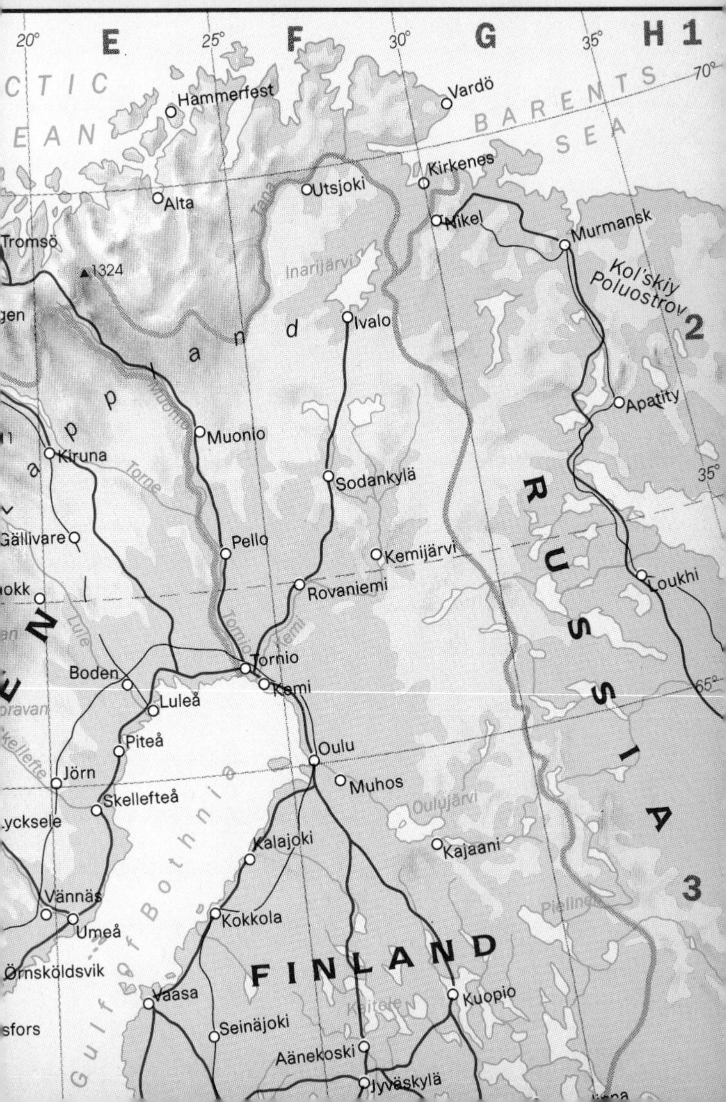

E
F
G
H
1
2
3
20°
25°
30°
35°
70°
65°
ARCTIC OCEAN
BARENTS SEA
Hammerfest
Vardö
Kirkenes
Alta
Utsjoki
Tana
Nikel
Murmansk
Tromsö
1324
Inarijärvi
Kol'skiy Poluostrov
Ivalo
Lappland
Apatity
Muonio
Kiruna
Torne
Sodankylä
Gällivare
Pello
Kemijärvi
Rovaniemi
Loukhi
RUSSIA
Tornio
Kemi
Boden
Luleå
Lule
Piteå
Oulu
Jörn
Muhos
Skellefteå
Oulujärvi
Lycksele
Kajaani
Kalajoki
Gulf of Bothnia
Vännäs
Umeå
Kokkola
Pielinen
FINLAND
Örnsköldsvik
Vaasa
Kuopio
Seinäjoki
Äänekoski
Jyväskylä

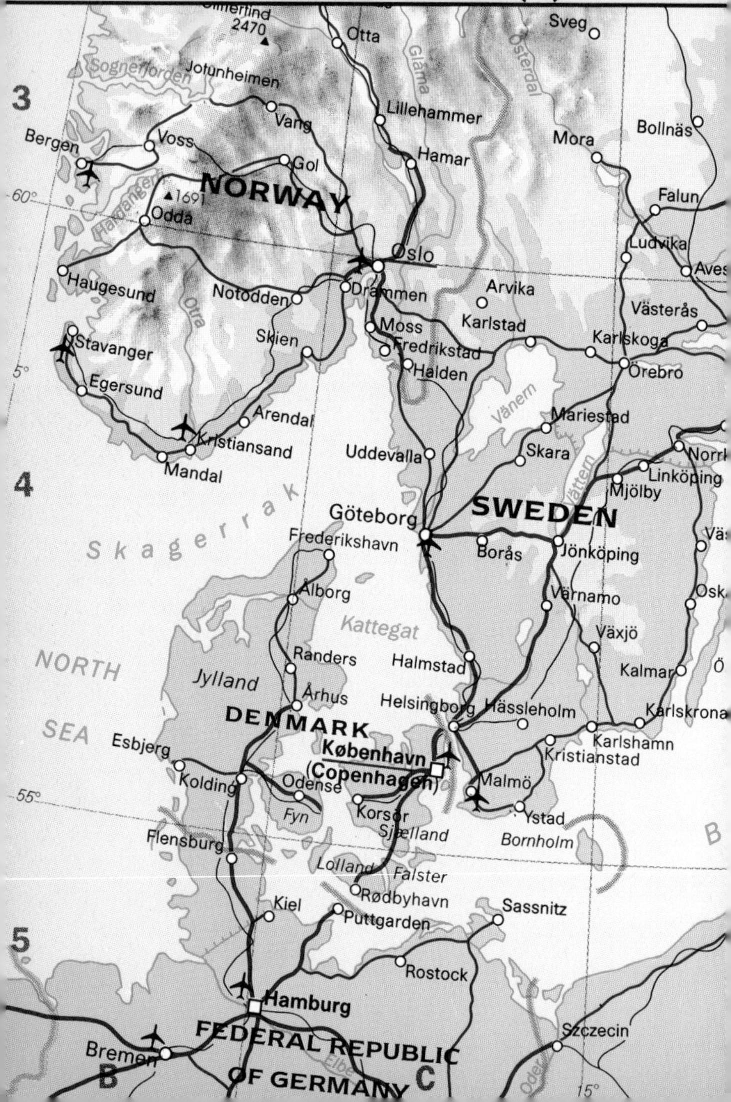
2470
Otta
Sveg
Glåma
Österdal
Sognefjorden
Jotunheimen
3
Vang
Lillehammer
Bollnäs
Bergen
Voss
Mora
Gol
Hamar
NORWAY
60°
1691
Falun
Hardanger
Odda
Ludvika
Oslo
Haugesund
Avesta
Drammen
Arvika
Notodden
Västerås
Otra
Moss
Karlstad
Skien
Karlskoga
Stavanger
Fredrikstad
Halden
Örebro
5°
Egersund
Vänern
Mariestad
Arendal
Kristiansand
Uddevalla
Skara
Mandal
Linköping
Vättern
4
Mjölby
Göteborg
SWEDEN
Skagerrak
Frederikshavn
Borås
Jönköping
Ålborg
Värnamo
Kattegat
Växjö
NORTH
Randers
Halmstad
Kalmar
Jylland
Århus
Helsingborg
Hässleholm
DENMARK
Karlskrona
SEA
Esbjerg
København
(Copenhagen)
Karlshamn
Kristianstad
Kolding
Odense
Malmö
55°
Fyn
Korsør
Ystad
Sjælland
Bornholm
Flensburg
B
Lolland
Falster
Rødbyhavn
Kiel
Sassnitz
Puttgarden
5
Rostock
Hamburg
FEDERAL REPUBLIC
OF GERMANY
Szczecin
Bremen
Elbe
Oder
B
C
15°

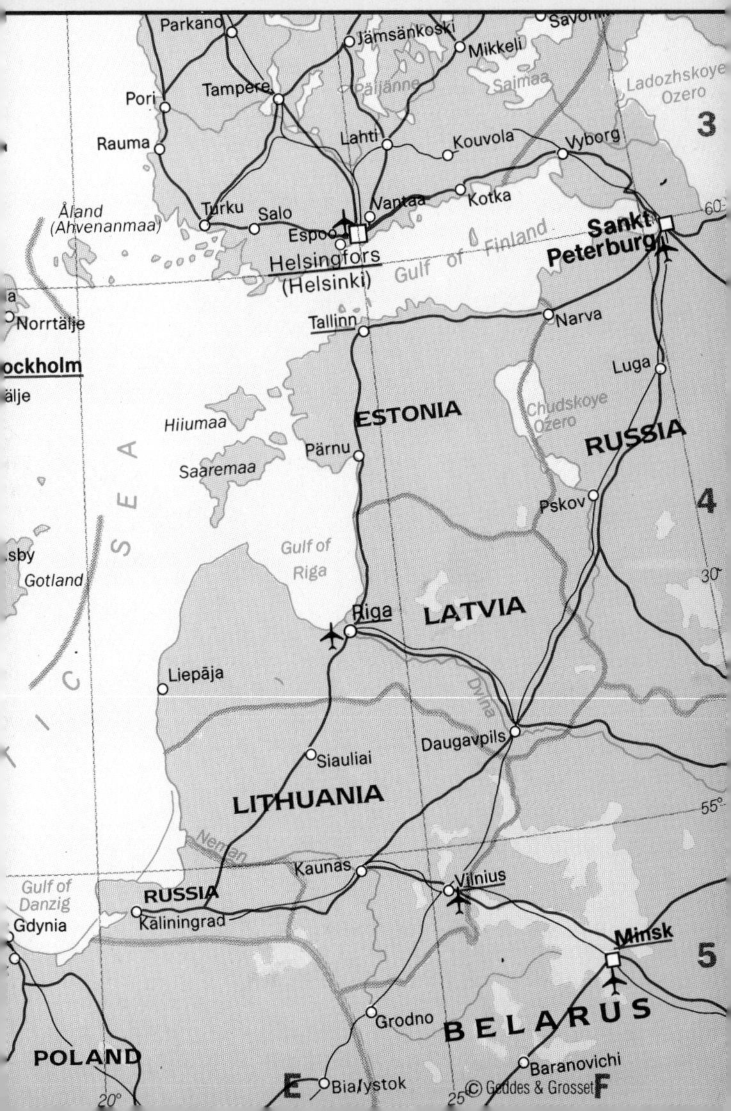
Parkano
Jämsänkoski
Mikkeli
Päijänne
Saimaa
Ladozhskoye Ozero
Pori
Tampere
Rauma
Lahti
Kouvola
Vyborg
3
Åland (Ahvenanmaa)
Turku
Salo
Vantaa
Kotka
Espoo
Helsingfors (Helsinki)
Gulf of Finland
Sankt Peterburg
60°
Norrtälje
ockholm
älje
Tallinn
Narva
Luga
ESTONIA
Hiiumaa
Chudskoye Ozero
RUSSIA
Pärnu
Saaremaa
Pskov
4
Gulf of Riga
sby
Gotland
30°
Riga
LATVIA
Liepāja
Dvina
Daugavpils
Siauliai
LITHUANIA
55°
Neman
Kaunas
Vilnius
Gulf of Danzig
RUSSIA
Kaliningrad
Gdynia
Minsk
5
Grodno
BELARUS
POLAND
Baranovichi
E
Bialystok
F
20°
25°
© Geddes & Grosset

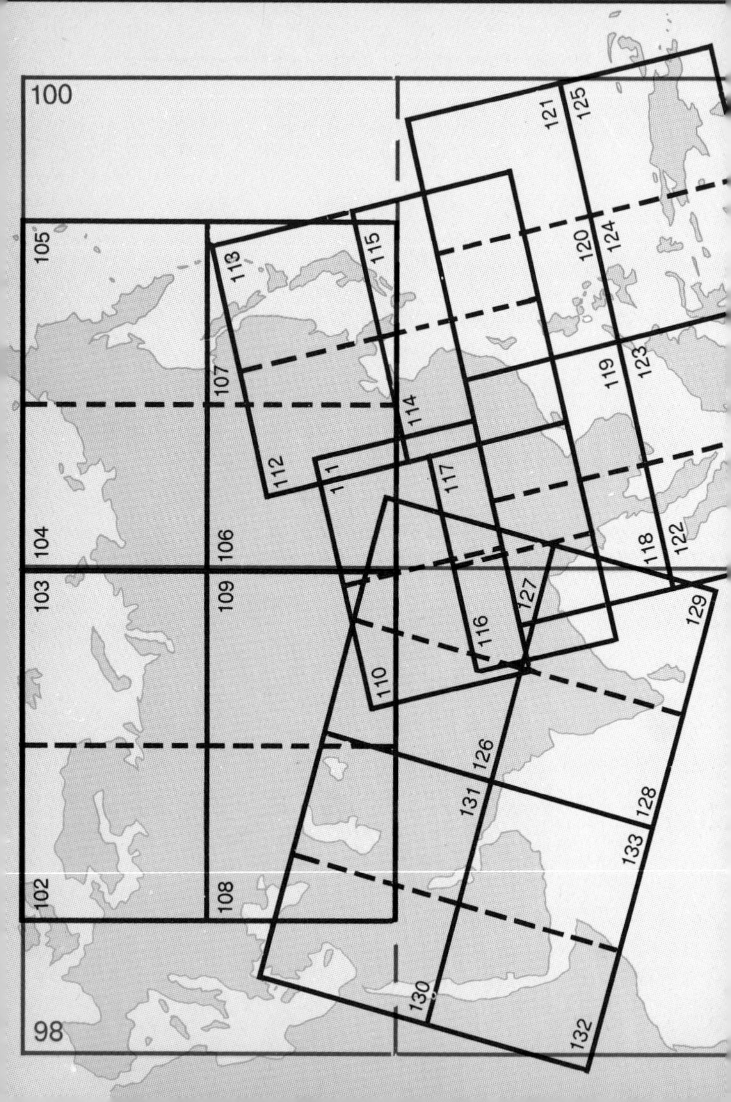
100
121
125
105
113
115
120
124
107
119
123
114
112
117
104
106
118
122
103
109
127
129
116
110
126
131
128
133
102
108
130
98
132

ARCTIC OCEAN
BARENTS SEA
BALTIC SEA
BLACK SEA
MEDITERRANEAN SEA
ARAL SEA
Novaya Zemlya
Yenisey
Ob
Irtysh
Volga
Don
Ural
Danube
Syrdar'ya
Ozero Balkhash
R U S S I A
E U R O P E
K A Z A K H S T A N
T U R K E Y
NORWAY
SWEDEN
FINLAND
ESTONIA
LATVIA
LITHUANIA
BELARUS
UKRAINE
MOL.
GEORGIA
ARMENIA
AZERBAIJAN
UZBEKISTAN
CYPRUS
Krasnoyarsk
Novosibirsk
Omsk
Yekaterinburg
Chelyabinsk
Ürümqi
Almaty
Bishkek
Tashkent
Murmansk
Archangel
Sankt Peterburg
Nizhniy Novgorod
Moskva
Rostov-na-Donu
Astrakhan
Tbilisi
Baku
Yerevan
Stockholm
Tallinn
Riga
Vilnius
Minsk
Khar'kov
Kiyev
Odessa
Chişinau
Bucureşti
Warszawa
Berlin
Praha
Bratislava
Budapest
Wien
Beograd
Istanbul
Ankara
Izmir
Beyrouth
London
Amsterdam
Bruxelles
Lux.
Paris
Bern
Roma
Tiranë
Athinai
100°
80°
60°
40°
20°
0°
20°
70°
60°
50°
40°
30°
© Geddes & Grosset

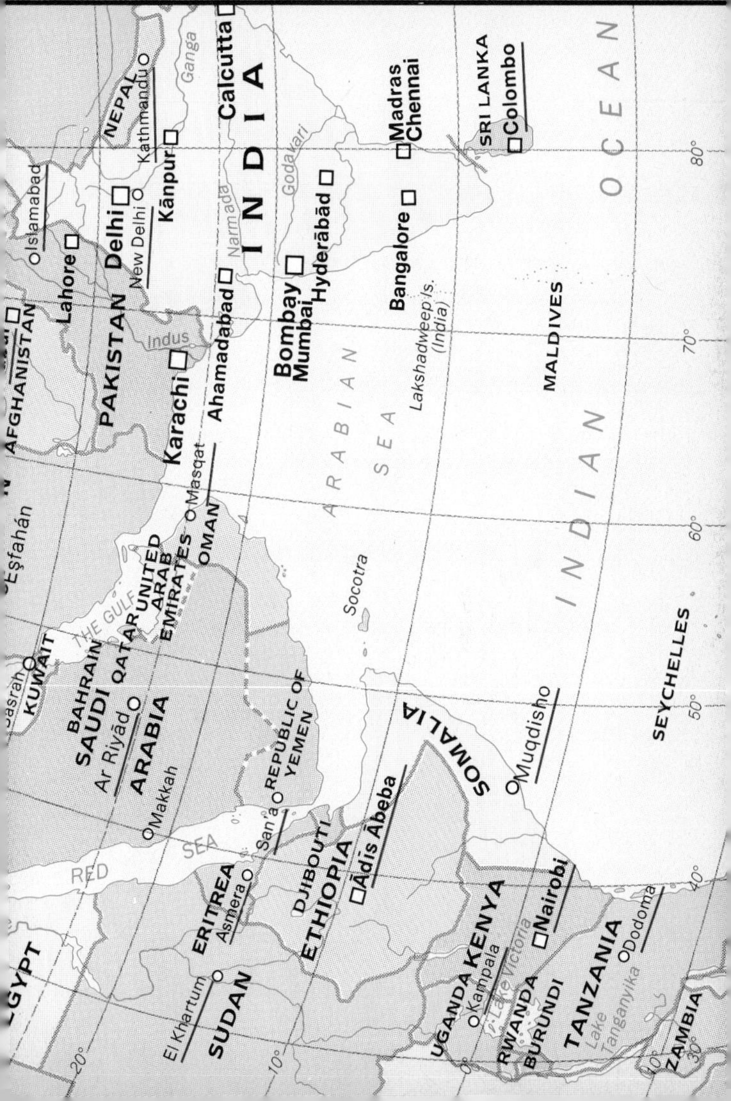
AFGHANISTAN
Islamabad
Lahore
PAKISTAN
Indus
Karachi
NEPAL
Kathmandu
Ganga
Calcutta
INDIA
Delhi
New Delhi
Kānpur
Narmada
Ahamadabad
Bombay
Mumbai
Godavari
Hyderābād
Bangalore
Madras
Chennai
SRI LANKA
Colombo
Lakshadweep Is.
(India)
MALDIVES
ARABIAN SEA
INDIAN OCEAN
Eşfahān
Masqat
OMAN
UNITED ARAB EMIRATES
THE GULF
QATAR
BAHRAIN
KUWAIT
SAUDI ARABIA
Ar Riyād
Makkah
REPUBLIC OF YEMEN
San'a
Socotra
SEYCHELLES
SOMALIA
Muqdisho
RED SEA
ERITREA
Asmera
DJIBOUTI
ETHIOPIA
Ādis Ābeba
EGYPT
SUDAN
El Khartum
KENYA
Nairobi
UGANDA
Kampala
Lake Victoria
RWANDA
BURUNDI
TANZANIA
Dodoma
Lake Tanganyika
ZAMBIA
80°
70°
60°
50°
40°
30°
20°
10°
0°
10°

RUSSIA
MONGOLIA
JAPAN
NORTH KOREA
SOUTH KOREA
ARCTIC OCEAN
BERING SEA
SEA OF OKHOTSK
SEA OF JAPAN
Aleutian Is.
Kuril Is.
Sakhalin
Hokkaidō
Honshū
Kyūshū
Sapporo
Tōkyō
Yokohama
Ōsaka
Kita-Kyūshū
Sŏul
P'yŏngyang
Vladivostok
Khabarovsk
Magadan
Yakutsk
Irkutsk
Ulaanbaatar
Harbin
Changchun
Shenyang
Beijing
Tianjin
Qingdao
Amur
Lena
Angara
Ozero Baykal
Arctic Circle
Tropic of Cancer
20°
30°
40°
50°
60°
70°
120°
140°
160°
180°
© Geddes & Grosset

P A C I F I C O C
PAPUA NEW GUINEA
New Guinea
Irian Jaya
Equator 0°
10°
AUSTRALIA
ARAFURA SEA
140°
130°
120°
110°
100°
90°
Halmahera
PHILIPPINES
Mindanao
Timor
I N D O N E S I A
Ujung Pandang
Sulawesi
CELEBES SEA
SULU SEA
Luzon
Manila
TAIWAN
T'ai-pei
SEA
HONG KONG
Guangzhou
Macau (Port.)
Hainan Dao
SOUTH CHINA SEA
JAVA SEA
Borneo
BRUNEI
Surabaya
Jawa
Jakarta
Palembang
SINGAPORE
Kuala Lumpur
M A L A Y S I A
Ho Chi Minh City
VIETNAM
Mekong
Chongqing
Kunming
Hanoi
LAOS
Vientiane
CAMBODIA
Phnom Penh
Gulf of Thailand
THAILAND
Bangkok
Sumatera
Medan
Rangoon
MYANMAR (BURMA)
Andaman Is. (India)
Nicobar Is. (India)
BENGAL
Lhasa
BHUTAN
Thimphu
BANGLA-DESH
Dhaka
Brahmaputra
C H

4
3
60°
70°
10°
0°
20°
50°
Arctic Circle
West from Greenwich
East from Greenwich
NORWEGIAN SEA
NORTH SEA
UNITED KINGDOM
Glasgow
Aberdeen
Bergen
Trondheim
NORWAY
Narvik
Oslo
Göteborg
SWEDEN
København (Copenhagen)
DENMARK
Malmö
Hamburg
FEDERAL REPUBLIC OF GERMANY
Berlin
Gulf of Bothnia
Stockholm
BALTIC SEA
Turku
Oulu
FINLAND
Kandalaksha
Tampere
Helsingfors (Helsinki)
Petrozavodsk
Severodvinsk
Ladozhskoye Ozero
Onezhskoye Ozero
Kaliningrad
Klaipeda
ESTONIA
Tallinn
LATVIA
Riga
LITHUANIA
Poznan
Lodz
POLAND
Wroclaw
Warszawa (Warsaw)
Kraków
Sankt Peterburg
Pskov
Daugavpils
Vilnius
Minsk
BELARUS
Vitebsk
Brest
L'viv
Chernovtsy
ROMANIA
UKRAINE
Zhitomir
Vinnitsa
Pripyat
Chernigov
Gomel
Mogilev
Dnepr
Dnestr
Kiyev
Desna
Smolensk
Bryansk
Serpukhov
Tula
Moskva (Moscow)
Tver'
Yaroslavl'
Cherepovets
Andropov
Vologda
Sukhona
Ivanovo
Vladimir
Volga

A
B
C
D
E
F
G
H
J
K
1
80°
10°
20°
30°
40°
50°
60°
70°
80°
Spitsbergen
Svalbard
(Norway)
Edgeøya
Nordaustlandet
ARCTIC OCEAN
Zemlya Frantsa Iosifa
BARENTS SEA
Novaya Zemlya
KARA SEA
O. Kolguyev
O. Vaygach
Poluostrov Yamal
Gydanskiy Poluostrov
RUSSIA
Pechora
Nar'yan Mar
Vorkuta
Labytnangi
Ob
Obskaya Guba
Noril'sk
Yenisey
Igarka
Ukhta
Syktyvkar
Uralskiy Khrebet
G. Narodnaya 1894

1
170°
80°
U
160°
T
150°
140°
S
130°
ARCTIC
OCEAN
120°
110°
100°
R
Q
P
O
N
M
L
Novosibirskiye
Ostrova
O. Faddeyevskiy
O. Novaya Sibir
EAST
O. Komsomolets
O. Oktyabr'skoy
Revolyutsii
Severnaya Zemlya
O. Bol'shevik
O. Bol'shoy
Lyakhovskiy
O. Kotel'nyy
LAPTEV
SEA
Gory
Byrranga
Ozero
Taymyr
oluostrov
Taymyr
Lena
Khrebet Orulgan
Gory
Putorana
RUSSIA
Verkhoyans
Sredne
Yakutsk

3
4
70°
60°
CHUKCHI SEA
Arctic Circle
Chukotskiy Poluostrov
St. Lawrence (U.S.A.)
O. Vrangelya
Chukotskiy Khrebet
BERING SEA
Koryakskiy Khrebet
Khrebet Kolymskiy
Kolyma
Ust'Kamchatsk
Klyuchevskaya Sopka
Klyuchevskaya 4750
Sredinnyy Khrebet
Kamchatka
Petropavlovsk Kamchatskiy
Zaliv Shelikhova
Cherskogo
Magadan
Okhotsk
Dzhugdzhur
SEA OF OKHOTSK
180°
170°
160°
50°

Tunguska
3
Suntar
Sibirskoye
Ald
Ploskogorye
RUSSIA
Stan
Yeniseysk
Angara
Bratsk
Krasnoyarsk
Ozero Baykal
Skovorod
Shilka
Yenisey
Tulun
Khrebet
Chita
Abakan
Zapadnyy Sayan
Vostochnyy Sayan
Cheremkhovo
Irkutsk
Angarsk
Ulan Ude
Yablonovyy
Borzya
Manzhouli
Kyzyl
Hövsgöl Nuur
Uvs Nuur
Ulaanbaatar
(Ulan Bator)
Choybalsan
Hovd
Tsetserleg
MONGOLIA
Altay
Saynshand
GOBI
Hohhot
Baotou
Lop Nur
Yumen
Taiyuan
CHINA
100°
110°

4
Khrebet
rebet
Aleksandrovsk-Sakhalinskiy
Sakhalin
Amur
Komsomol'sk na-Amure
Sovetskaya Gavan'
Yuzhno-Sakhalinsk
Kuril'skiye
Ost
(Kuril Is.)
Belogorsk
Blagoveshchensk
Birobidzhan
Khabarovsk
Sikhote–Alin'
Xiao Hinggan Ling
Wakkanai
Hokkaidō
Sapporo
Hakodate
Aomori
Ussuri
Qiqihar
Harbin
Oz. Khanka
Ussuriysk
Nakhodka
Vladivostok
Sendai
Jilin
Ch'ŏngjin
SEA OF JAPAN
Niigata
140
Changchun
Tōkyō
Yokohama
JAPAN
Fushun
NORTH KOREA
Shenyang
Anshan
Hamhŭng
Honshū
Kyoto
Nagoya
Wŏnsan
SOUTH KOREA
Ōsaka
Jinzhou
Sŏul (Seoul)
Kobe
P'yŏngyang
Taegu
Lüda
Pusan
Shikoku
Bo Hai
Taejŏn
Kwangju
Kita-Kyūshū
Kyūshū
Fukuoka
Qingdao
Mokp'o
YELLOW SEA
azhuang
Jinan
Huang
Kagoshima
30
120°
130°
O
P
7

MOL.
Kishinev
Odessa
Krivoy Rog
UKRAINE
Nikolayev
Dnepropetrovsk
Melitopol'
Zaporozh'ye
Donetsk
Zhdanov
Sevastopol'
Kerch
Azovskoye More
BLACK SEA
Novorossiysk
Krasnodar
Sumy
Poltava
Khar'kov
Kursk
Orel
Tambov
Voronezh
Voroshilovgrad
Shakhty
Rostov-na-Donu
Don
Ryazan'
Gor'kiy
Cheboksary
Penza
Ul'yanovsk
Syzran'
Saratov
Samara
Ural'sk
Orenburg
Volgograd
Volga
Astrakhan'
Ural
Atyrau
Stavropol'
Samsun
Sukhumi
Batumi
Elbrus
5642
GEORGIA
Caucasus
Groznyy
Makhachkala
TURKEY
Erzurum
Yerevan
Tbilisi
ARMENIA
Kirovabad
Diyarbakir
SYRIA
AZERBAIJAN
Baku
Araks
Tabriz
CASPIAN SEA
Plato Ustyurt
Al Mawsil
Krasnovodsk
Karakumy
TURKMENISTAN
Nukus
Urgench
IRAQ
Baghdād
Tehrān
Amudarya
Ashkhabad
Chardzhou
Mashhad
Mary
Eşfahān
Al Basrah
IRAN
KUWAIT
THE GULF
Herat
AFGHANISTAN
30°
40°
50°
60°
5
6
7
F
G
H

Zapadno
Sibirskaya
Nizmennost
RUSSIA
KAZAKHSTAN
KYRGYZSTAN
TAJIKISTAN
CHINA
TIAN SHAN
Tarim Pendi
Sergino
Surgut
Ob
Perm
Serov
Uralskiy Khrebet
Nizhniy Tagil
Tyumen'
Tobol'sk
Irtysh
Zlatoust
Yekaterinburg
Chelyabinsk
Petropavlovsk
Tobol
Ishim
Omsk
Tomsk
Novosibirsk
Kemerovo
Prokop'yevsk
Novokuznetsk
Barnaul
Pavlodar
Akmola
Semipalatinsk
Karaganda
Oz. Zaysan
Balkhash
Zaysan
Ozero Balkhash
Kzyl Orda
Syrdar'ya
Aulie Ata
Chimkent
Bishkek
Tashkent
Almaty
Ürümqi
Namangan
Andizhan
Fergana
Samarkand
Pik Pobedy 7439
Turfan Depression
-154
Tarim
Kashi
Pik Kommunizma 7495
Pamir
Mazār-e Sharīf
70°
80°
© Geddes & Grosset

A
B
1
2
3
70°
50°
80°
40°
Semipalatinsk
Irtysh
KAZAKHSTAN
Balkhash
Ozero Balkhash
Oz. Zaysan
Zaysan
Aulie Ata.
Bishkek
Almaty
KYRGYZSTAN
Namangan
Andizhan
rgana
Oz. Issyk Kul
Pik Pobedy 7439
TIAN SHAN
Ürümqi
Turfan Depression
Kashi
Yarkant
Tarim
XINJIANG UY
ZIZHIQU
Bosten Hu
Tarim Pendi
Taklimakan Shamo
Hotan
Ruoqiang
Altun Shan
K2 8611
Karakoram
Indus
Kunlun
Xizang Gaoyuan
H

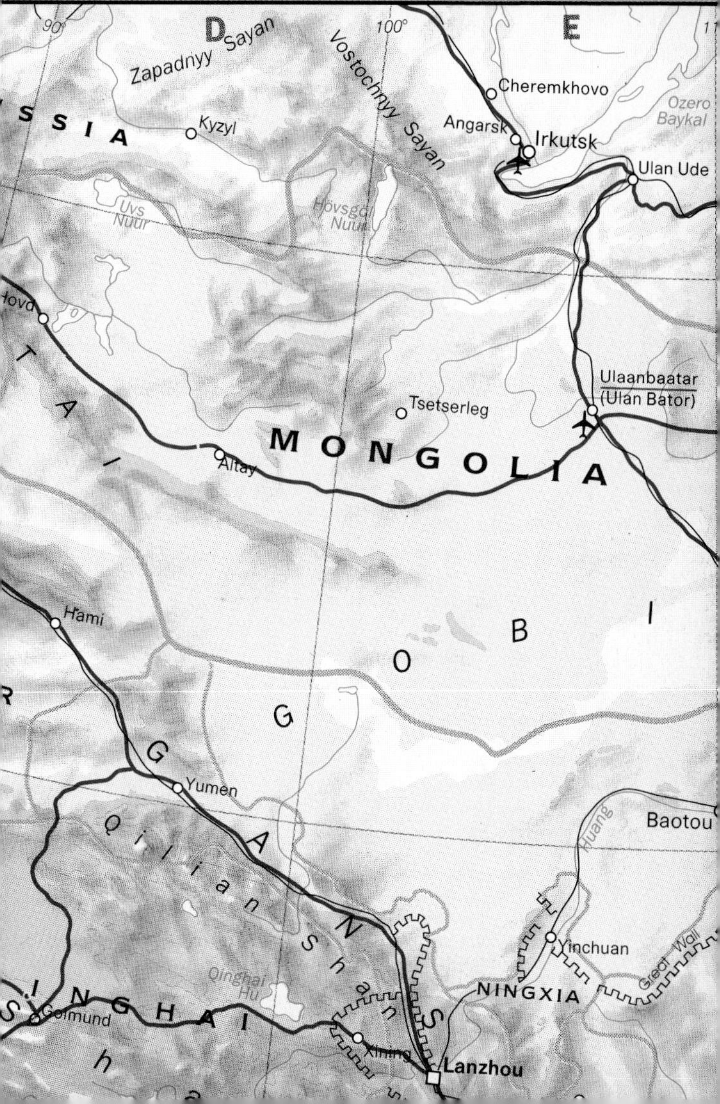
90°
D
Zapadnyy Sayan
Vostochnyy Sayan
100°
E
Cheremkhovo
Ozero Baykal
SSIA
Kyzyl
Angarsk
Irkutsk
Ulan Ude
Uvs Nuur
Hövsgöl Nuur
Hovd
Ulaanbaatar
(Ulan Bator)
Tsetserleg
MONGOLIA
Altay
Hami
G O B I
Yumen
Baotou
Huang
Qilian Shan
NINGXIA
Yinchuan
Great Wall
Qinghai Hu
Golmund
Xining
Lanzhou

F
G
120°
130°
Skovorodino
Yablonovyy Khrebet
Shilka
Amur
Chita
Belogorsk
Blagoveshchens
Ergun
Da Hinggan Ling
Borzya
Manzhouli
Hailar
Xiao Hinggan Ling
HEILONGJ
Nen
Choybalsan
Qiqihar
Jiamu
Songhua
Harbin
A
Baicheng
JILIN
Saynshand
Changchun
Jilin
Siping
Liaoyuan
Erenhot
NEI MONGOL ZIZHIQU
(INNER MONGOLIA)
Tonghua
Chifeng
Shenyang
Fushun
Fuxin
LIAONING
Benxi
Liaoyang
Jinzhou
Anshan
Dandong
Zhangjiakou
Yingkou
Liaodong
Hohhot
BEIJING
Qinhuangdao
Datong
Pyŏngyang
Tangshan
Beijing
(Peking)
Tianjin
Lüda
Kae
Baoding
Bo Hai
HEBEI
Cangzhou
Yantai
Shijiazhuang
Taiyuan
Yangquan
Dezhou
Tae
Xingtai
Huang
Weifang
Handan
SHANXI
Jinan
Zibo
Qingdao
YELLOW SEA
Changzhi
SHANDONG
Anyang
Linfen

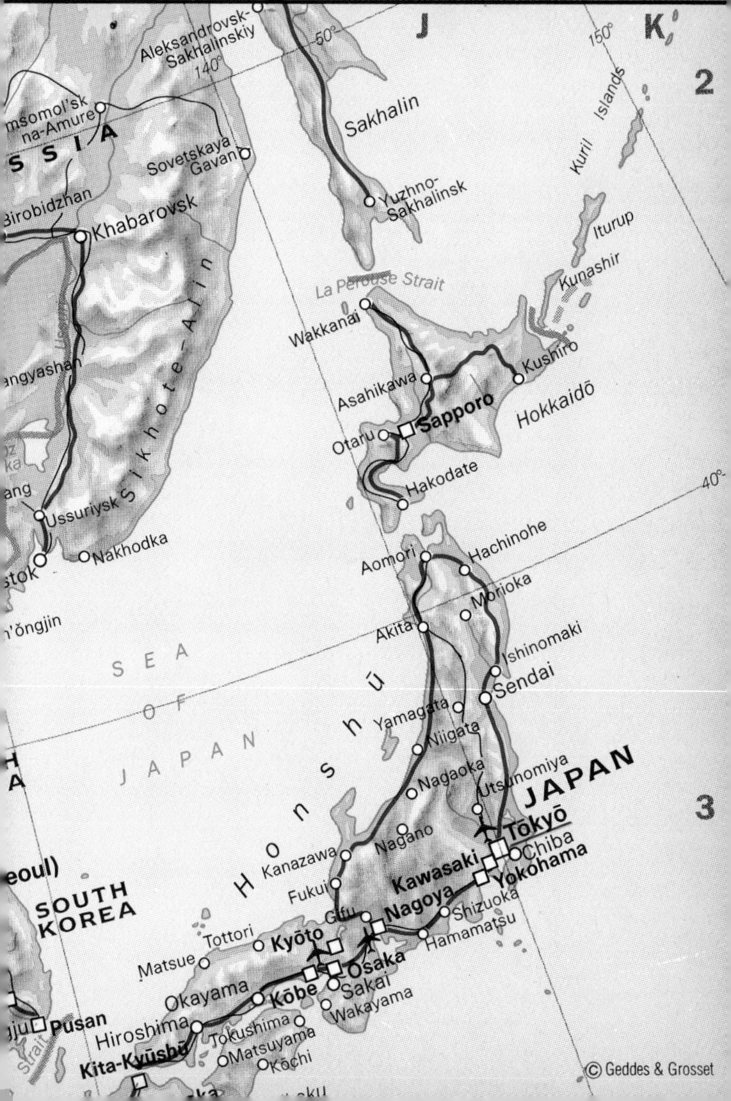
Aleksandrovsk-Sakhalinskiy
Sakhalin
Kuril Islands
Sovetskaya Gavan
Yuzhno-Sakhalinsk
Birobidzhan
Khabarovsk
Sikhote-Alin
Iturup
Kunashir
La Perouse Strait
Wakkanai
Kushiro
Asahikawa
Hokkaidō
Sapporo
Otaru
Hakodate
Ussuriysk
Nakhodka
Hachinohe
Aomori
Morioka
Akita
Ishinomaki
Sendai
SEA OF JAPAN
Honshū
Yamagata
Niigata
Nagaoka
Utsunomiya
JAPAN
Tōkyō
Nagano
Chiba
Kanazawa
Kawasaki
Yokohama
SOUTH KOREA
Fukui
Nagoya
Shizuoka
Gifu
Tottori
Kyōto
Hamamatsu
Matsue
Ōsaka
Okayama
Kōbe
Sakai
Wakayama
Pusan
Hiroshima
Tokushima
Matsuyama
Kita-Kyūshū
Kōchi
J
K
2
3
140°
150°
50°
40°
© Geddes & Grosset

EASTERN ASIA (S.E.), CENTRAL JAPAN

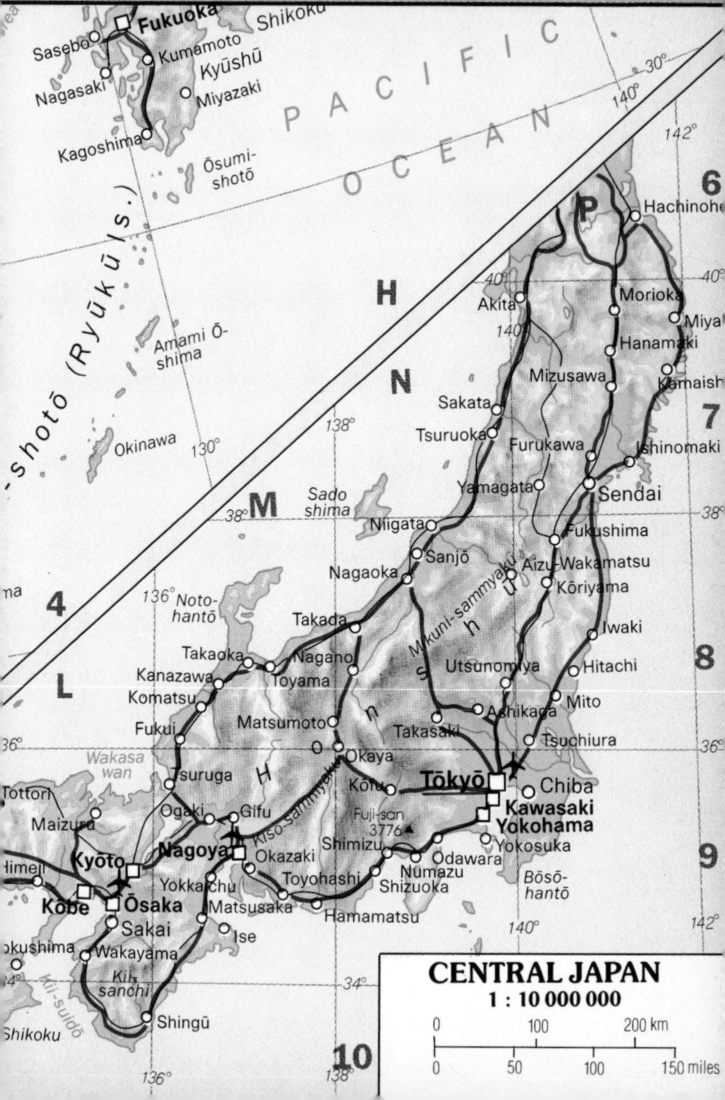
Fukuoka
Shikoku
Sasebo
Kumamoto
Kyūshū
Nagasaki
Miyazaki
Kagoshima
Ōsumi-shotō
PACIFIC
OCEAN
-shotō (Ryūkyū Is.)
Amami Ō-shima
Okinawa
Hachinohe
Akita
Morioka
Miya
Hanamaki
Mizusawa
Kamaish
Sakata
Tsuruoka
Furukawa
Ishinomaki
Yamagata
Sendai
Sado shima
Niigata
Fukushima
Sanjō
Aizu-Wakamatsu
Nagaoka
Kōriyama
Mikuni-sammyaku
Noto-hantō
Takada
Iwaki
Takaoka
Nagano
Utsunomiya
Hitachi
Kanazawa
Toyama
Komatsu
Mito
Ashikaga
Matsumoto
Fukui
Takasaki
Tsuchiura
Wakasa wan
Okaya
Tsuruga
Kōfu
Tōkyō
Chiba
Tottori
Ogaki
Gifu
Kawasaki
Maizuru
Yokohama
Fuji-san 3776
Kiso-sammyaku
Shimizu
Yokosuka
Kyōto
Nagoya
Okazaki
Odawara
Himeji
Toyohashi
Numazu
Shizuoka
Bōsō-hantō
Yokkaichi
Kobe
Ōsaka
Matsusaka
Hamamatsu
Sakai
Ise
Tokushima
Wakayama
Kii-sanchi
Kii-suidō
Shingū
Shikoku
H
O
N
S
H
Ū
M
L
P
H
N
4
6
7
8
9
10
CENTRAL JAPAN
1 : 10 000 000
0
100
200 km
0
50
100
150 miles

XIZANG ZIZHIQU
(TIBET)
Tanggula
Gangdise Shan
HIMALAYA
NEPAL
INDIA
BHUTAN
BANGLADESH
BAY OF BENGAL
Dehra Dūn
Moradabad
Bareilly
Shahjahanpur
Lucknow
Kānpur
Ghaghara
Ganga
Gorakhpur
Allāhābād
(Ganges)
Vārānasi
Mirzapur
Son
Patna
Tropic of Cancer
Annapurna
8078
Mt Everest
8848
Kathmandu
Kangchenjunga
8598
Thimphu
Lhasa
Yarlung Zangbo
Nam Co
Siling Co
Dibru
Brahmaputra
Bhagalpur
Rangpur
Shillong
Gauhati
Mymensingh
Imphāl
Ranchi
Asansol
Bilaspur
Jamshedpur
Hāora
Calcutta
Dhākā
(Dacca)
Raipur
Kharagpur
Khulna
Chittagong
Chin Hills
MY
(BU
Myingya
Arakan Yoma
Cuttack
Sittwe
Meikt
Irrawaddy
Vishakhapatnam
Pro
Henzada
3
4
5
C
D
30°
20°
90°

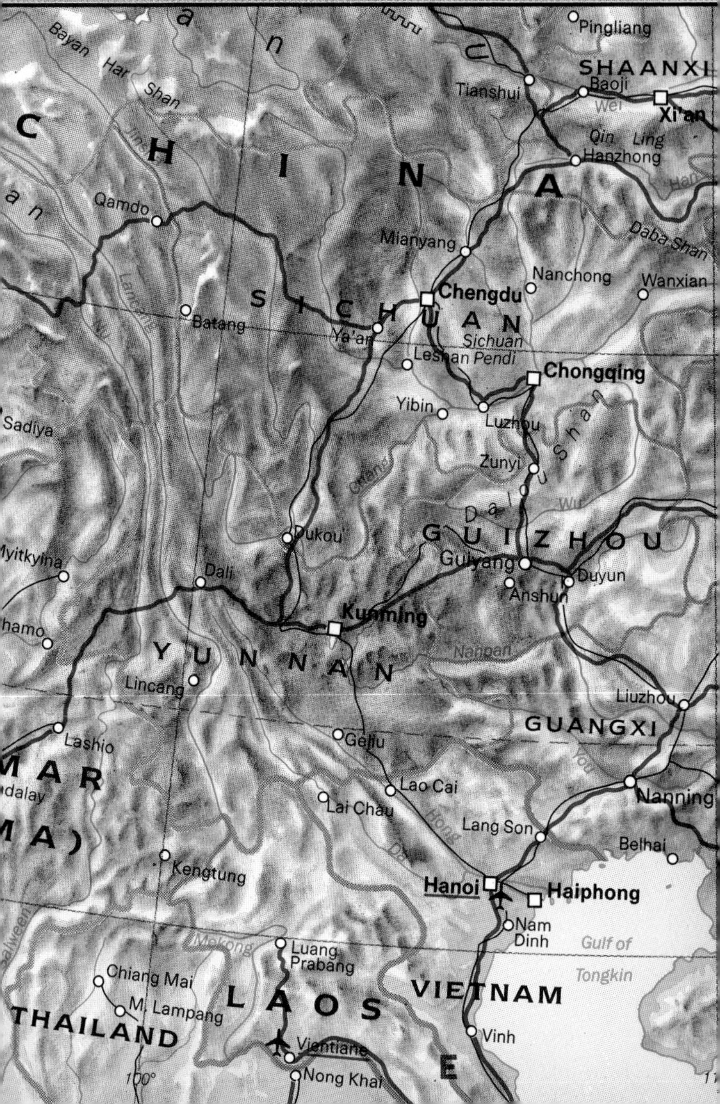
Pingliang
SHAANXI
Tianshui
Baoji
Wei
Xi'an
Qin Ling
Hanzhong
Han
Bayan Har Shan
CHINA
Qamdo
Mianyang
Daba Shan
Nanchong
Wanxian
Chengdu
SICHUAN
Batang
Ya'an
Sichuan Pendi
Leshan
Chongqing
Yibin
Luzhou
Sadiya
Zunyi
Dalou Shan
Wu
GUIZHOU
Dukou
Guiyang
Duyun
Anshun
Myitkyina
Dali
Kunming
Nanpan
YUNNAN
Lincang
Liuzhou
GUANGXI
Lashio
Gejiu
You
Nanning
Lao Cai
Lai Chau
Hong
Lang Son
Beihai
Da
Kengtung
Hanoi
Haiphong
Nam Dinh
Mekong
Luang Prabang
Gulf of Tongkin
Chiang Mai
M. Lampang
THAILAND
LAOS
VIETNAM
Vinh
Vientiane
Nong Khai
100°

NEPAL
A
B
1
2
3
90°
100°
20°
10°
Thimphu
BHUTAN
Sadiya
Bhāgalpur
Rangpur
Brahmaputra
Dibrugarh
Gauhati
Shillong
BANGLADESH
Ganga
INDIA
Naga Hills
Myitkyina
Dukou
Dali
Mymensingh
Imphāl
Dhākā
(Dacca)
Hāora
Khulna
Calcutta
Kunmi
Bhamo
Chin
Hills
Chittagong
Lincang
Lashio
MYANMAR
(BURMA)
Myingyan
Mandalay
Arakan
Kengtung
Sittwe
Meiktila
Irrawaddy
Pegu
Yoma
BAY
OF
BENGAL
Salween
Mekong
Prome
Chiang
Mai
Henzada
M. Lampang
Bassein
Pegu
Dawna Ra.
Ping
Nan
Yangon
(Rangoon)
C. Negrais
M. Phitsanulok
Moulmein
THAILAN
Ye
M. Nakhon
Sawan
Nakhon
Ratchasima
North Andaman
Tavoy
Thon
Buri
Middle Andaman
ANDAMAN
SEA
Bangkok
(Krung Thep)
Andaman
Islands
(India)
South Andaman
Mergui
Archipelago
Little Andaman
Gulf
of
Thailand
Phnom
Ten Degree Channel
Isthmus
of Kra
Chumphon
Kompong
Som
Nicobar
Islands
(India)
Phuket
Nakhon Si
Thammarat

Chongqing
Luzhou
110°
Dongting Hu
Poyang Hu
Nanchang
Jingdezhen
Changsha
Guiyang
Hengyang
CHINA
Fuzhou
Guilin
Quanzhou
Liuzhou
Shaoguan
Xiamen
Wuzhou
Xi
Nanning
Shantou
Lao Cai
Foshan
Guangzhou
Kowloon
Macau (Macao) (Port)
Victoria
HONG KONG
Lang Son
Hanoi
Haiphong
Zhanjiang
Nam Dinh
Gulf of Tongkin
Haikou
Vinh
Hainan Dao
VIETNAM
Hue
Savannakhet
Da Nang
Paracel Is.
Pakse
Mekong
Qui Nhon
SOUTH CHINA SEA
Kompong Cham
Da Lat
Nha Trang
Calamian Group
Ho Chi Minh City (Saigon)
My Tho
Spratly Islands
Palawan

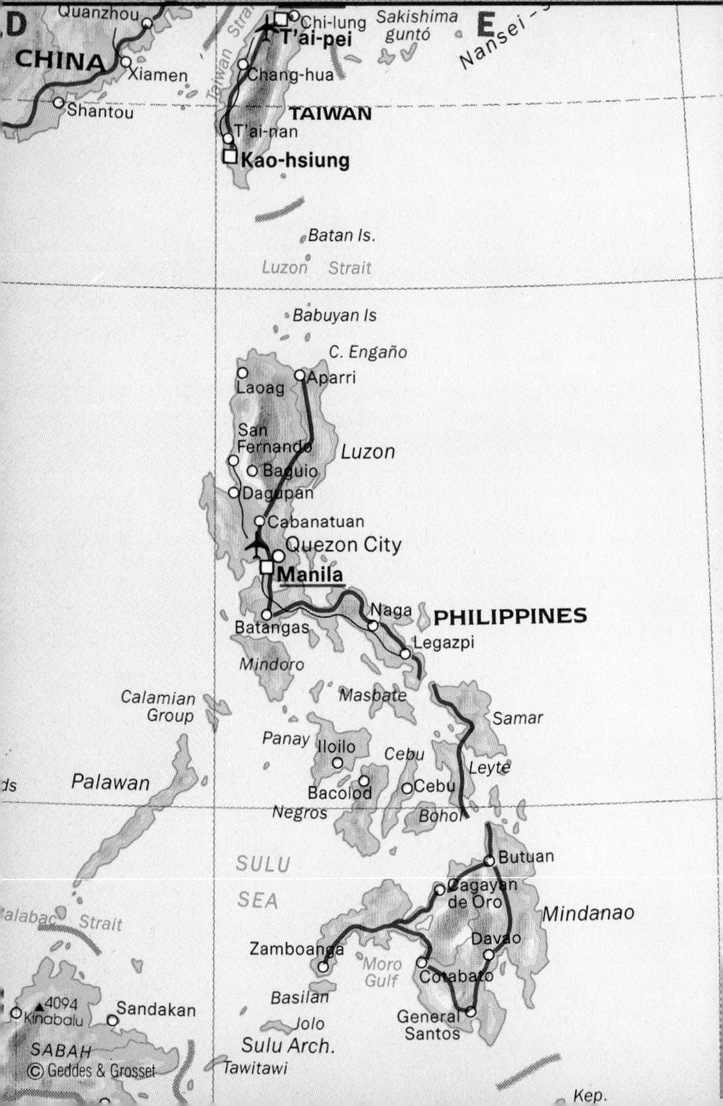
D
E
Quanzhou
CHINA
Xiamen
Shantou
Taiwan Strait
Chi-lung
T'ai-pei
Sakishima guntó
Nansei
Chang-hua
TAIWAN
T'ai-nan
Kao-hsiung
Batan Is.
Luzon Strait
Babuyan Is
C. Engaño
Laoag
Aparri
San Fernando
Luzon
Baguio
Dagupan
Cabanatuan
Quezon City
Manila
Naga
PHILIPPINES
Batangas
Legazpi
Mindoro
Calamian Group
Masbate
Samar
Panay
Iloilo
Cebu
Leyte
Palawan
Bacolod
Cebu
Negros
Bohol
SULU SEA
Butuan
Cagayan de Oro
Mindanao
Strait
Zamboanga
Moro Gulf
Davao
Cotabato
Basilan
4094
Kinabalu
Sandakan
Jolo
General Santos
SABAH
Sulu Arch.
Tawitawi
Kep.

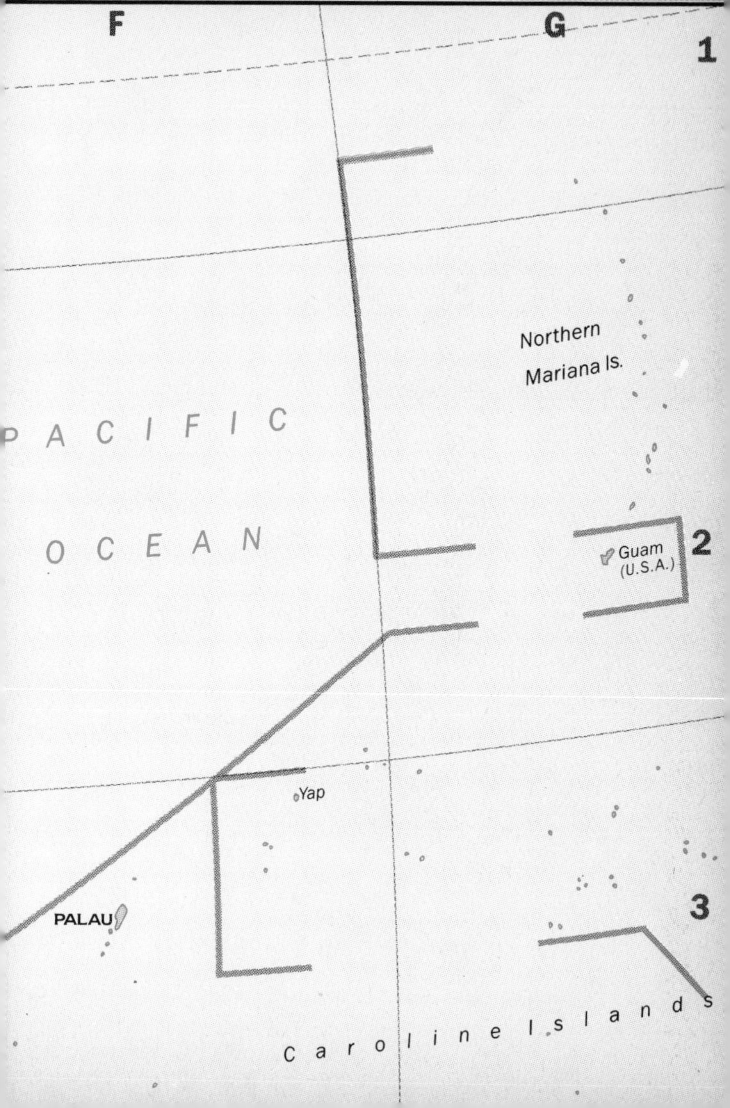
F
G
1
2
3
Northern
Mariana Is.
PACIFIC
OCEAN
Guam
(U.S.A.)
Yap
PALAU
Caroline Islands

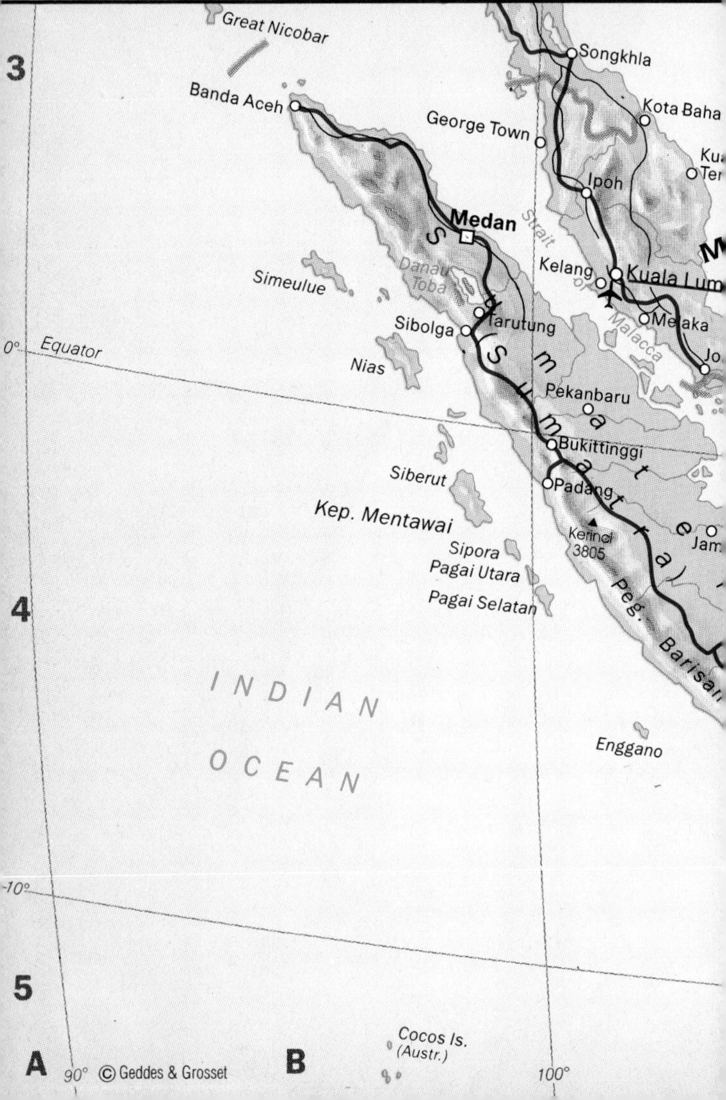
Great Nicobar
Banda Aceh
Songkhla
Kota Baha
George Town
Ipoh
Medan
Strait of Malacca
Simeulue
Danau Toba
Kelang
Kuala Lum
Sibolga
Tarutung
Melaka
Equator
0°
Nias
Sumatera
Pekanbaru
Bukittinggi
Siberut
Padang
Kep. Mentawai
Kerinci 3805
Sipora
Pagai Utara
Pagai Selatan
Peg. Barisan
INDIAN OCEAN
Enggano
-10°
Cocos Is. (Austr.)
90°
100°
3
4
5
A
B

Con Son
Balabac Strait
Kota Kinabalu
4094 Kinabalu
Sandakan
Bandar Seri Begawan
BRUNEI
SABAH
LAYSIA
Miri
Natuna Besar
Tawau
Kep. Anambas
Kep. Natuna
SARAWAK
Tarakan
Sibu
Rajang
Peg. Iran
ORE
Singkawang
Kuching
G. Menyapa 2000
KALIMANTAN
Pontianak
Borneo
Samarinda
Balikpapan
Bangka
Peg. Schwaner
Makassar Strait
Palu
Pangkalpinang
Palangkaraya
Kandangan
bang
Belitung
Majene
Banjarmasin
Tg. Puting
Laut
INDONESIA
Parepare
ukbetung
JAVA SEA
Ujung Pandang
Jakarta
Bogor
Cirebon
Semarang
Madura
andung
3428
Surakarta
FLORES
Surabaya
Lesser Sunda
Yogyakarta
Kediri
Bali
Lombok
Malang
Banyuwangi
Raba
Jawa (Java)
Mataram
Sumbawa
Christmas I. (Austr.)
Sumba
D
110°
12

SULU SEA
Butuan
Cagayan de Oro
Mindanao
PALAU
Zamboanga
Davao
PHILIPPINES
Moro Gulf
Cotabato
Basilan
Jolo
General Santos
Sulu Arch.
Tawitawi
Kep. Talaud
CELEBES SEA
Kep. Sangihe
Morotai
Manado
Halmahera
Gorontalo
MOLUCCA SEA
Waigeo
Teluk Tomini
Kep. Togian
MALUKU (MOLUCCAS)
Manok
Sorong
Obi
Poso
Kep. Banggai
Kep. Sula
SERAM SEA
Misoöl
Sulawesi (Celebes)
Fakfak
Seram
Buru
Ambon
Kendari
INDONESIA
Muna
Butung
Kep. Kai
Salayar
BANDA SEA
SEA
Islands
Yamdena
Tran
Wetar
Babar
Kepulauan Tanimbar
Alor
Flores
Ruteng
Ende
Dili
Kep. Leti
ARAFUR
SAWU SEA
Timor
Kupang
Roti
E
120°
130°

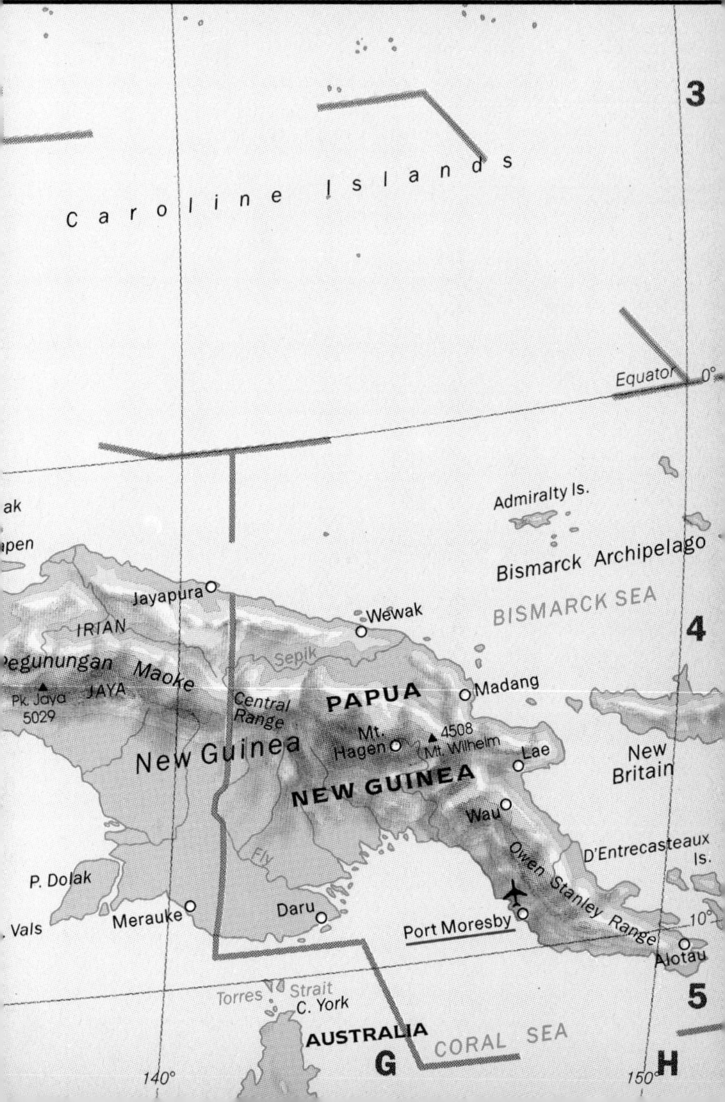

3
Caroline Islands
Equator
0°
ak
apen
Admiralty Is.
Bismarck Archipelago
BISMARCK SEA
Jayapura
Wewak
IRIAN
4
Sepik
Pegunungan Maoke
JAYA
Pk. Jaya
5029
Central Range
PAPUA
Madang
Mt. Hagen
4508
Mt. Wilhelm
New Guinea
Lae
New Britain
NEW GUINEA
Wau
Fly
D'Entrecasteaux Is.
Owen Stanley Range
P. Dolak
Merauke
Daru
Port Moresby
10°
Vals
Alotau
Torres Strait
C. York
5
AUSTRALIA
CORAL SEA
G
H
140°
150°

NORTHERN INDIA & THE HIMALAYAS

MONGOLIA
Hami
Turfan Depression
−154
Lop Nur
Yumen
Qilian Shan
Altun Shan
Qinghai Hu
Golmund
Kunlun Shan
Bayan Har Shan
Jinsha
Xizang Gaoyuan
CHINA
Tanggula Shan
Nu
Lancang
Nam Co
Lhasa
Yarlung Zangbo
Annapurna 8078
Kangchenjunga 8598
Mt Everest 8848
NEPAL
Kathmandu
Thimphu
BHUTAN
Sadiya
Dibrugarh
Brahmaputra
Naga Hills
Gauhati
Shillong
Myitkyina
MYANMAR (BURMA)
Gorakhpur
Patna
Bhagalpur
Vārānasi
Mirzapur
Rangpur
Mymensingh
Imphāl
BANGLADESH
Dhāka (Dacca)
Tropic of Cancer
1
2
3
H

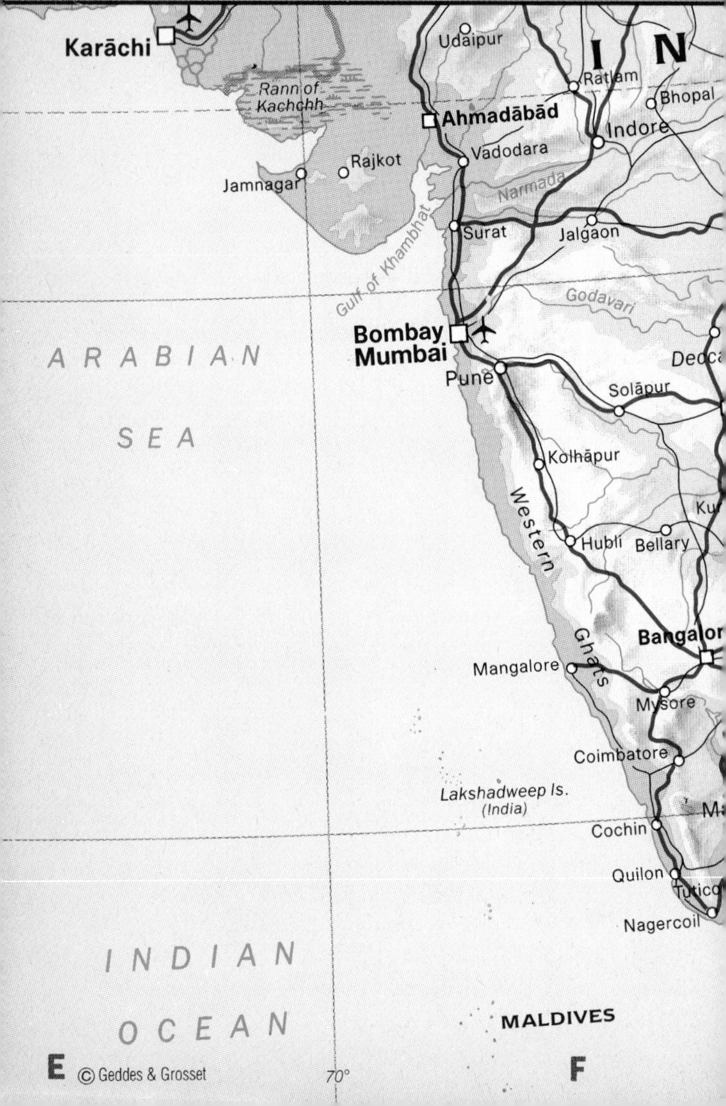
Karāchi
Udaipur
I N
Ratlam
Bhopal
Rann of Kachchh
Ahmadābād
Indore
Vadodara
Rajkot
Jamnagar
Narmada
Surat
Jalgaon
Gulf of Khambhat
Godavari
Bombay
Mumbai
ARABIAN
SEA
Pune
Solāpur
Kolhāpur
Western
Ghats
Hubli
Bellary
Bangalor
Mangalore
Mysore
Coimbatore
Lakshadweep Is.
(India)
Cochin
Quilon
Nagercoil
INDIAN
OCEAN
MALDIVES
E
F
70°

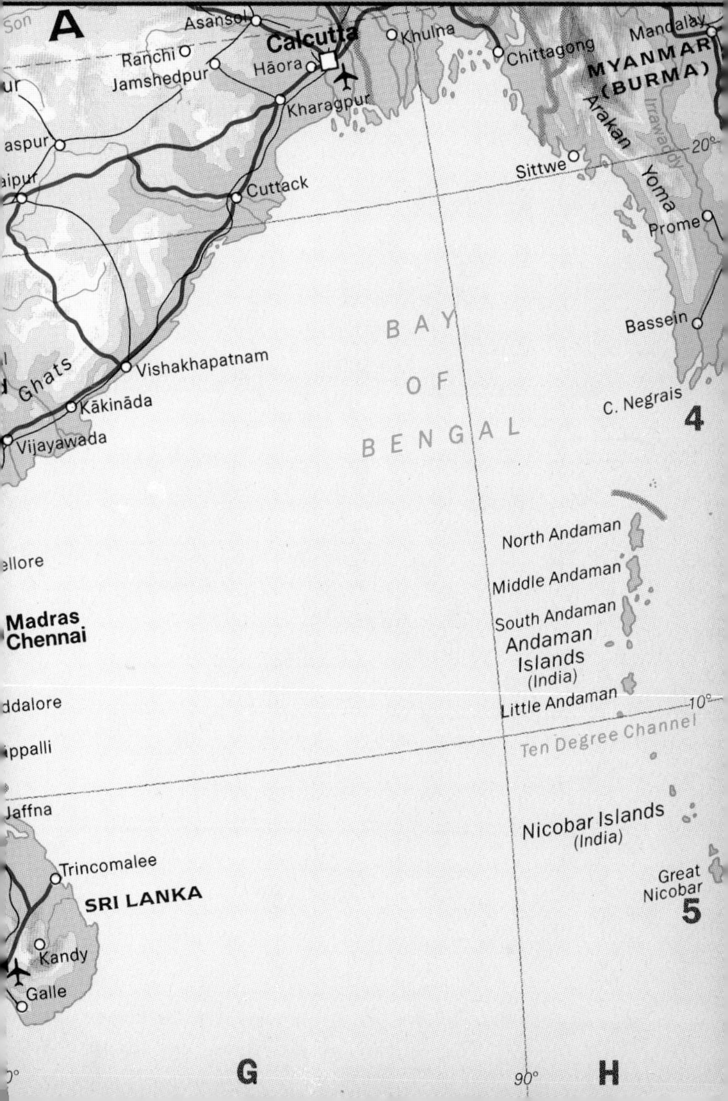
A
Son
Asansol
Calcutta
Khulna
Chittagong
Mandalay
MYANMAR (BURMA)
Ranchi
Jamshedpur
Hāora
Kharagpur
Arakan Yoma
Irrawaddy
20°
aspur
Sittwe
aipur
Cuttack
Prome
BAY OF BENGAL
Bassein
Ghats
Vishakhapatnam
Kākināda
C. Negrais
4
Vijayawada
North Andaman
ellore
Middle Andaman
South Andaman
Madras
Chennai
Andaman Islands (India)
ddalore
Little Andaman
10°
Ten Degree Channel
ippalli
Jaffna
Nicobar Islands (India)
Trincomalee
Great Nicobar
SRI LANKA
5
Kandy
Galle
G
90°
H

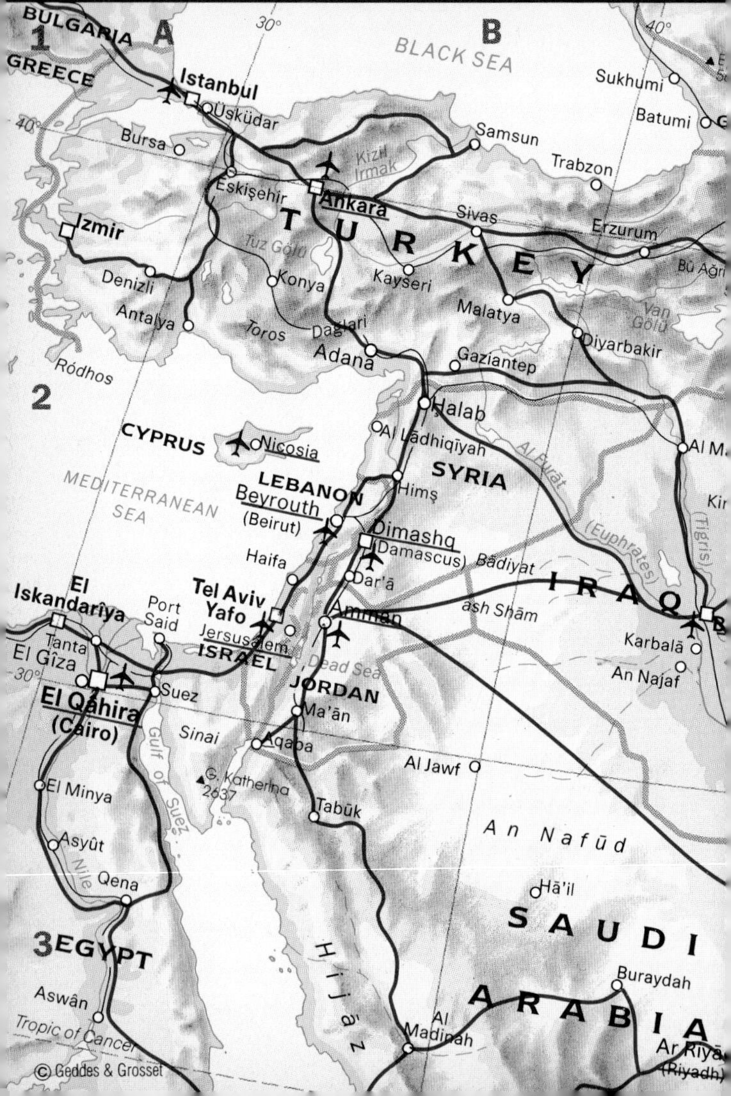
BULGARIA
GREECE
A
B
1
2
3
30°
40°
BLACK SEA
Istanbul
Üsküdar
Bursa
Sukhumi
Batumi
Samsun
Trabzon
Kizil Irmak
Eskişehir
Ankara
Izmir
TURKEY
Sivas
Erzurum
Tuz Gölü
Konya
Kayseri
Denizli
Antalya
Malatya
Van Gölü
Toros Dağlari
Adana
Diyarbakir
Gaziantep
Ródhos
Halab
CYPRUS
Nicosia
Al Lādhiqīyah
SYRIA
Al Furāt
(Euphrates)
(Tigris)
MEDITERRANEAN SEA
LEBANON
Beyrouth
(Beirut)
Ḥimṣ
Dimashq
(Damascus)
Bādiyat ash Shām
Haifa
Dar'ā
IRAQ
El Iskandarîya
Port Said
Tel Aviv Yafo
Jerusalem
ISRAEL
Amman
Tanta
El Gîza
Karbalā
An Najaf
Dead Sea
El Qâhira
(Cairo)
Suez
JORDAN
Ma'ān
Sinai
Aqaba
Gulf of Suez
Al Jawf
G. Katherina 2637
El Minya
Tabūk
An Nafūd
Asyût
Nile
Qena
Ḥā'il
SAUDI ARABIA
EGYPT
Hijāz
Buraydah
Aswân
Al Madinah
Tropic of Cancer
Ar Riyāḍ
(Riyadh)
© Geddes & Grosset

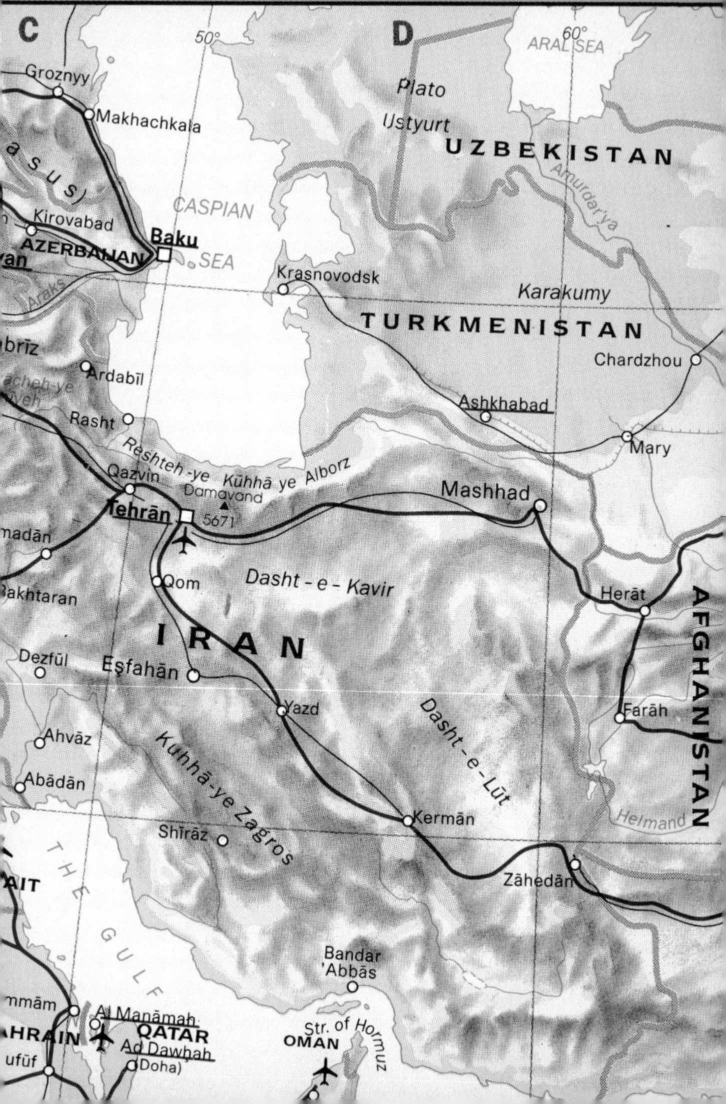

C
D
50°
60°
ARAL SEA
Groznyy
Makhachkala
Plato
Ustyurt
UZBEKISTAN
Amudar'ya
CASPIAN
SEA
Kirovabad
Baku
AZERBAIJAN
Araks
Krasnovodsk
Karakumy
TURKMENISTAN
Chardzhou
Ardabīl
Ashkhabad
Rasht
Mary
Reshteh-ye Kūhhā ye Alborz
Qazvīn
Damavand
5671
Mashhad
Tehrān
Qom
Dasht-e-Kavir
Herāt
AFGHANISTAN
IRAN
Dezfūl
Eşfahān
Yazd
Dasht-e-Lūt
Farāh
Ahvāz
Kūhhā-ye Zagros
Abādān
Kermān
Helmand
Shīrāz
Zāhedān
THE GULF
Bandar 'Abbās
Al Manāmah
QATAR
Ad Dawḩah (Doha)
Str. of Hormuz
OMAN

Lake Nasser
Nubian Desert
20°
Nile
SUDAN
Port Sudan
Atbara
Atbara
El Khartum (Khartoum)
Kassala
4
Wad Medani
Gedaref
ERITREA
Mits'iwa
Asmera
Jiddah
Makkah
At Ta'if
RED SEA
ASIR
San'ā
Al Ḥudaydah
Ta'izz
Aden
Danakil ▼ -116
Ras Dashen ▲ 4620
Gonder
L. Tana
Bahr el Azraq
Ethiopian Highlands
Debre Mark'os
Desē
Āseb
DJIBOUTI
Djibouti
Gulf
10°
Ādīs Ābeba (Addis Ababa)
Dirē Dawa
Berbera
Hargeysa
Hārer
Jima
ETHIOPIA
SO
5
L. Abaya
Shebele
KENYA
B
L. Turkana
40°
C

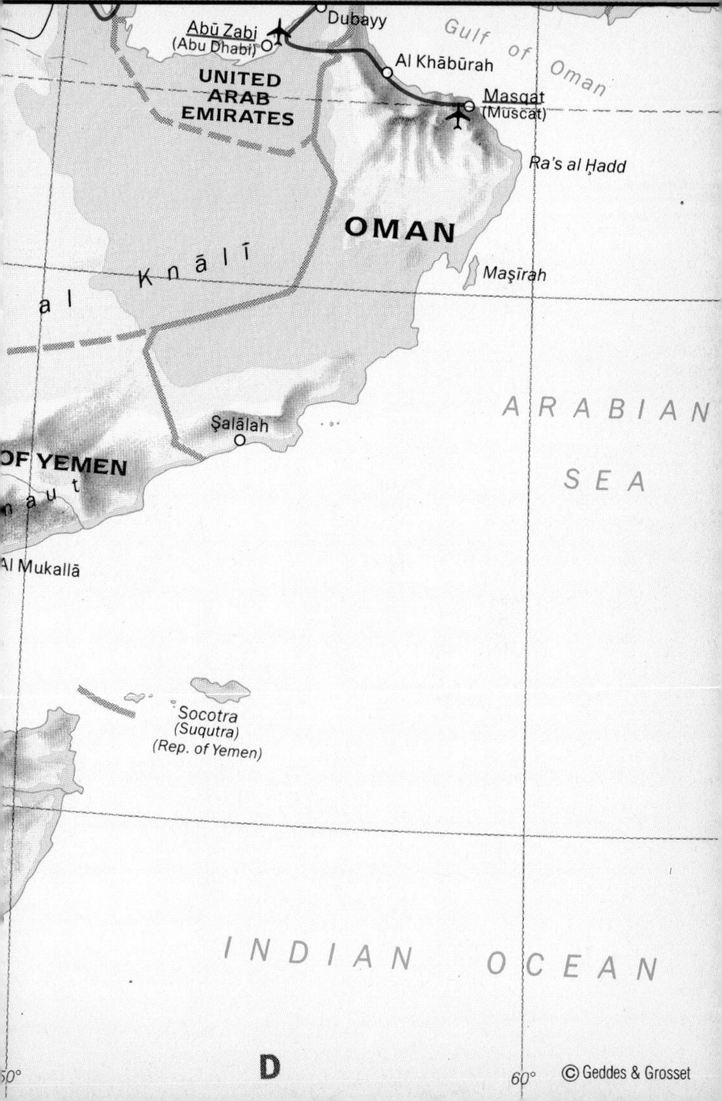

Dubayy
Abū Zabi
(Abu Dhabi)
Gulf of Oman
Al Khābūrah
UNITED ARAB EMIRATES
Masqat
(Muscat)
Ra's al Ḩadd
OMAN
Kn ā l ī
Maşīrah
a l
ARABIAN
SEA
Şalālah
OF YEMEN
a u t
Al Mukallā
Socotra
(Suqutra)
(Rep. of Yemen)
INDIAN OCEAN
D
50°
60°

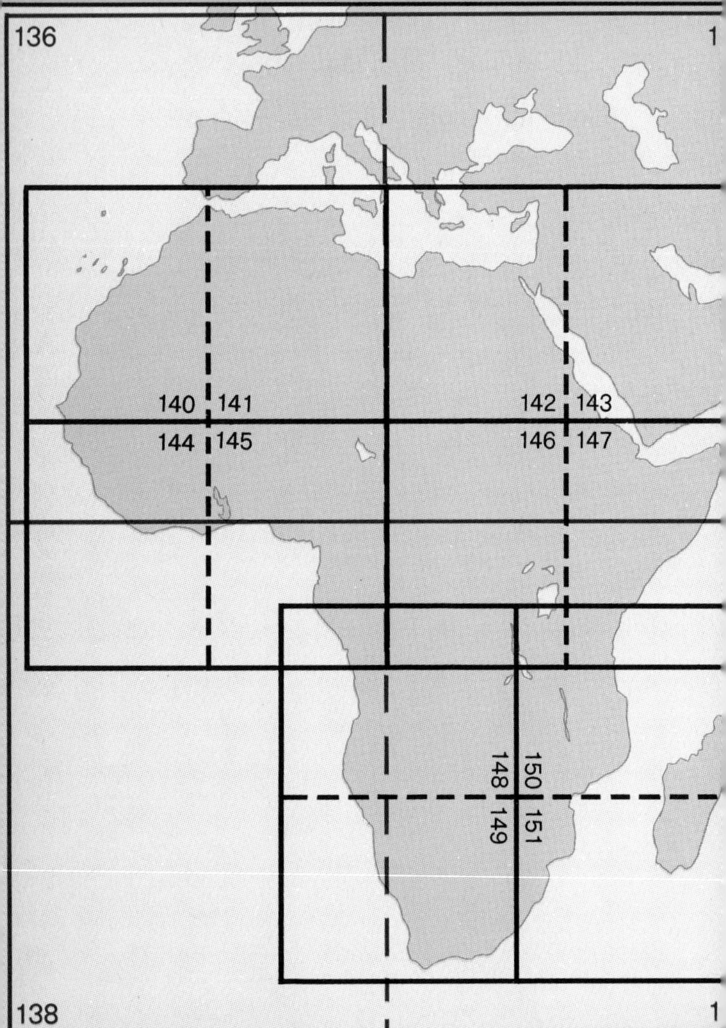
136
1
140
141
142
143
144
145
146
147
148
149
150
151
138
1

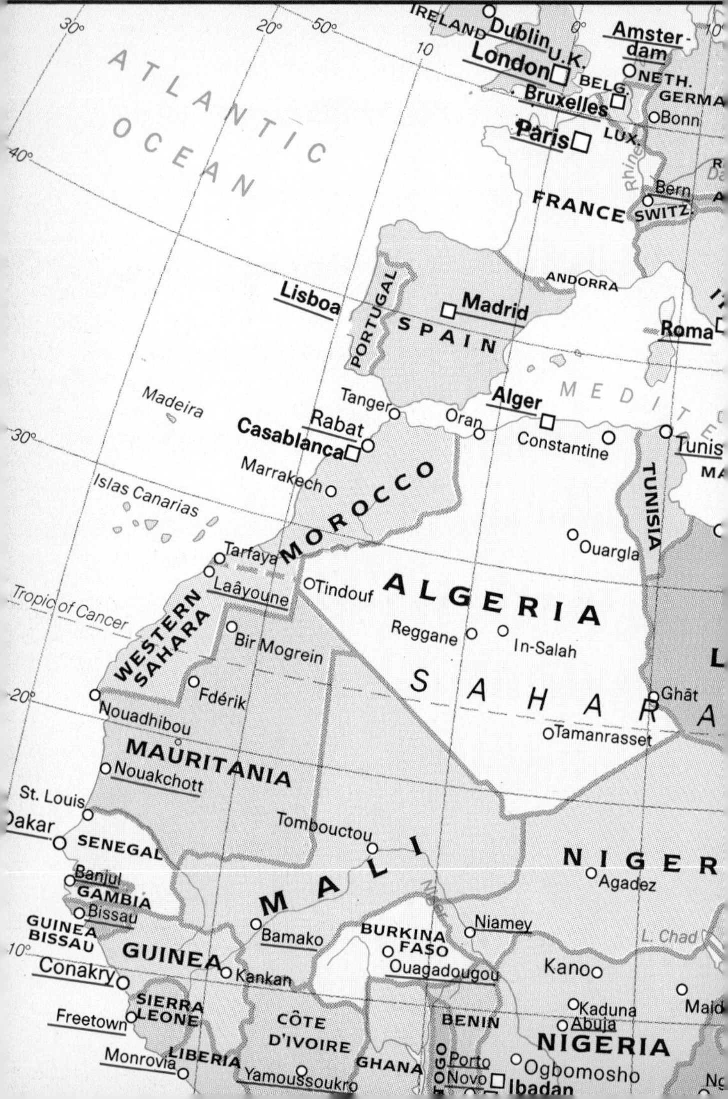
ATLANTIC OCEAN
IRELAND
Dublin
U.K.
London
Amsterdam
NETH.
BELG.
Bruxelles
GERMA
Bonn
LUX.
Paris
Rhine
Bern
SWITZ.
FRANCE
ANDORRA
Lisboa
PORTUGAL
Madrid
SPAIN
Roma
Madeira
Tanger
Rabat
Casablanca
Oran
Alger
Constantine
MEDIT
Tunis
TUNISIA
Marrakech
MOROCCO
Islas Canarias
Tarfaya
Laâyoune
Tindouf
ALGERIA
Ouargla
Tropic of Cancer
WESTERN SAHARA
Bir Mogrein
Reggane
In-Salah
SAHARA
Fdérik
Nouadhibou
Ghât
Tamanrasset
MAURITANIA
Nouakchott
St. Louis
Dakar
SENEGAL
Tombouctou
MALI
NIGER
Agadez
Banjul
GAMBIA
Bissau
GUINEA BISSAU
Bamako
BURKINA FASO
Niamey
L. Chad
GUINEA
Conakry
Kankan
Ouagadougou
Kano
Niger
SIERRA LEONE
Freetown
CÔTE D'IVOIRE
BENIN
Kaduna
Abuja
Maid
NIGERIA
Monrovia
LIBERIA
Yamoussoukro
GHANA
TOGO
Porto Novo
Ogbomosho
Ibadan
30°
20°
50°
10
0°
10°
40°
30°
20°
10°

LITH.
Minsk
BELARUS
RUSSIA
KAZAKHSTAN
Warszawa
Kiyev
UKRAINE
SLOVAKIA
MOLDOVA
ARAL SEA
CASPIAN SEA
UZBEK.
Budapest
Chisinau
ROMANIA
Beograd
Bucureşti
TURKMENISTAN
BLACK SEA
GEOR.
Tbilisi
YUGOS.
Sofiya
BULGARIA
Baku
Ashkabad
ARM.
AZER.
MAC
Tiranë
Ankara
Yerevan
TURKEY
Tehrān
GREECE
Athínai
Tigris
SYRIA
Baghdád
IRAN
CYPRUS
LEB.
Dimashq
Euphrates
IRAQ
Beyrouth
Jerusalem
'Ammān
KUWAIT
Al Kuwayt
Banghāzī
El Iskandarîya
ISR.
JORDAN
The Gulf
BAHRAIN
El Qâhira
As Suez
Ad Dawhah
Nile
SAUDI ARABIA
QATAR
Abū Zabī
U.A.E.
EGYPT
Ar Riyād
Aswân
RED SEA
Wadī Halfa
Port Sudan
'Atbara
ERITREA
San'ā
REP. OF YEMEN
El Khartum
Asmera
Wad Medanī
El Obeid
Gulf of Aden
Bahr el Azraq
(Blue Nile)
DJIBOUTI
Djibouti
SUDAN
SOMALIA
(White Nile)
Bahr el Abiad
Ādis Ābeba
ETHIOPIA

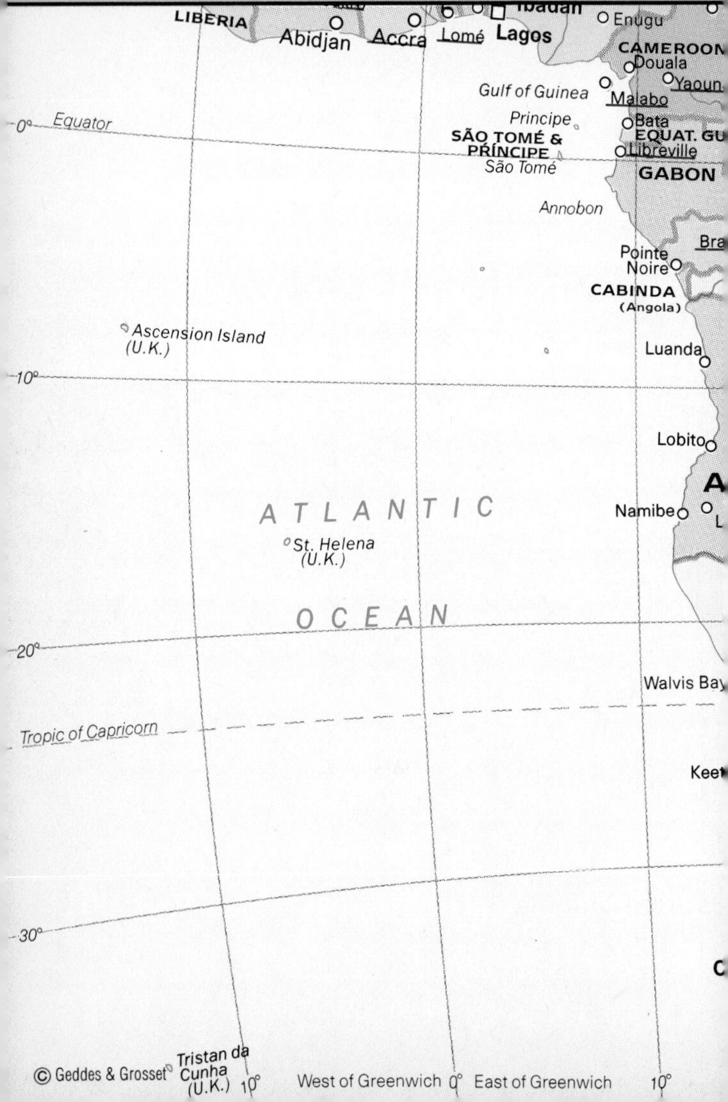
LIBERIA
Abidjan
Accra
Lomé
Lagos
Enugu
CAMEROON
Douala
Gulf of Guinea
Malabo
0° Equator
Principe
Bata
EQUAT. GU
SÃO TOMÉ & PRÍNCIPE
São Tomé
Libreville
GABON
Annobon
Pointe Noire
CABINDA (Angola)
Ascension Island (U.K.)
Luanda
10°
Lobito
ATLANTIC
Namibe
St. Helena (U.K.)
OCEAN
20°
Walvis Bay
Tropic of Capricorn
30°
Tristan da Cunha (U.K.)
10°
West of Greenwich
0°
East of Greenwich
10°

ENTRAL
N REPUBLIC
Wau
SUDAN
ETHIOPIA
SOMALIA
Bangassou
Jūbā
Turkana
Zaïre
UGANDA
Muqdisho
Mbandaka
Kisangani
Kampala
KENYA
0°
Kismaayo
L. Victoria
Nairobi
DEMOCRATIC
REPUBLIC
OF CONGO
RWANDA
Kigali
Mwanza
Kindu
BURUNDI
Bujumbura
Arusha
Mombasa
Kasai
Kananga
Kigoma
Dodoma
Zanzibar
L. Tanganyika
Kalemie
TANZANIA
Dar es Salaam
Lualaba
Kamina
Mbeya
10°
Likasi
COMOROS
MALAWI
Lubumbashi
Antsiranana
Ndola
L. Malawi
Pemba
Lichinga
ZAMBIA
Lilongwe
MOZAMBIQUE
Moçambique
Mozambique Channel
Lusaka
Blantyre
Nampula
MADAGASCAR
Zambezi
Livingstone
Harare
ZIMBABWE
Antananarivo
Beira
Bulawayo
20°
Limpopo
BOTSWANA
Gaborone
Toliara
Inhambane
Pretoria
Maputo
Johannesburg
Mbabane
SWAZILAND
Bloemfontein
Maseru
Durban
LESOTHO
INDIAN
OCEAN
SOUTH AFRICA
30°
East London
Port Elizabeth
20°
30°
40°
50°

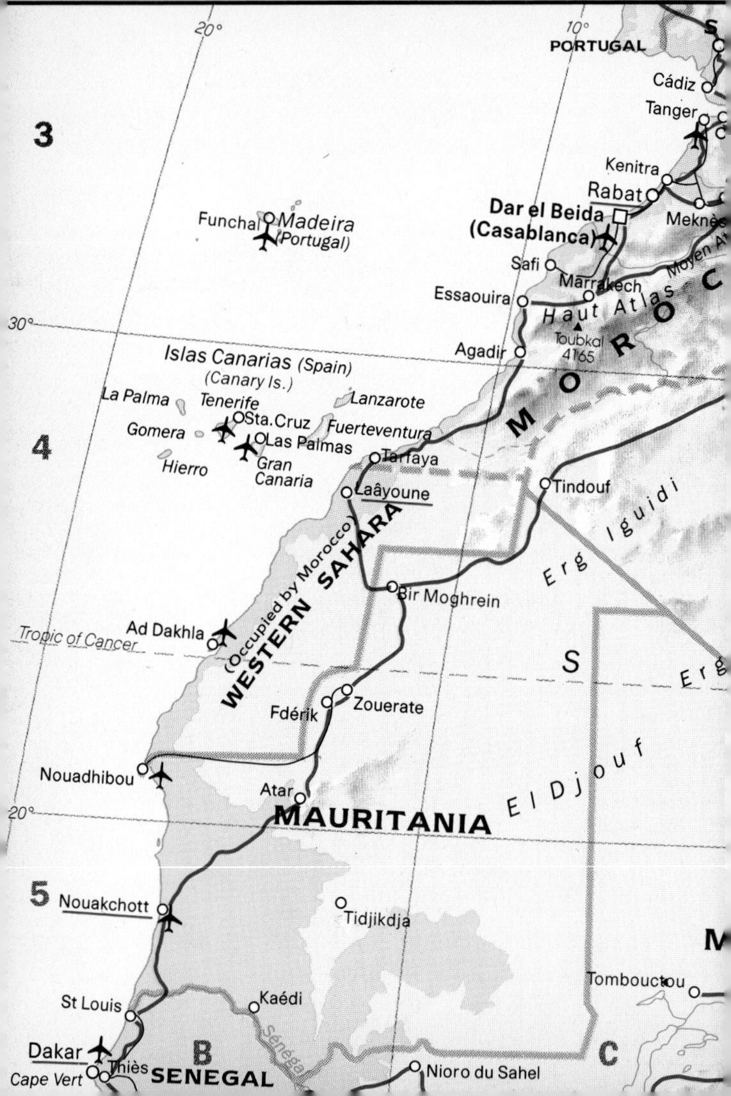
20°
10°
PORTUGAL
Cádiz
Tanger
3
Kenitra
Rabat
Dar el Beida
(Casablanca)
Meknès
Funchal
Madeira
(Portugal)
Safi
Marrakech
Moyen At
Essaouira
Haut Atlas
Toubkal
4165
30°
Agadir
Islas Canarias (Spain)
(Canary Is.)
La Palma
Tenerife
Lanzarote
Sta.Cruz
Gomera
Fuerteventura
Las Palmas
4
Hierro
Gran
Canaria
Tarfaya
MOROC
Laâyoune
Tindouf
Erg Iguidi
WESTERN SAHARA
(Occupied by Morocco)
Bir Moghrein
Ad Dakhla
Tropic of Cancer
S
Erg
Fdérik
Zouerate
Nouadhibou
El Djouf
Atar
20°
MAURITANIA
5
Nouakchott
Tidjikdja
M
Tombouctou
St Louis
Kaédi
Sénégal
Dakar
Thiès
Cape Vert
B
SENEGAL
C
Nioro du Sahel

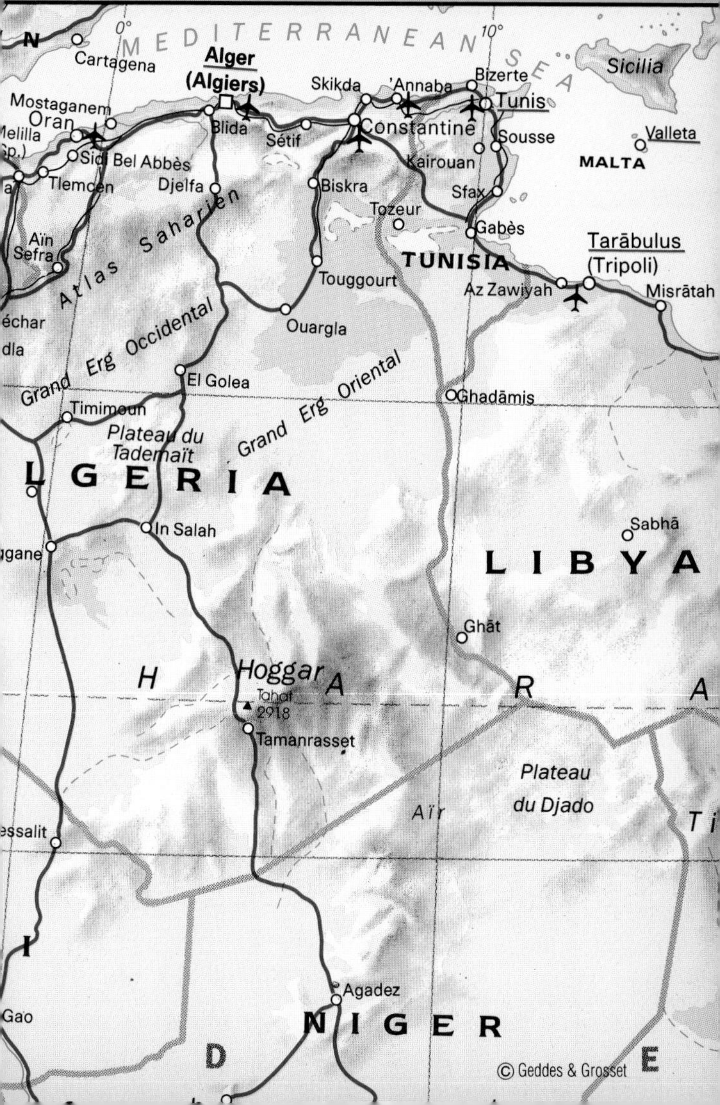
MEDITERRANEAN SEA
0°
10°
Cartagena
Alger
(Algiers)
Skikda
'Annaba
Bizerte
Tunis
Sicilia
Mostaganem
Oran
Melilla
Blida
Sétif
Constantine
Sousse
Valleta
MALTA
Sidi Bel Abbès
Kairouan
Tlemcen
Djelfa
Biskra
Sfax
Atlas Saharien
Tozeur
Gabès
Aïn Sefra
TUNISIA
Tarābulus
(Tripoli)
Touggourt
Az Zawiyah
Misrātah
échar
Ouargla
Grand Erg Occidental
El Golea
Grand Erg Oriental
Ghadāmis
Timimoun
Plateau du Tademaït
LGERIA
In Salah
Sabhā
LIBYA
Ghāt
Hoggar
H A R A
Tahat
2918
Tamanrasset
Plateau du Djado
Aïr
essalit
Agadez
Gao
NIGER
© Geddes & Grosset

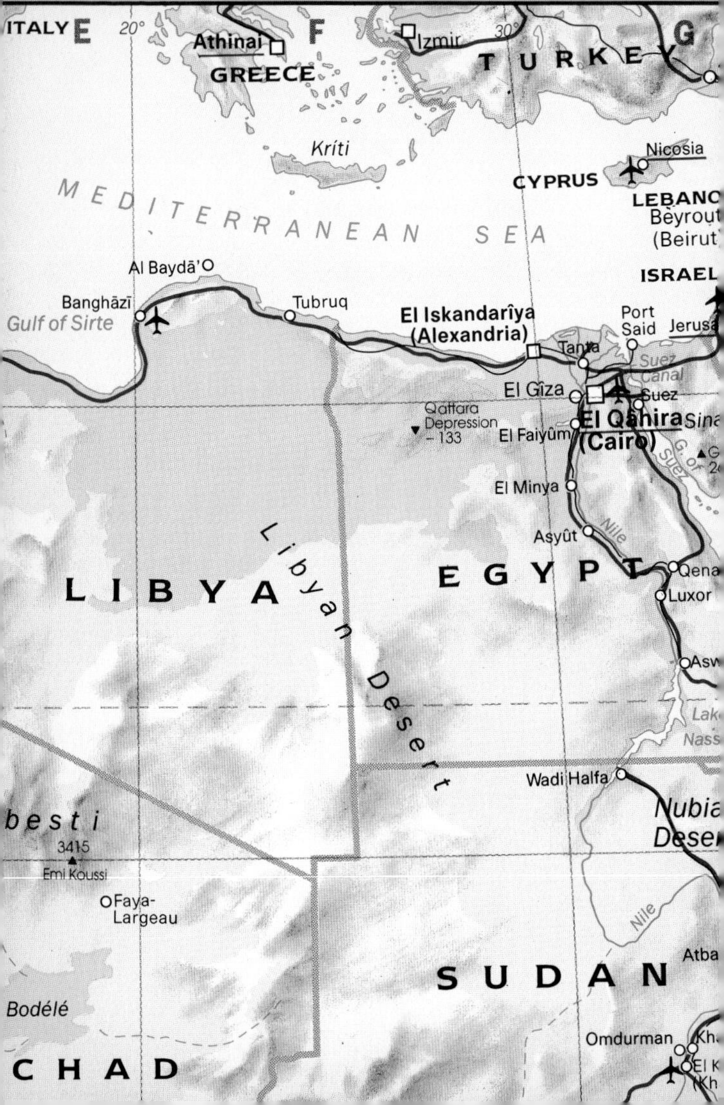
ITALY
E
20°
F
G
30°
Athinai
GREECE
Izmir
TURKEY
Kríti
Nicosia
CYPRUS
LEBANO
Beyrout
(Beirut)
MEDITERRANEAN SEA
ISRAEL
Al Baydā'
Banghāzī
Gulf of Sirte
Tubruq
El Iskandarîya
(Alexandria)
Port
Said
Jerus
Tanta
Suez
Canal
El Gîza
Suez
Qattara
Depression
-133
El Qâhira
(Cairo)
El Faiyûm
El Minya
Asyût
Nile
LIBYA
Libyan Desert
EGYPT
Qena
Luxor
Asw
Wadi Halfa
Nubia
Deser
besti
3415
Emi Koussi
Faya-
Largeau
Nile
Atba
SUDAN
Bodélé
Omdurman
CHAD

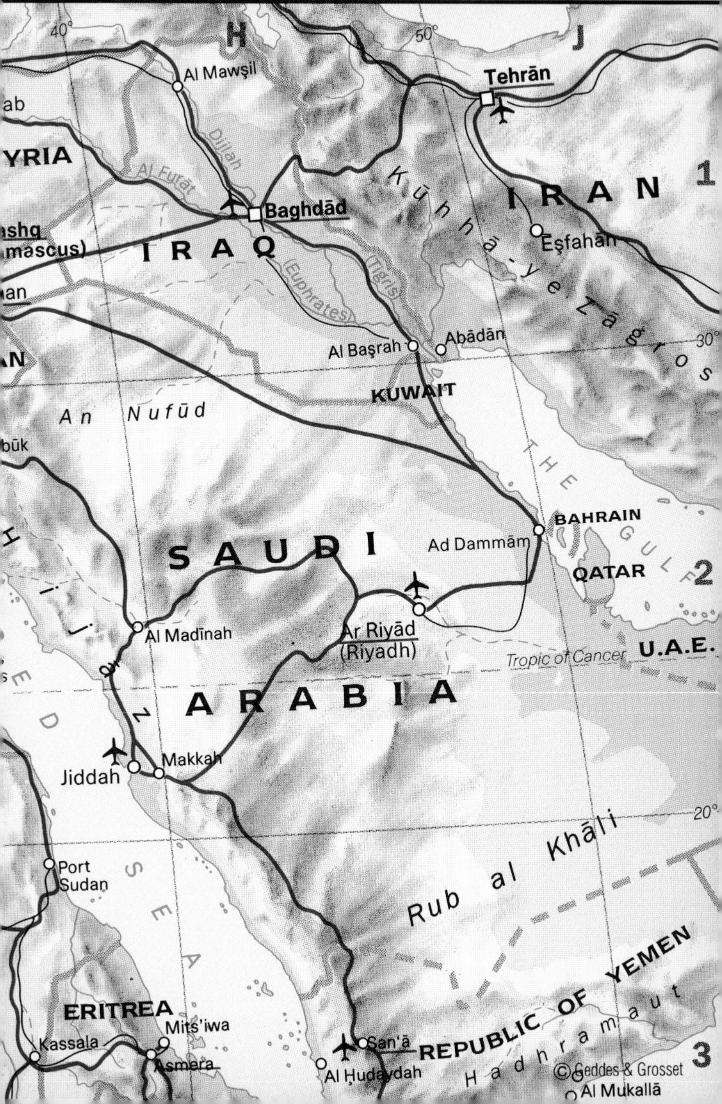
H
J
40°
50°
30°
20°
1
2
3
Al Mawşil
Tehrān
YRIA
Dijlah
Al Furāt
Baghdād
IRAN
Eşfahān
Kūhhā-ye Zāgros
IRAQ
ashq
mascus)
Euphrates
Tigris
Al Başrah
Abādān
KUWAIT
An Nufūd
būk
THE GULF
BAHRAIN
Ad Dammām
QATAR
SAUDI ARABIA
Al Madīnah
Ar Riyād
(Riyadh)
Tropic of Cancer
U.A.E.
Hijaz
RED SEA
Makkah
Jiddah
Rub al Khāli
Port
Sudan
REPUBLIC OF YEMEN
ERITREA
Mits'iwa
Kassala
Asmera
San'ā
Al Ḩudaydah
Hadhramaut
© Geddes & Grosset
Al Mukallā

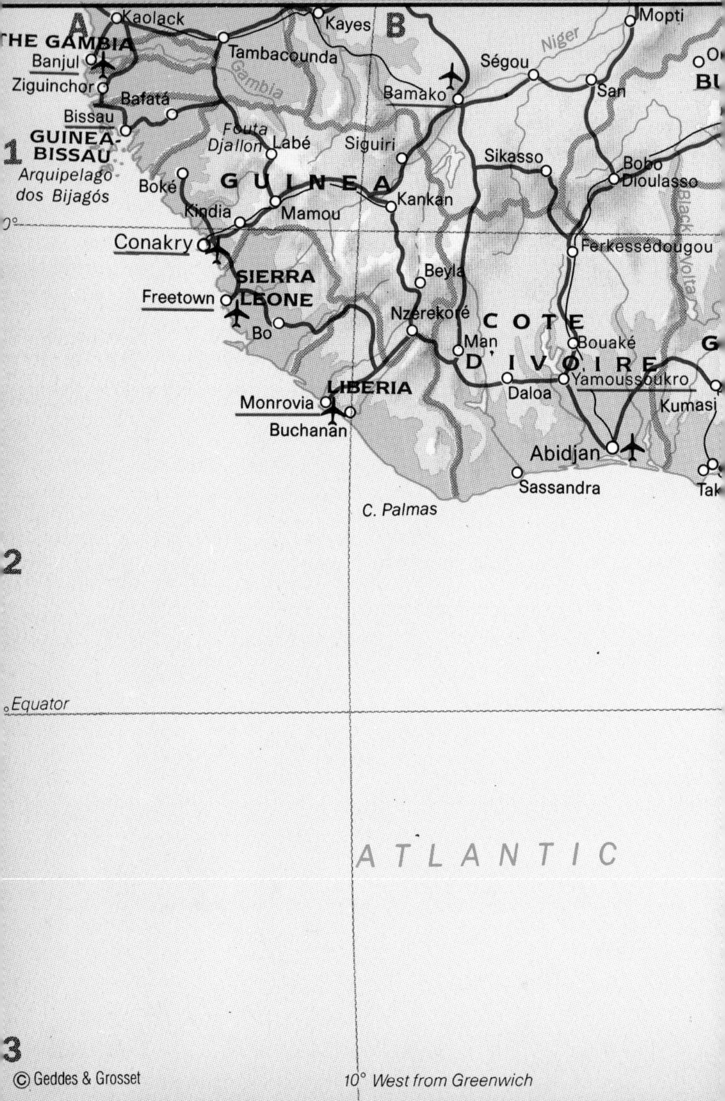
A
B
1
2
3
THE GAMBIA
Kaolack
Kayes
Mopti
Banjul
Tambacounda
Ségou
Niger
Gambia
Ziguinchor
Bafatá
Bamako
San
Bissau
GUINEA-BISSAU
Fouta Djallon
Labé
Siguiri
Sikasso
Bobo Dioulasso
Arquipelago dos Bijagós
Boké
GUINEA
Kindia
Mamou
Kankan
Black Volta
Conakry
Ferkessédougou
SIERRA LEONE
Beyla
Freetown
Nzerekoré
COTE D'IVOIRE
Bo
Man
Bouaké
Yamoussoukro
Daloa
LIBERIA
Kumasi
Monrovia
Buchanan
Abidjan
Sassandra
C. Palmas
Equator
ATLANTIC
10° West from Greenwich

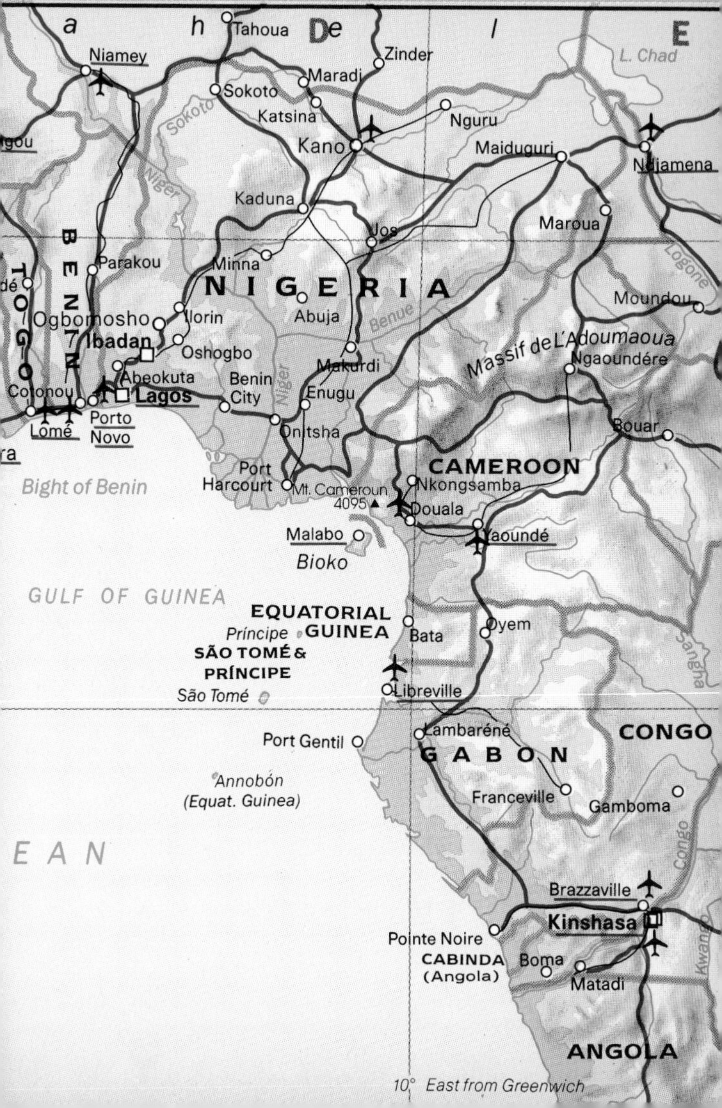
a
h
Tahoua
De
l
E
Niamey
Zinder
L. Chad
Maradi
Sokoto
Sokoto
Katsina
Nguru
gou
Kano
Maiduguri
Ndjamena
Niger
Kaduna
Maroua
BENIN
Jos
Logone
Parakou
Minna
TOGO
NIGERIA
Moundou
Abuja
Benue
Ogbomosho
Ilorin
Ibadan
Oshogbo
Massif de L'Adoumaoua
Makurdi
Ngaoundére
Abeokuta
Benin City
Niger
Enugu
Cotonou
Lagos
Porto Novo
Lomé
Onitsha
Bouar
ra
Port Harcourt
CAMEROON
Bight of Benin
Mt. Cameroun 4095
Nkongsamba
Douala
Malabo
Yaoundé
Bioko
GULF OF GUINEA
EQUATORIAL GUINEA
Príncipe
Bata
Oyem
Sangha
SÃO TOMÉ & PRÍNCIPE
São Tomé
Libreville
CONGO
Port Gentil
Lambaréné
GABON
Annobón (Equat. Guinea)
Franceville
Gamboma
Congo
EAN
Brazzaville
Kinshasa
Pointe Noire
CABINDA (Angola)
Boma
Matadi
Kwango
ANGOLA
10° East from Greenwich

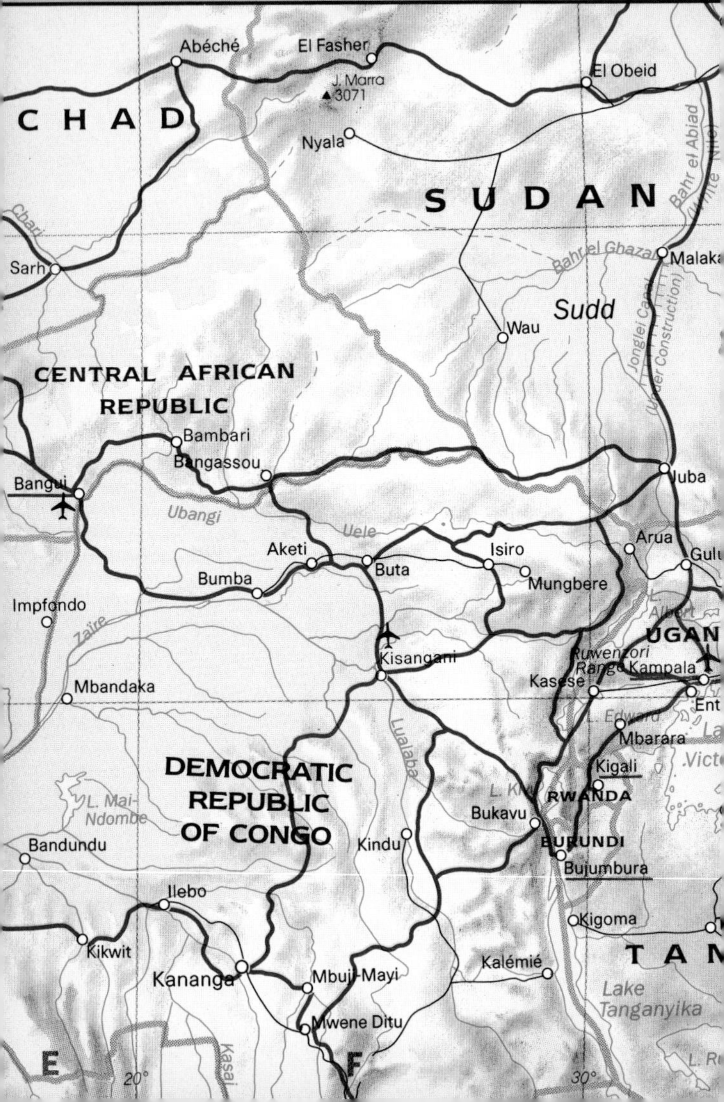
Abéché
El Fasher
J. Marra
3071
El Obeid
CHAD
Nyala
SUDAN
Bahr el Abiad (White Nile)
Chari
Sarh
Bahr el Ghazal
Malaka
Sudd
Wau
Jonglei Canal (Under Construction)
CENTRAL AFRICAN REPUBLIC
Bambari
Bangassou
Bangui
Juba
Ubangi
Uele
Arua
Aketi
Buta
Isiro
Mungbere
Gulu
Bumba
L. Albert
Impfondo
Zaïre
UGAN
Kisangani
Ruwenzori
Rango
Kampala
Kasese
Mbandaka
Ent
L. Edward
Mbarara
Lualaba
DEMOCRATIC REPUBLIC OF CONGO
Kigali
Vict
L. Mai-Ndombe
L. Kivu
RWANDA
Bukavu
Kindu
BURUNDI
Bandundu
Bujumbura
Ilebo
Kigoma
Kikwit
TAN
Kananga
Kalémié
Mbuji-Mayi
Lake Tanganyika
Mwene Ditu
E
F
20°
Kasai
30°

Gedaref
Ras Dashen 4620
Dandkil -116
Ta'izz
Āseb
'Adan
Gulf of Aden
Gonder
L. Tana
DJIBOUTI
Djibouti
Desē
Debre Mark'os
Berbera
Burco
Ethiopian
Dirē Dawa
Hārer
Hargeysa
ETHIOPIA
Ādīs Ābeba
(Addis Ababa)
Jima
Highlands
Abaya
Shebele
SOMALIA
Lake Turkana
Jubba
Muqdisho
(Mogadishu)
KENYA
Eldoret
Mt. Kenya 5200
Equator
Nakuru
Kismaayo
Nairobi
Kilimanjaro 5895
INDIAN
OCEAN
Arusha
Moshi
Mombasa
Masai Steppe
Tanga
Pemba
Zanzibar
Dodoma
Dar es Salaam
40°
50°
10°
0°
3
4
5
H
J

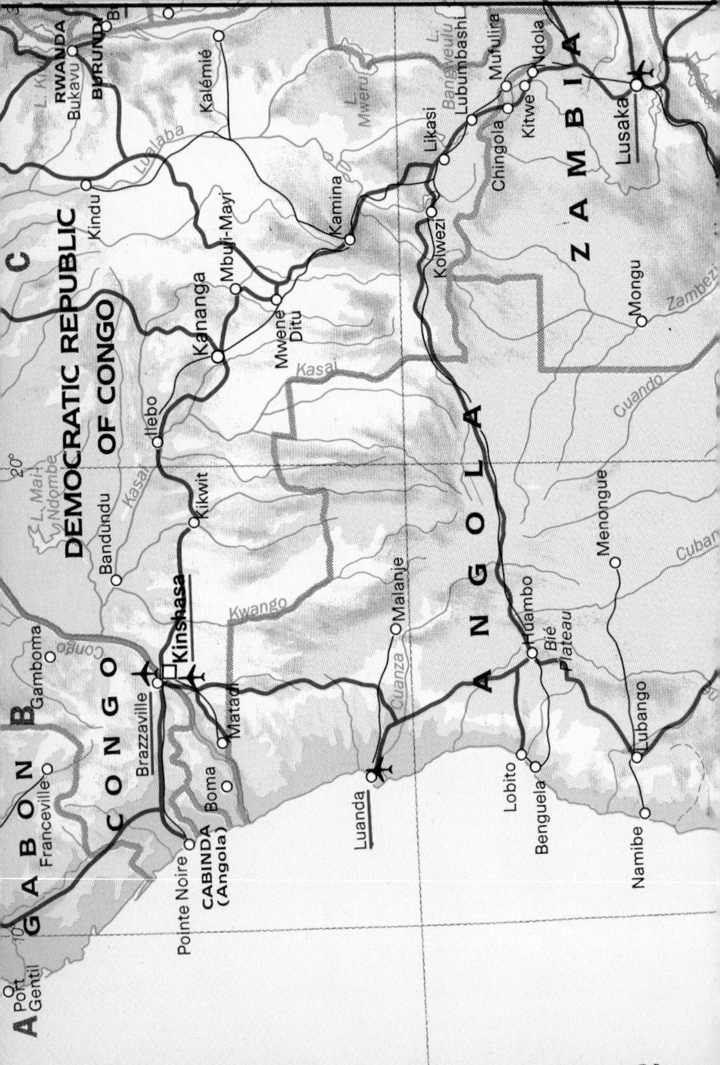
A
B
C
1
2
RWANDA
Bukavu
BURUNDI
Kalémié
Lualaba
L. Mweru
L. Bangweulu
Lubumbashi
Mufulira
Ndola
Kitwe
Chingola
Likasi
Lusaka
ZAMBIA
Kindu
DEMOCRATIC REPUBLIC OF CONGO
Mbuji-Mayi
Kamina
Kolwezi
Mongu
Zambezi
Kananga
Mwene Ditu
Kasai
Ilebo
Cuando
Kikwit
Bandundu
L. Mai-Ndombe
20°
Menongue
Cubango
Kinshasa
Kwango
Malanje
ANGOLA
Huambo
Bié Plateau
Congo
Gamboma
Brazzaville
CONGO
Matadi
Cuanza
Luanda
Lobito
Benguela
Lubango
Namibe
GABON
Franceville
Boma
Pointe Noire
CABINDA (Angola)
Port Gentil
10°

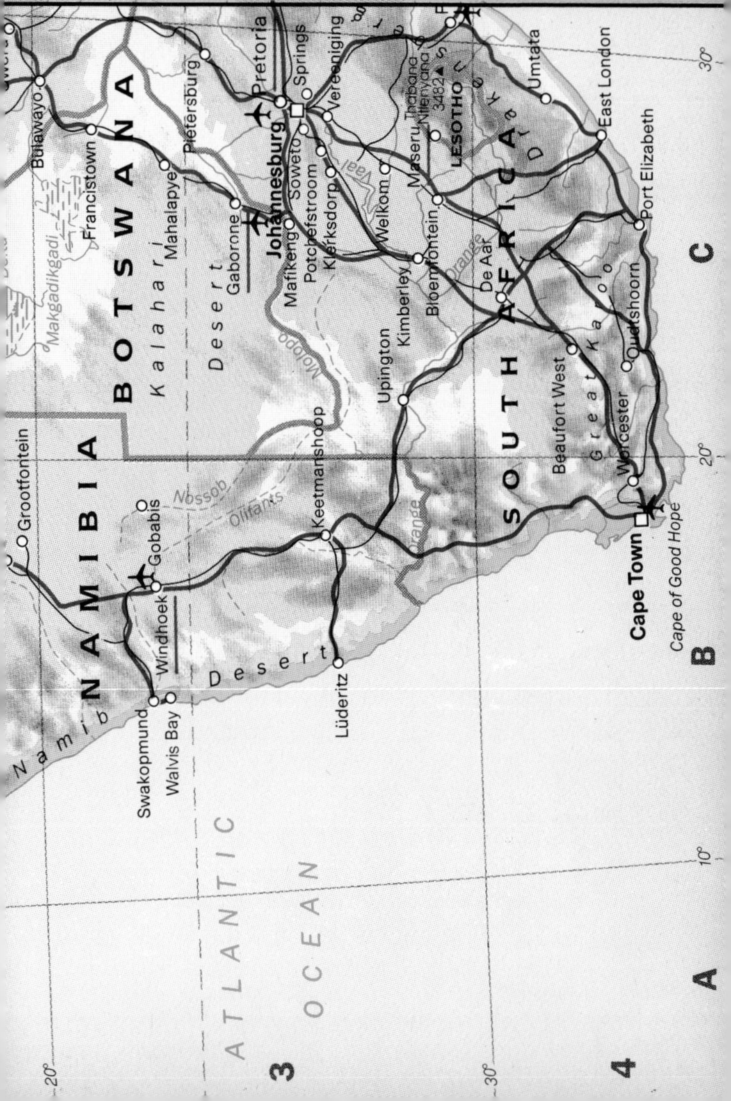
NAMIBIA
BOTSWANA
SOUTH AFRICA
LESOTHO
ATLANTIC OCEAN
Kalahari Desert
Namib Desert
Great Karoo
Makgadikgadi
Bulawayo
Francistown
Mahalapye
Pietersburg
Pretoria
Springs
Vereeniging
Johannesburg
Soweto
Gaborone
Mafikeng
Potchefstroom
Klerksdorp
Vaal
Welkom
Maseru
Thabana Ntlenyana 3482
Umtata
East London
Port Elizabeth
Bloemfontein
Kimberley
Orange
De Aar
Upington
Molopo
Beaufort West
Oudtshoorn
Worcester
Cape Town
Cape of Good Hope
Grootfontein
Gobabis
Nossob
Olifants
Keetmanshoop
Windhoek
Swakopmund
Walvis Bay
Lüderitz
20°
30°
10°
3
4
A
B
C

D
E
F
1
2
50°
40°
10°
Amirante Is.
SEYCHELLES
Farquhar Is.
INDIAN
OCEAN
Antsirañana
Massif du Tsaratanana
Mayotte (France)
COMOROS
Mahajanga
Moroni
Cape Delgado
Mtwara
Pemba
Moçambique
Nampula
KENYA
Nairobi
Mombasa
Pemba
Zanzibar
Dar es Salaam
Mafia I.
Rufiji
Kilimanjaro 5895
Moshi
Arusha
Masai Steppe
TANZANIA
Dodoma
Iringa
Mbeya
Rungwe 2959
Ruvuma
Lichinga
Lake Malawi
MALAWI
Zomba
Blantyre
Lilongwe
Cabora Bassa Dam
Tete
Zambezi
Shire
Lake Victoria
Mwanza
Tabora
Kigoma
Lake Tanganyika
L. Rukwa
Kasama
Muchinga Mts
Luangwa
ZAMBIA
Kigali
RWANDA
BURUNDI
Bujumbura

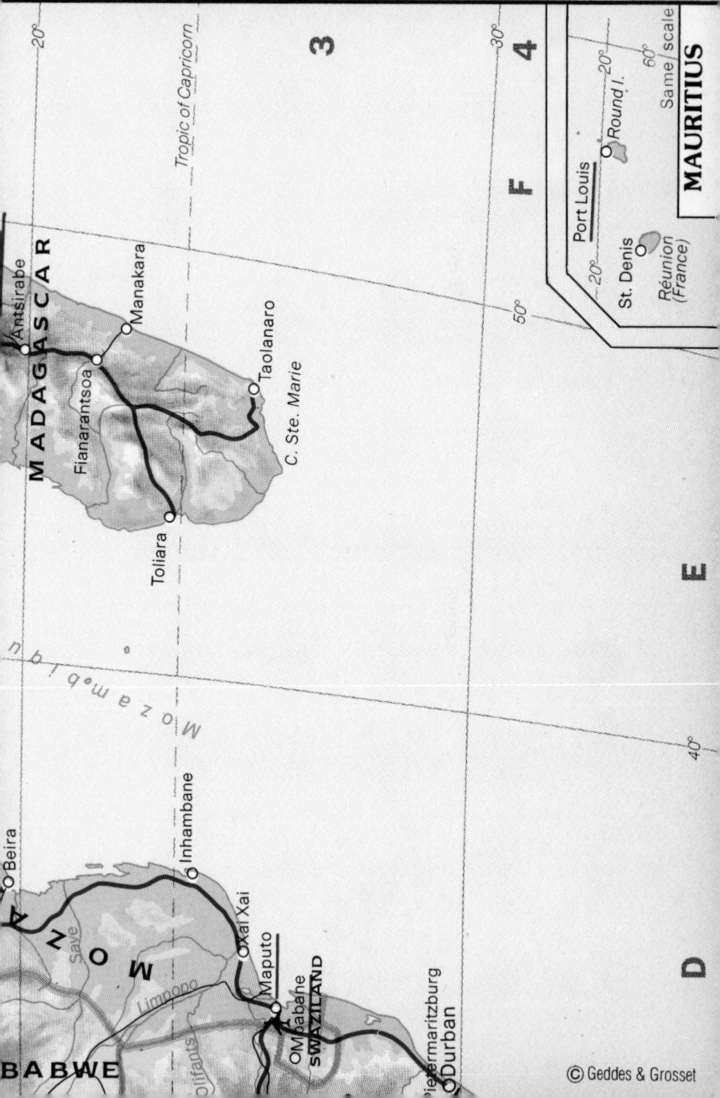

MADAGASCAR
Antsirabe
Manakara
Fianarantsoa
Taolanaro
C. Ste. Marie
Toliara
Tropic of Capricorn
Mozambique
Beira
Inhambane
Xai Xai
Maputo
Mbabane
SWAZILAND
Pietermaritzburg
Durban
Save
Limpopo
Olifants
BABWE
MAURITIUS
Port Louis
Round I.
St. Denis
Réunion (France)
Same scale
20°
30°
40°
50°
60°
3
4
D
E
F
© Geddes & Grosset

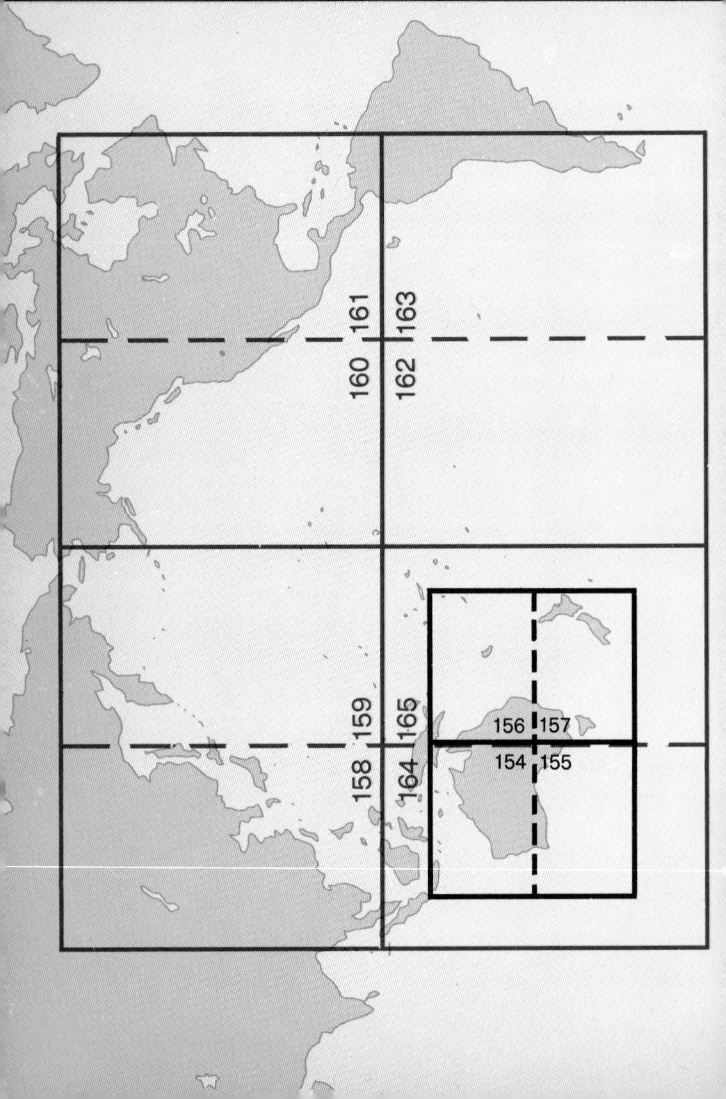

161
163
160
162
159
165
158
164
156
157
154
155

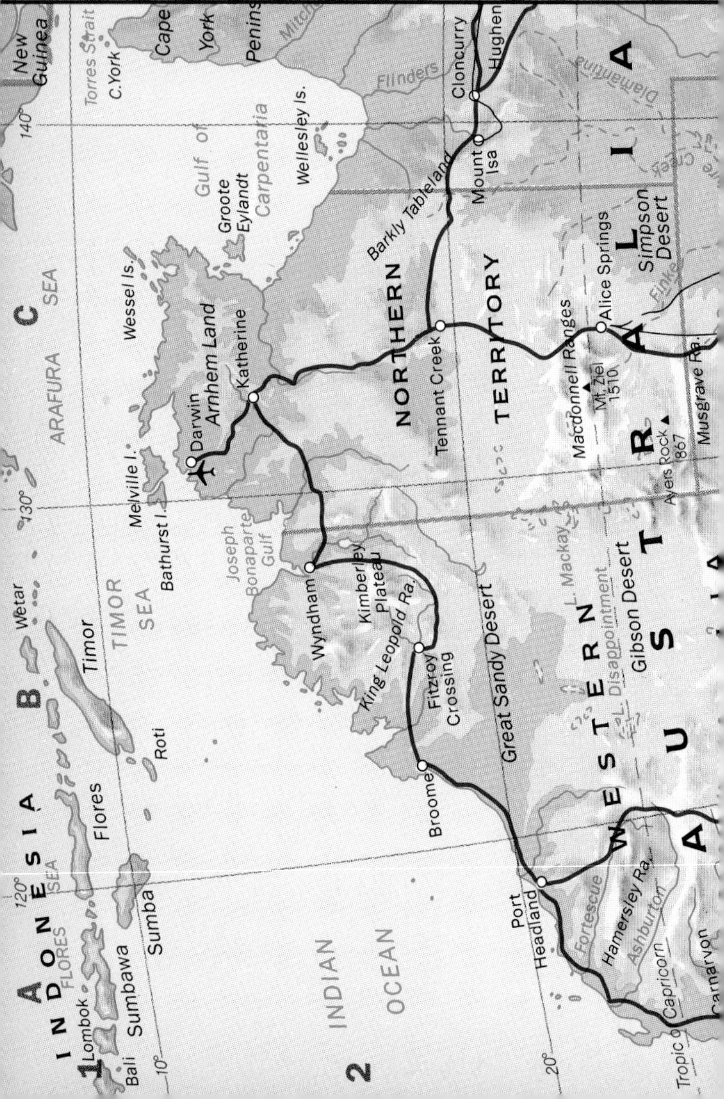
INDONESIA
ARAFURA SEA
TIMOR SEA
FLORES SEA
INDIAN OCEAN
NORTHERN TERRITORY
WESTERN AUSTRALIA
New Guinea
Torres Strait
C.York
Cape York Penins
Gulf of Carpentaria
Groote Eylandt
Wellesley Is.
Flinders
Cloncurry
Hughenden
Mount Isa
Barkly Tableland
Diamantina
Simpson Desert
Alice Springs
Finke
Macdonnell Ranges
Mt. Ziel 1510
Ayers Rock 867
Musgrave Ra.
Tennant Creek
Wessel Is.
Arnhem Land
Katherine
Darwin
Melville I.
Bathurst I.
Joseph Bonaparte Gulf
Wyndham
Kimberley Plateau
King Leopold Ra.
Fitzroy Crossing
Great Sandy Desert
L. Mackay
L. Disappointment
Gibson Desert
Broome
Port Headland
Fortescue
Hamersley Ra.
Ashburton
Carnarvon
Tropic of Capricorn
Wetar
Timor
Roti
Flores
Sumba
Sumbawa
Lombok
Bali
140°
130°
120°
10°
20°
A
B
C
1
2

Geraldton
Perth
Fremantle
Bunbury
C. Leeuwin
Augusta
Albany
L. Moore
L. Barlee
Kalgoorlie
Norseman
Esperance
Nullarbor Plain
Great Australian Bight
Tarcoola
L. Torrens
L. Gairdner
Gawler Ra.
Whyalla
Eyre Pen.
Spencer Gulf
Kangaroo I.
Port Augusta
Port Pirie
Adelaide
Broken Hill
Mildura
Murray
Mount Gambier
Warrnambool
A
B
C
4
5
30°
40°
110°
120°
130°
140°

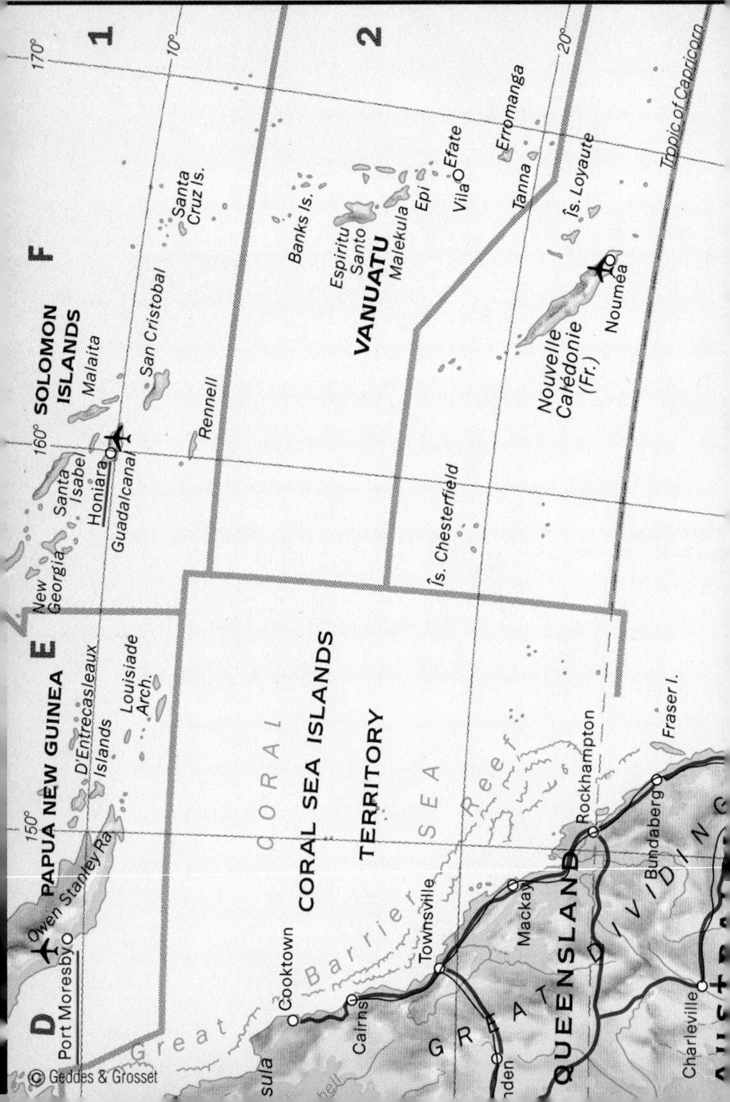

SOLOMON ISLANDS
Malaita
Santa Isabel
Honiara
Guadalcanal
New Georgia
San Cristobal
Rennell
Santa Cruz Is.
Banks Is.
Espiritu Santo
VANUATU
Malekula
Epi
Vila
Efate
Erromanga
Tanna
Îs. Loyauté
Nouméa
Nouvelle Calédonie (Fr.)
Îs. Chesterfield
Tropic of Capricorn
PAPUA NEW GUINEA
D'Entrecasteaux Islands
Louisiade Arch.
Owen Stanley Ra.
Port Moresby
CORAL SEA ISLANDS TERRITORY
CORAL SEA
Great Barrier Reef
Cooktown
Cairns
Townsville
Mackay
Rockhampton
Bundaberg
Fraser I.
Charleville
QUEENSLAND
GREAT DIVIDING
1
2
D
E
F
150°
160°
170°
10°
20°
© Geddes & Grosset

4
5
D
E
F
G
30°
40°
150°
160°
170°
180°
Three Kings Is.
North Cape
Whangarei
Bay of Plenty
Gisborne
Hastings
Palmerston North
Wellington
NEW ZEALAND
North Island
Auckland
Hamilton
Ruapehu 2797
Wanganui
Cook Str.
Norfolk I. (Austr.)
C. Farewell
Nelson
Christchurch
Hokitika
Southern Alps
Mt. Cook 3764
Dunedin
Invercargill
South Island
Stewart I.
Lord Howe I. (Austr.)
TASMAN SEA
NEW SOUTH WALES
Tamworth
Maitland
Newcastle
Sydney
Wollongong
Canberra
A.C.T.
Mt. Kosciusko 2230
Nyngan
Orange
Goulburn
Wagga Wagga
Albury
Bendigo
Lachlan
VICTORIA
Melbourne
Morwell
Geelong
Bass Strait
Furneaux Group
Launceston
TASMANIA
Hobart
Mt. Ossa 1617

30°
40°
50°
60°
70°
80°
90°
100°
East of Greenwich
Ob
Yenisey
60°
RUSSIA
Yekaterinburg
Krasnoyarsk
Omsk
Novosibirsk
Oz. Baykal
Irkutsk
Chita
50°
KAZAKHSTAN
Karaganda
Oz. Balkhash
Ulaanbaatar
MONGOLIA
Harbin
Changchun
Ürümqi
Almaty
Shenyang
NORTH KOREA
Beijing
40°
Tianjin
Lüda
Pyŏn
Huang
Jinan
Sŏul
Lanzhou
Qingdao
SOUTH KOREA
Xi'an
YELLOW SEA
CHINA
Nanjing
Kita-Kyūshū
Chengdu
Wuhan
Shanghai
Ky
30°
Chang
Chongqing
EAST CHINA SEA
NEPAL
BHUTAN
INDIA
Brahmaputra
Fuzhou
Ryūkyū Is.
Irrawaddy
Salween
Mekong
BANG.
Kunming
T'ai-pei
Dhākā
Guangzhou
TAIWAN
Calcutta
MYANMAR (BURMA)
Hanoi
MACAU (Port.)
HONG KONG
20°
Vientiane
LAOS
Hainan Dao
Luzon
Rangoon
VIETNAM
THAILAND
Manila
Andaman Is. (India)
Bangkok
CAMB.
SOUTH CHINA SEA
Mindoro
PHILIPPINES
Samar
Phnom Penh
Ho Chi Minh City
Palawan
10°
Gulf of Thailand
Nicobar Is. (India)
SULU SEA
Mindanao
Palau
BRUNEI

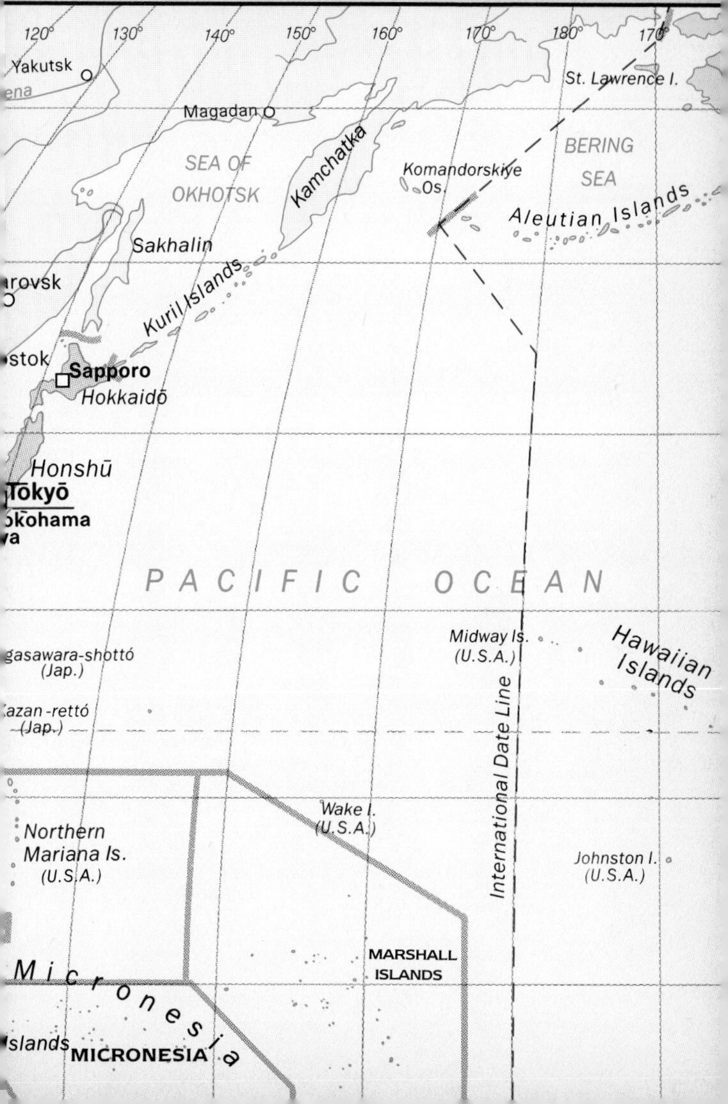
120°
130°
140°
150°
160°
170°
180°
170°
Yakutsk
ena
Magadan
St. Lawrence I.
SEA OF OKHOTSK
Kamchatka
Komandorskiye Os.
BERING SEA
Aleutian Islands
Sakhalin
rovsk
Kuril Islands
stok
Sapporo
Hokkaidō
Honshū
Tōkyō
okohama
va
PACIFIC OCEAN
Midway Is. (U.S.A.)
Hawaiian Islands
gasawara-shottó (Jap.)
International Date Line
azan-rettó (Jap.)
Wake I. (U.S.A.)
Northern Mariana Is. (U.S.A.)
Johnston I. (U.S.A.)
MARSHALL ISLANDS
Micronesia
slands
MICRONESIA

160°
150°
140°
130°
120°
110°
100°
90°
Yukon
Anchorage
Great Bear Lake
Mackenzie
Great Slave Lake
L. Athabasca
Gulf of Alaska
Kodiak I.
Alexander Arch.
CANAD
Edmonton
Queen Charlotte Is.
Calgary
Regin
Vancouver
Vancouver I.
Seattle
Missou
Portland
Snake
UNITE
San Francisco
Colorado
Los Angeles
San Diego
Guadalupe (Mex.)
PACIFIC
Hawaiian Islands
Honolulu
OCEAN
Hawaii
Revilla
(M
P
O
Palmyra (U.S.A.)

60°
50°
40°
30°
20°
10°
0°
10°
West of Greenwich
GREENLAND
(Den.)
Davis Str.
ICELAND
Reykjavik
60°
LABRADOR
SEA
50°
Newfoundland
St. Lawrence
L. Superior
L. Huron
L. Michigan
Montréal
Ottowa
polis
L. Ontario
Detroit
Toronto
Boston
Chicago
L. Erie
New York
A T E S
Pittsburgh
Philadelphia
Cincinnati
40°
ver
Baltimore
St. Louis
Ohio
Washington
ATLANTIC
M E R I C A
Dallas
Mississippi
Atlanta
New
Orleans
Bermuda
(U.K.)
Houston
30°
OCEAN
avo del Norte
GULF OF
MEXICO
Miami
nterrey
THE
BAHAMAS
MEXICO
La Habana
Tropic of Cancer
CUBA
Guadalajara
Greater Antilles
DOMINICAN
REPUBLIC
México
HAITI
20°
BELIZE
JAMAICA
Puerto
Rico
(U.S.A.)
Lesser Antilles
GUATEMALA
Guatemala
HONDURAS
Tegucigalpa
CARIBBEAN SEA
San Salvador
EL SALVADOR
NICARAGUA
Managua
Clipperton I.
(Fr.)
COSTA RICA
San José
Panamá
Caracas
10°
PANAMA
VENEZUELA
Medellín
de Coco
(C.R.)
Bogotá

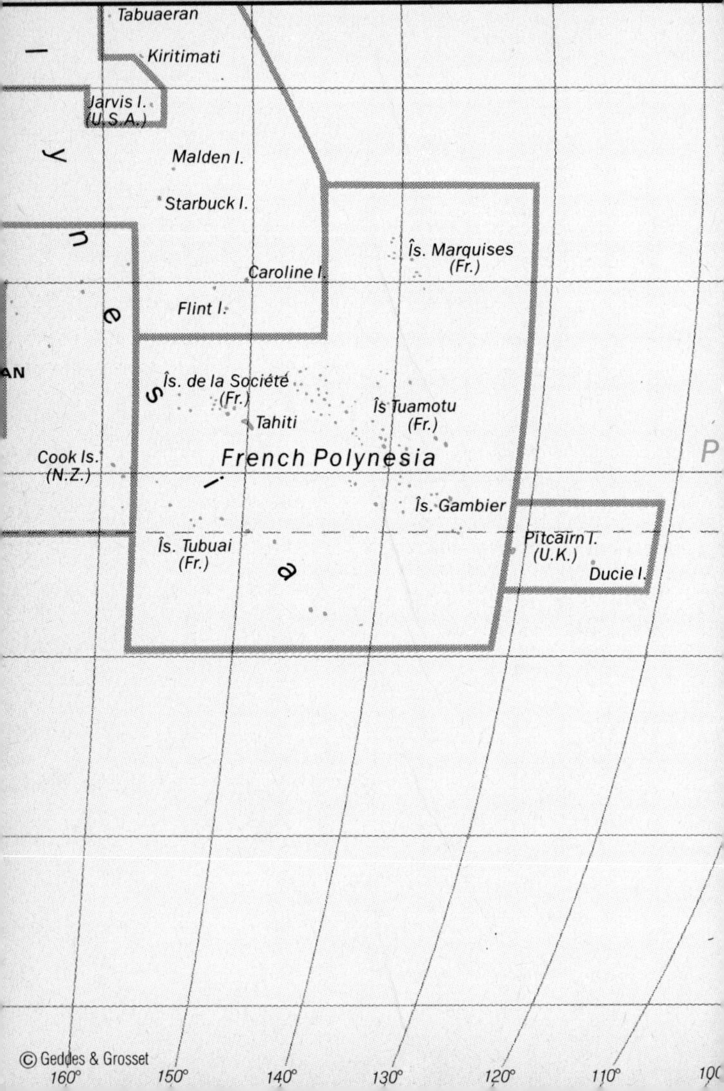
Tabuaeran
Kiritimati
Jarvis I.
(U.S.A.)
Malden I.
Starbuck I.
Caroline I.
Flint I.
Îs. Marquises
(Fr.)
Îs. de la Société
(Fr.)
Tahiti
Îs Tuamotu
(Fr.)
French Polynesia
Cook Is.
(N.Z.)
Îs. Gambier
Pitcairn I.
(U.K.)
Ducie I.
Îs. Tubuai
(Fr.)
AN
P
160°
150°
140°
130°
120°
110°

COLOMBIA
Equator
0°
Quito
Islas Galápagos
(Ecuador)
Guayaquil
ECUADOR
Amazonas
Trujillo
BRAZIL
PERU
10°
Callao
Lima
Titicaca
Arequipa
La Paz
BOLIVIA
IC OCEAN
Sucre
20°
PAR.
Tropic of Capricorn
Antofagasta
Asunción
Sala-y-Gomez (Ch.)
Pascua
Ch.)
30°
Córdoba
URUGUAY
Rosario
Montevideo
Santiago
Is. Juan Fernández
(Ch.)
Buenos
Aires
CHILE
Concepción
ARGENTINA
Bahía Blanca
40°
Puerto Montt
Patagonia
50°
Falkland Is.
(Islas Malvinas)
(U.K.)
Punta Arenas
Tierra del
Fuego
South Georgia
(U.K.)
80°
70°
60°
50°
40°
20°

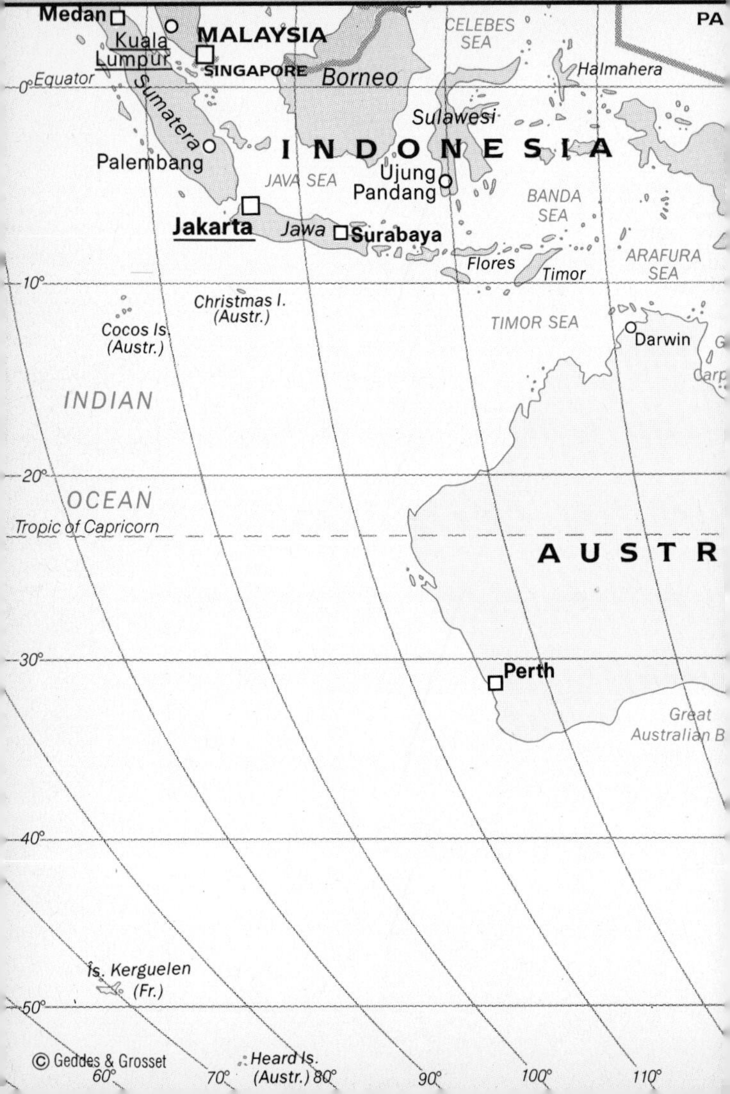
Medan
Kuala Lumpur
MALAYSIA
SINGAPORE
Borneo
CELEBES SEA
Halmahera
PA
0° Equator
Sumatera
Sulawesi
INDONESIA
Palembang
JAVA SEA
Ujung Pandang
BANDA SEA
Jakarta
Jawa
Surabaya
ARAFURA SEA
Flores
Timor
10°
Christmas I. (Austr.)
Cocos Is. (Austr.)
TIMOR SEA
Darwin
INDIAN
20°
OCEAN
Tropic of Capricorn
AUSTR
30°
Perth
Great Australian B
40°
Îs. Kerguelen (Fr.)
50°
Heard Is. (Austr.)
60°
70°
80°
90°
100°
110°
© Geddes & Grosset

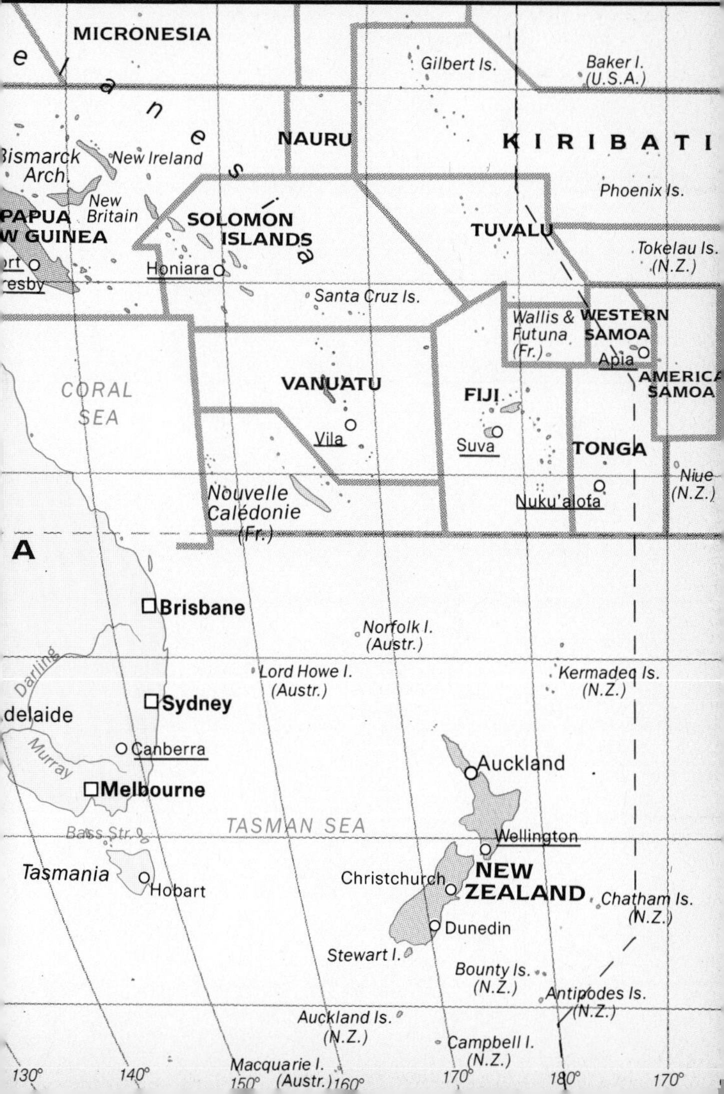
MICRONESIA
e l a n e s i a
Gilbert Is.
Baker I. (U.S.A.)
NAURU
K I R I B A T I
Bismarck Arch.
New Ireland
New Britain
PAPUA NEW GUINEA
Port Moresby
SOLOMON ISLANDS
Honiara
Phoenix Is.
TUVALU
Tokelau Is. (N.Z.)
Santa Cruz Is.
Wallis & Futuna (Fr.)
WESTERN SAMOA
Apia
AMERICAN SAMOA
CORAL SEA
VANUATU
Vila
FIJI
Suva
TONGA
Nuku'alofa
Niue (N.Z.)
Nouvelle Calédonie (Fr.)
A
Brisbane
Norfolk I. (Austr.)
Darling
Lord Howe I. (Austr.)
Kermadec Is. (N.Z.)
Adelaide
Sydney
Canberra
Murray
Melbourne
Auckland
TASMAN SEA
Bass Str.
Wellington
Tasmania
Hobart
Christchurch
NEW ZEALAND
Chatham Is. (N.Z.)
Dunedin
Stewart I.
Bounty Is. (N.Z.)
Antipodes Is. (N.Z.)
Auckland Is. (N.Z.)
Campbell I. (N.Z.)
Macquarie I. (Austr.)
130°
140°
150°
160°
170°
180°
170°

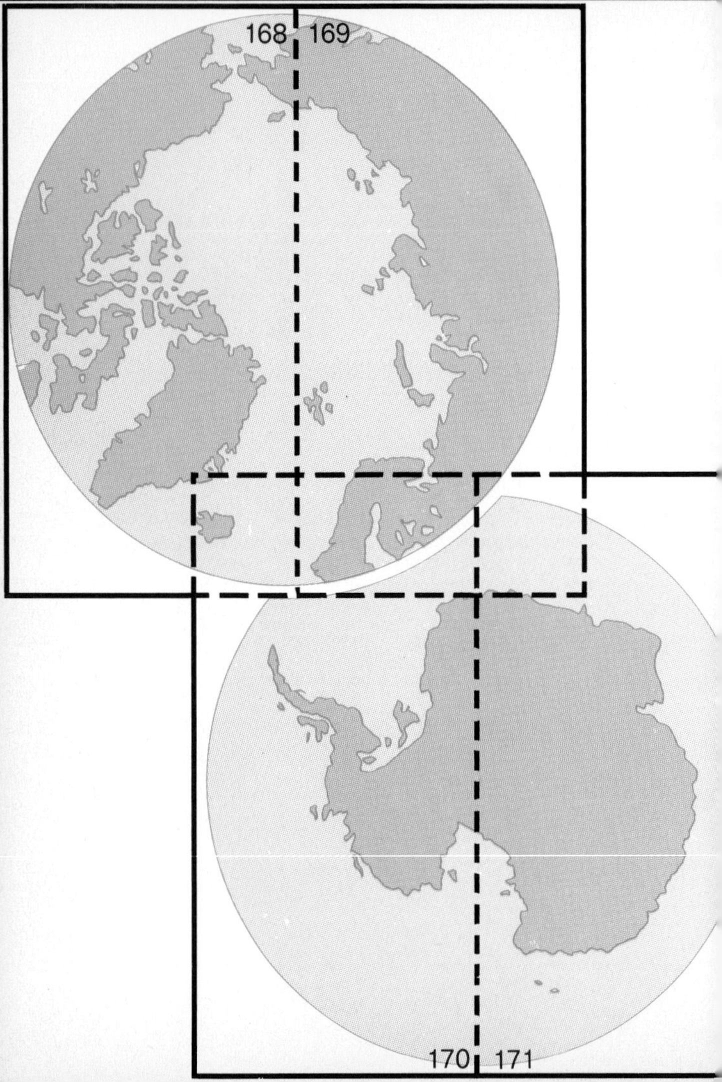
168
169
170
171

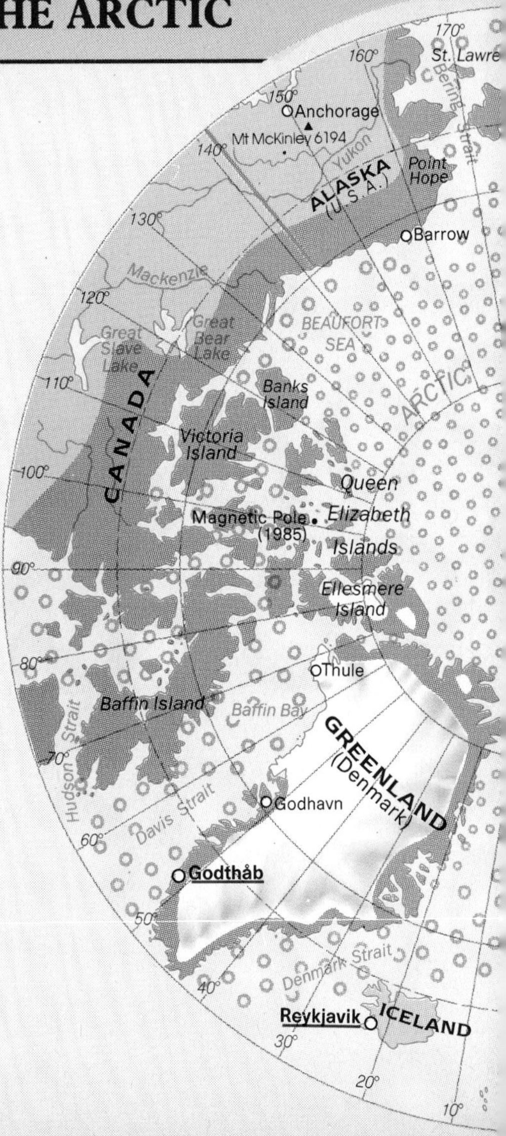
St. Lawre
Bering Strait
Anchorage
Mt McKinley 6194
Yukon
ALASKA
(U.S.A.)
Point Hope
Barrow
Mackenzie
Great Bear Lake
Great Slave Lake
BEAUFORT SEA
ARCTIC
CANADA
Banks Island
Victoria Island
Queen Elizabeth Islands
Magnetic Pole (1985)
Ellesmere Island
Thule
Baffin Island
Baffin Bay
Hudson Strait
GREENLAND
(Denmark)
Davis Strait
Godhavn
Godthåb
Denmark Strait
Reykjavik
ICELAND
170°
160°
150°
140°
130°
120°
110°
100°
90°
80°
70°
60°
50°
40°
30°
20°
10°

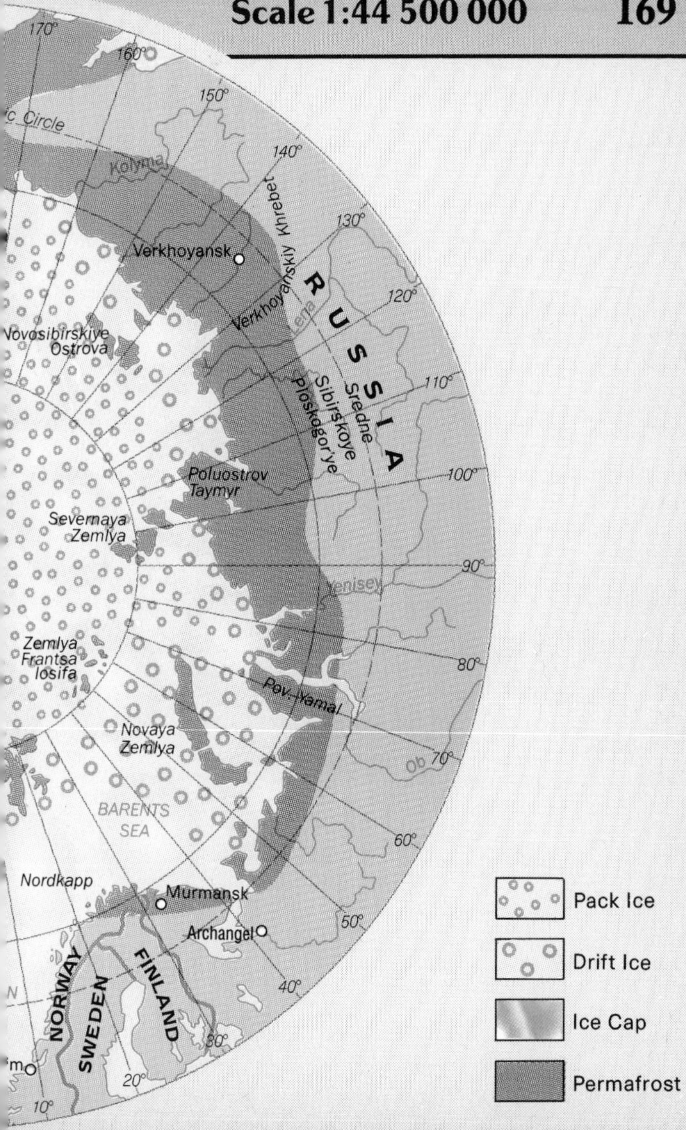
RUSSIA
Verkhoyansk
Verkhoyanskiy Khrebet
Kolyma
Lena
Novosibirskiye Ostrova
Sredne Sibirskoye Ploskogor'ye
Poluostrov Taymyr
Severnaya Zemlya
Yenisey
Zemlya Frantsa Iosifa
Pov. Yamal
Novaya Zemlya
Ob
BARENTS SEA
Nordkapp
Murmansk
Archangel
NORWAY
SWEDEN
FINLAND
Arctic Circle
170°
160°
150°
140°
130°
120°
110°
100°
90°
80°
70°
60°
50°
40°
30°
20°
10°
Pack Ice
Drift Ice
Ice Cap
Permafrost

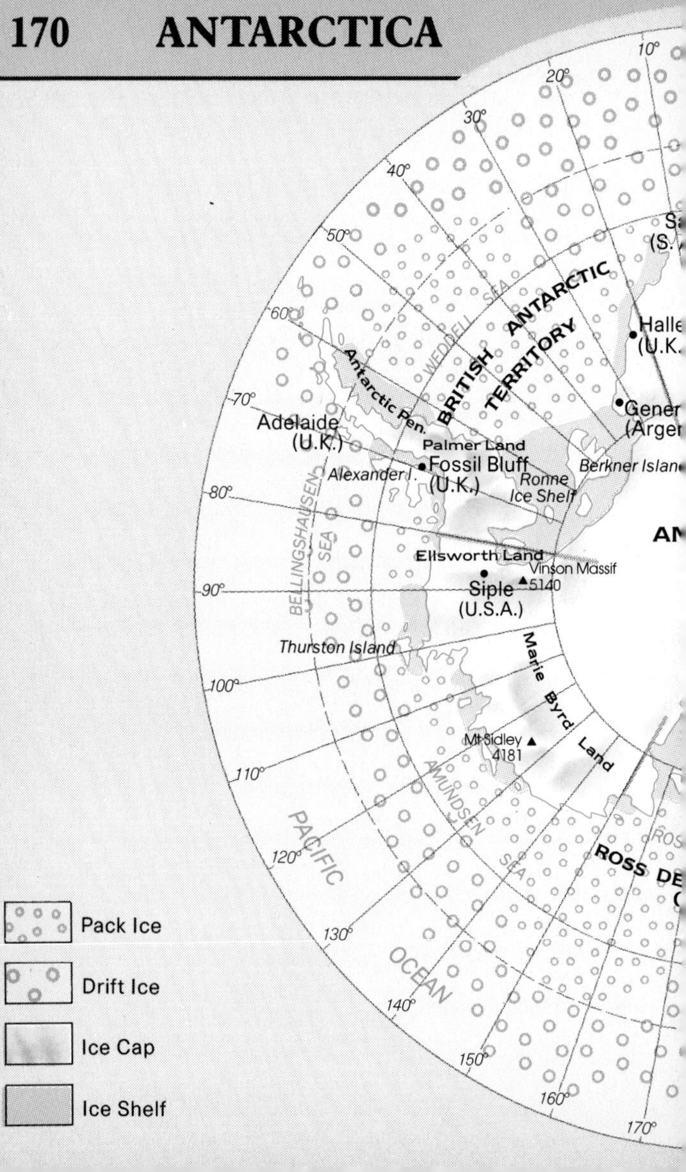
10°
20°
30°
40°
50°
60°
70°
80°
90°
100°
110°
120°
130°
140°
150°
160°
170°
BRITISH ANTARCTIC TERRITORY
WEDDELL SEA
Antarctic Pen.
Adelaide (U.K.)
Palmer Land
Fossil Bluff (U.K.)
Alexander I.
Ronne Ice Shelf
Berkner Island
BELLINGSHAUSEN SEA
Ellsworth Land
Vinson Massif 5140
Siple (U.S.A.)
Thurston Island
Marie Byrd Land
Mt Sidley 4181
AMUNDSEN SEA
PACIFIC OCEAN
ROSS
Pack Ice
Drift Ice
Ice Cap
Ice Shelf

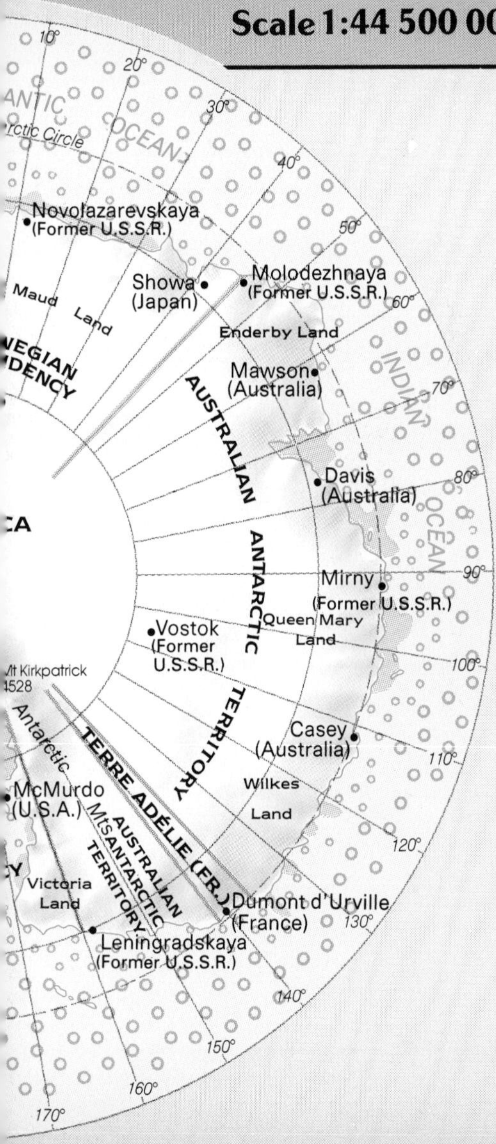

OCEAN
Antarctic Circle
Novolazarevskaya (Former U.S.S.R.)
Maud Land
Showa (Japan)
Molodezhnaya (Former U.S.S.R.)
Enderby Land
Mawson (Australia)
INDIAN OCEAN
AUSTRALIAN ANTARCTIC TERRITORY
Davis (Australia)
Mirny (Former U.S.S.R.)
Queen Mary Land
Vostok (Former U.S.S.R.)
Mt Kirkpatrick
Casey (Australia)
Wilkes Land
TERRE ADÉLIE (FR.)
McMurdo (U.S.A.)
AUSTRALIAN ANTARCTIC TERRITORY
Victoria Land
Dumont d'Urville (France)
Leningradskaya (Former U.S.S.R.)
10° 20° 30° 40° 50° 60° 70° 80° 90° 100° 110° 120° 130° 140° 150° 160° 170°

Index

In the index, the first number refers to the page, and the following letter and number to the section of the map in which the index entry can be found. For example London 56G6 means that London can be found on page 56 where column G and row 6 meet.

Abbreviations used in the Index

Afghan	Afghanistan
Alb	Albania
Alg	Algeria
Arg	Argentina
Aust	Australia
Bang	Bangladesh
Belg	Belgium
Bol	Bolivia
Bos.Herz.	Bosnia Herzegovina
Bulg	Bulgaria
Camb	Cambodia
Can	Canada
CAR	Central African Republic
Cro.	Croatia
Czech.Rep.	Czech.Republic
Dem.Rep.of Congo	Democratic Republic of Congo
Den	Denmark
Dom Rep.	Dominican Republic
El Sal	El Salvador
Eng	England
Eq Guinea	Equatorial Guinea
Est	Estonia
Eth	Ethiopia
FRG	Federal Republic of Germany
Fin	Finland
Hung	Hungary
Indon.	Indonesia
Lat	Latvia
Leb	Lebanon
Lib	Liberia
Liech	Leichtenstein
Lith	Lithuania
Lux	Luxembourg
Madag	Madagascar
Malay	Malaysia
Maur	Mauritania
Mor	Morocco
Mozam	Mozambique
N.Ire	Northern Ireland
N.Korea	North Korea
NZ	New Zealand
Neth	Netherlands
Nic	Nicaragua
Nig	Nigeria
Nor	Norway
PNG	Papua New Guinea
Pak	Pakistan
Par	Paraguay
Phil	Phillipines
Pol	Poland
Port	Portugal
Rep.Yemen	Republic of Yemen
Rom	Romania
S.Africa	South Africa
S.Arabia	Saudi Arabia
S.Korea	South Korea
Scot	Scotland
Sen	Senegal
Slo	Slovenia
Switz	Switzerland
Tanz	Tanzania
Thai	Thailand
Turk	Turkey
UAE	United Arab Emirates
UK	United Kingdom
USA	United States of America
Urug	Uruguay
Ven	Venezuela
Viet	Vietnam
Yugos	Yugoslavia
Zim	Zimbabwe

A

B

C

D

E

F

G

H

I

J

K

L

M

O

P

T

U

V

Gazetteer

Afghanistan

Area 652,225 sq km (251,773 sq miles); *population* 18,052,000; *capital* Kabul; *other major cities* Herat, Kandahar,; Mazar-i-Sharif; *form of government* Republic; *religions* Sunni Islam, Shia Islam; *currency* Afghani

Afghanistan is a landlocked country in southern Asia. The greater part of the country is mountainous with several peaks over 6000 m (19,686 ft) in the central region. The climate is generally arid with great extremes of temperature. There is considerable snowfall in winter which may remain on the mountain summits the year round. The main economic activity is agriculture and although predominantly pastoral, successful cultivation takes place in the fertile plains and valleys. Natural gas is produced in northern Afghanistan and over 90% of this is piped across the border to the former USSR. Other mineral resources are scattered and so far underdeveloped. The main exports are Karakuls (Persian lambskins), raw cotton and foodstuffs. Since the Russian withdrawal from Afghanistan in 1989, the country has still been troubled by, mainly ethnic, conflict.

Albania

Area 28,748 sq km (11,100 sq miles); *population* 3,422,000 (estimate prior to 1997, when significant numbers of refugees were leaving the country); *capital* Tirana (Tiranë); *other major cities* Durrës, Shkodër, Elbasan; *form of government* Socialist Republic; *religion* Constitutionally atheist but mainly Sunni Islam; *currency* Lek

Albania is a small mountainous country in the eastern Mediterranean. Its immediate neighbours are Greece, Serbia and The Former Yugoslav Republic of Macedonia, and it is bounded to the west by the Adriatic Sea. The climate is typically Mediterranean and although most rain falls in winter, severe thunderstorms frequently occur on the plains in summer. Winters are severe in the highland areas and heavy snowfalls are common. All land is state owned, with the main agricultural areas lying along the Adriatic coast and in the Korce Basin. Industry is also nationalized and output is small. The principal industries are agricultural product processing, textiles, oil products and cement. Most trade is with neighbouring Serbia and The Former Yugoslav Republic of Macedonia. Albania has been afflicted by severe economic problems and in late 1996 public dissatisfaction with the government erupted into civil unrest, leading to a major revolt by citizen militias during which the government forces lost control, particularly in the south of the country. By March 1997 the country was on the brink of collapse and large numbers of refugees were leaving.

Algeria

Area 2,381,741 sq km (919,590 sq miles); *population* 27,940,000; *capital* Algiers (Alger); *other major cities* Oran, Constantine, Annaba; *form of government* Republic; *religion* Sunni Islam; *currency* Algerian dinar

Algeria is a huge country in northern Africa, which fringes the Mediterranean Sea in the north. Over four-fifths of Algeria is covered by the Sahara Desert to the south. Near the north coastal area the Atlas Mountains run east-west in parallel ranges. The climate in the coastal areas is warm and temperate with most of the rain falling in winter. The summers are dry and hot with temperatures rising to over 32°C. Inland beyond the Atlas Mountains conditions become more arid and temperatures range from 49°C during the day to 10°C at night. Most of Algeria is unproductive agriculturally, but it does possess one of the largest reserves of natural gas and oil in the world. Algeria's main exports are oil-based products, and some fruit and vegetables.

Andorra

Area 457 sq km (170 sq miles); *population* 65,000; *capital* Andorra-la-Vella; *form of government* Co-principality; *religion* RC; *currency* Franc, Peseta

Andorra is a tiny state, situated high in the eastern Pyrénées, between France and Spain. The state consists of deep valleys and high mountain peaks which reach heights of 3000 m/9843 ft. Although only 20 km/12 miles wide and 30 km/19 miles long, the spectacular scenery and climate attract many tourists. About 10 million visitors arrive each year, during the cold weather when heavy snowfalls makes for ideal skiing, or in summer when the weather is mild and sunny and the mountains are used for walking. Tourism and the duty-free trade are now Andorra's chief sources of income. Natives who are not involved in the tourist industry may raise sheep and cattle on the high pastures.

Angola

Area: 1,246,700 sq km (481,351 sq miles); *population* 10,844,000; *capital* Luanda; *other major cities* Huambo, Lobito, Benguela; *form of government* People's Republic; *religions* RC, Animism; *currency* Kwanza

Angola is situated on the Atlantic coast of west central Africa, Angola lies about 10°S of the equator. It shares borders with Congo, Zaïre, Zambia and Namibia. Its climate is tropical with temperatures constantly between 20°C and 25°C. The rainfall is heaviest in inland areas where there are vast equatorial forests. The country is also rich in minerals, however deposits of manganese, copper and phosphate are as yet unexploited. Diamonds are mined in the north-east and oil is produced near Luanda. Oil production is the most important aspect of the economy, making up about 80% of export revenue. However, the Angolan economy has been severely damaged by the civil war of the 80s and early 90s.

Antigua and Barbuda

Area 442 sq km (170 sq miles); *population* 66,000; *capital* St John's; *form of government* Constitutional Monarchy; *religion* Christianity (mainly Anglicanism); *currency* East Caribbean dollar

Antigua and Barbuda is located on the eastern side of the Leeward Islands, a tiny state comprising three islands—Antigua, Barbuda and the uninhabited Redonda Antigua's strategic position was recognized by the British in the 18th century when it was an important naval base, and later by the USA who built the island's airport during World War II to defend the Caribbean and the Panama Canal. The climate is tropical although its average rainfall of 100 mm (4 inches) makes it drier than most of the other islands of the West Indies. On Antigua, many sandy beaches make it an ideal tourist destination, and tourism is the main industry. Barbuda is surrounded by coral reefs and the island is home to a wide range of wildlife.

Argentina

Area 2,766,889 sq km (1,302,296 sq miles); *population* 34,663,000; *capital* Buenos Aires; *other major cities* Cordoba, Rosaria, Mendoza, La Plata; *form of government* Federal Republic; *religion* RC; *currency* Peso

Argentina, the world's 8th largest country, stretches from the Tropic of Capricorn to Cape Horn on the southern tip of the South American continent. To the west a massive mountain chain, the Andes, forms the border with Chile. The climate ranges from warm temperate over the Pampas in the central region, to a more arid climate in the north and west, while in the extreme south conditions although also dry are much cooler. The vast fertile plains of the Pampas once provided Argentina with its main source of wealth, but as manufacturing industries were established in the early 20th century agriculture suffered badly and food exports were greatly reduced. A series of military regimes has resulted in an unstable economy which fails to provide reasonable living standards for the population.

Armenia

Area 29,800 sq km (11,500 sq miles); *population* 3,603,000; *capital* Yerevan; Other major city : Kumayri (Leninakan); *form of government* Republic; *religion* Armenian Orthodox; *currency* Dram

Armenia is the smallest republic of the former USSR and part of the former kingdom of Armenia which was divided between Turkey, Iran and the former USSR. It declared independence from the USSR in 1991. It is a landlocked Transcaucasian republic, and its neighbours are Turkey, Iran, Georgia and Azerbaijan. The country is very mountainous with many peaks over 3000 m (9900 ft). Agriculture is mixed in the lowland areas. The main crops grown are grain, sugar beet and potatoes, and livestock reared include cattle, pigs and sheep. Mining of copper, zinc and lead is important, and industrial development is increasing. Hydro-electricity is produced from stations on the river Razdan as it falls 1000 m (3281 ft) from Lake Sevan to its confluence with the River Araks.

Australia

Area 7,300,848 sq km (2,966,150 sq miles); *population* 18,114,000; *capital* Canberra; *other major cities* Adelaide, Brisbane, Melbourne, Perth, Sydney; *form of government* Federal Parliamentary State; *religion* Christianity; *currency* Australian dollar

Australia, the world's smallest continental landmass, is a vast and sparsely populated island state in the southern hemisphere. The most mountainous region is the Great Dividing Range which runs down the entire east coast. Because of its great size, Australia's climates range from tropical monsoon to cool temperate and also large areas of desert. Central and south Queensland are subtropical while north and central New South Wales are warm temperate. Much of Australia's wealth comes from agriculture, with huge sheep and cattle stations extending over large parts of the interior. These have helped maintain Australia's position as the world's leading producer of wool. Cereal growing is dominated by wheat. Mineral extraction is also very important.

Austria

Area 83,855 sq km (32,367 sq miles); *population* 8,015,000; *capital* Vienna (Wien); *other major cities* Graz, Linz, Salzburg; *form of government* Federal Republic; *religion* RC; *currency* Schilling

Austria is a landlocked country in central Europe and is surrounded by seven nations. The wall of mountains which runs across the centre of the country dominates the scenery. In the warm summers tourists come to walk in the forests and mountains and in the cold winters skiers come to the mountains which now boast over 50 ski resorts. Agriculture in Austria is based on small farms, many of which are run by single families. Dairy products, beef and lamb from the hill farms contribute to exports. More then 37% of Austria is covered in forest, resulting in the paper-making industry near Graz. Unemployment is very low in Austria and its low strike record has attracted multinational companies in recent years. Attachment to local customs is still strong and in rural areas men still wear lederhosen and women the traditional dirndl skirt on feast days and holidays.

Azerbaijan

Area 86,600 sq km (33,400 sq miles); *population* 7,559,000; *capital* Baku; *other major cities* Kirovabad, Sumgait; *form of government* Republic; *religions* Shia Islam, Sunni Islam, Russian Orthodox; *currency* Manat

Azerbaijan, a republic of the former USSR, declared itself independent in 1991. It is situated on the south-west coast of the Caspian Sea and shares borders with Iran, Armenia, Georgia and the Russian Federation. The Araks river separates Azerbaijan from the region known as Azarbaijan in northern Iran. The country is semi-arid, and 70% of the land is irrigated for the production of cotton, wheat, maize, potatoes, tobacco, tea and citrus fruits. It has rich mineral deposits of oil, natural gas, iron and aluminium. The most important mineral is oil, which is found in the Baku area from where it is piped to Batumi on the Black Sea. There are steel, synthetic rubber and aluminium works at Sumgait just north of the capital Baku.

Bahamas

Area 13,939 sq km (5382 sq miles); *population* 277,000; *capital* Nassau; *other major cities* Freeport; *form of government* Constitutional Monarchy; *religion* Christianity; *currency* Bahamian dollar

The Bahamas consist of an archipelago of 700 islands located in the Atlantic Ocean off the south-east coast of Florida. The largest island is Andros (4144 sq km/1600 sq miles), and the two most populated are Grand Bahama and New Providence where the capital Nassau lies. Winters in the Bahamas are mild and summers warm. Most rain falls in May, June, September and October, and thunderstorms are frequent in summer. The islands have few natural resources, and for many years fishing and small-scale farming was the only way to make a living. Now, however tourism, which employs over two-thirds of the workforce, is the most important industry and has been developed on a vast scale. About three million tourists, mainly from North America, visit the Bahamas each year.

Bahrain

Area 691 sq km (267 sq miles); *population* 539,000; *capital* Manama; *form of government* Monarchy (Emirate); *religions* Shia Islam, Sunni Islam; *currency* Bahraini dollar

Bahrain is a Gulf State comprising 33 low-lying islands situated between the Qatar peninsula and the mainland of Saudi Arabia. Bahrain Island is the largest, and a causeway linking it to Saudi Arabia was opened in 1986. The highest point in the state is only 122.4 m (402 ft) above sea level. The climate is pleasantly warm between December and March, but very hot from June to November. Most of Bahrain is sandy and too saline to support crops but drainage schemes are now used to reduce salinity and fertile soil is imported from other islands. Oil was discovered in 1931 and revenues from oil now account for about 75% of the country's total revenue. Bahrain is being developed as a major manufacturing state, the first important enterprise being aluminum smelting. Traditional industries include pearl fishing, boat building, weaving and pottery.

Bangladesh

area 143,998 sq km (55,598 sq miles); *population* 118,342,000; *capital* Dacca (Dhaka); *other major cities* Chittagong, Khulna; *form of government* Republic; *religion* Sunni Islam; *currency* aka

Bangladesh was formerly the Eastern Province of Pakistan. It is bounded almost ntirely by India and to the south by the Bay of Bengal. The country is extremely flat and is virtually a huge delta formed by the Ganges, Brahmaputra and Meghna rivers. he country is subject to devastating floods and cyclones which sweep in from the Bay of Bengal. Most villages are built on mud platforms to keep them above water. he climate is tropical monsoon with heat, extreme humidity and heavy rainfall in the monsoon season. The short winter season is mild and dry. The combination of rainfall, sun and silt from the rivers makes the land productive, and it is often possible to grow three crops a year. Bangladesh produces about 70% of the world's jute and the production of jute-related products is a principal industry.

Barbados

area 430 sq km (166 sq miles); *population* 264,000; *capital* Bridgetown; *form of government* Constitutional Monarchy; *religions* Anglicanism, Methodism; *currency* Barbados dollar

Barbados is the most easterly island of the West Indies and lies well outside the group of islands which makes up the Lesser Antilles. Most of the island is low-lying and only in the north does it rise to over 340 m/1116 ft at Mount Hillaby. The climate is tropical, but the cooling effect of the North-east Trade winds prevents the temperatures rising above 30°C (86°F). There are only two seasons, the dry and the wet, when rainfall is very heavy. At one time the economy depended almost exclusively on the production of sugar and its by-products molasses and rum, and although the industry is now declining, sugar is still the principal export. Tourism has now taken over as the main industry and it employs approximately 40% of the island's labour force. The island is surrounded by pink and white sandy beaches and coral reefs which are visited by almost 400 000 tourists each year.

Belarus (Belorussia, Byelorussia)

area 207,600 sq km (80,150 sq miles); *population* 10,355,000; *capital* Minsk; *other major cities* Gomel, Mogilev, Vitebsk; *form of government* Republic; *religions* Russian Orthodox, RC; *currency* Rouble

Belarus, a republic of the former USSR, declared itself independent in 1991. It borders Poland to the west, Ukraine to the south, Latvia and Lithuania to the north, and the Russian Federation to the east. The country consists mainly of a low-lying plain, and forests cover approximately one third of the country. The climate is ontinental with long severe winters and short warm summers. Although the conomy is overwhelmingly based on industry, including oil refining, food processing, woodworking, chemicals, textiles and machinery, output has gradually declined ince 1991 and problems persist in the supply of raw materials from other republics that previously formed parts of the USSR. Agriculture, although seriously affected by contamination from the Chernobyl nuclear accident of 1986, accounts for approximately 20% of employment, the main crops being flax, potatoes and hemp. The main livestock raised are cattle and pigs. Extensive forest areas also contribute in the upply raw materials for woodwork and paper-making.

Belgium

Area 30,519 sq km (11,783 sq miles); *population* 10,100,630; *capital* Brussels; *other major cities* Antwerp, Charleroi, Ghent, Liege; *form of government* Constitutional Monarchy; *religion* RC; *currency* Belgian franc

Belgium is a relatively small country in north-west Europe with a short coastline o the North Sea. The Meuse river divides Belgium into two distinct geographica regions. To the north of the river the land slopes continuously for 150 km/93 mile until it reaches the North Sea where the coastlands are flat and grassy. To the sout of the river is the forested plateau area of the Ardennes. Between these two region lies the Meuse valley. Belgium is a densely populated industrial country with fe natural resources. Agriculture is based on livestock production but employs only 3% of the workforce. The metal-working industry, originally based on the small miner deposits in the Ardennes, is the most important industry, and in the northern citie new textile industries are producing carpets and clothing. Nearly all raw materials ar now imported through the main port of Antwerp.

Belize

Area 22,965 sq km (8867 sq miles); *population* 205,000; *capital* Belmopan; Other major city : Belize City; *form of government* Constitutional Monarchy; *religion* RC; *currency* Belize dollar

Belize is a small Central American country on the south-east of the Yucata Peninsula in the Caribbean Sea. Its coastline on the Gulf of Honduras is approache through some 550 km/342 miles of coral reefs and keys (cayo). The coastal area an north of the country are low-lying and swampy with dense forests inland. In the sout the Maya Mountains rise to 1100 m/3609 ft. The subtropical climate is warm an humid and the trade winds bring cooling sea breezes. Rainfall is heavy, particularl in the south, and hurricanes may occur in summer. The dense forests which cove most of the country provide valuable hardwoods such as mahogany. Most of th population make a living from forestry, fishing or agriculture. The main crops grow for export are sugar cane, citrus fruits (mainly grapefruit), bananas and coconuts Despite this approximately only 5% of Belize's total land area is cultivated an industry is very underdeveloped, causing many people to emigrate to find work.

Benin

Area 112,622 sq km (43,483 sq miles); *population* 5,160,000; *capital* Porto-Novo; Other major city : Cotonou; *form of government* Republic; *religions* Animism, RC, Sunni Islam, Christian; *currency* CFA Franc

Benin on the southern coast of West Africa is an ice cream cone-shaped country wit a very short coastline on the Bight of Benin. The coastal area has white sand beaches backed by lagoons and low-lying fertile lands. In the north-west the Atakor Mountains are grassy plateaux which are deeply cut into steep forested valleys. Th climate in the north is tropical and in the south equatorial. There are nine rainy month each year so crops rarely fail. Farming is predominantly subsistence, with yams cassava, maize, rice, groundnuts and vegetables forming most of the produce. Th country is very poor, although since the late '80s economic reforms have bee towards a market economy and Western financial aid has been sought. The mai exports are palm oil, palm kernels, and cotton. Tourism is now being developed bu as yet facilities for this are few except in some coastal towns.

Bermuda

Area 54 sq km (21 sq miles); *population* 61,000; *capital* Hamilton; *form of government* Colony under British administration; *religion* Protestantism; *currency* Bermuda dollar

Bermuda consists of a group of 150 small islands in the western Atlantic Ocean. It lies about 920 km/572 miles east of Cape Hatteras on the coast of the USA. The hilly limestone islands are the caps of ancient volcanoes rising from the sea-bed. The main island, Great Bermuda, is linked to the other islands by bridges and causeways. The climate is warm and humid with rain spread evenly throughout the year. Bermuda's chief agricultural products are fresh vegetables, bananas and citrus fruit. Many foreign banks and financial institutions operate from the island, taking advantage of the lenient tax laws. Its proximity to the USA and the pleasant climate have led to a flourishing tourist industry.

Bhutan

Area 46,500 sq km (17,954 sq miles); *population* 1,442,000; *capital* Thimpu; *form of government* Constitutional Monarchy; *religion* Buddhism, Hinduism; *currency* Ngultrum

Bhutan is surrounded by India to the south and China to the north. It rises from foothills overlooking the Brahmaputra river to the southern slopes of the Himalayas. The Himalayas, which rise to over 7500 m/24,608 ft in Bhutan, make up most of the country. The climate is hot and wet on the plains but temperatures drop progressively with altitude, resulting in glaciers and permanent snow cover in the north. The valleys in the centre of the country are wide and fertile and about 95% of the workforce are farmers. Yaks reared on the high pasture land provide milk, cheese and meat. Rice is grown on the lowest ground. Vast areas of the country still remain forested as there is little demand for new farmland. Bhutan is one of the world's poorest and least developed countries; it has little contact with the rest of the world and the number of visitors is limited to 1500 each year.

Bolivia

Area 1,098,581 sq km (424,164 sq miles); *population* 7,715,000; *capital* La Paz (administrative *capital*), Sucre (legal *capital*); Other major city : Cochabamba; *form of government* Republic; *religion* RC; *currency* Boliviano

Bolivia is a landlocked republic of Central South America through which the great mountain range of the Andes runs. It is in the Andes that the highest navigable lake in the world, Lake Titicaca, is found. On the undulating depression south of the lake, the Altiplano, is the highest capital city in the world, La Paz. To the east and north-east of the mountains is a huge area of lowland containing tropical rainforests (the Llanos) and wooded savanna (the Chaco). The north-east has a heavy rainfall while in the south-west it is negligible. Temperatures vary with altitude from extremely cold on the summits to cool on the Altiplano, where at least half of the population lives. Although rich in natural resources, e.g. oil, tin, Bolivia remains a poor country because of lack of funds for their extraction, lack of investment and political instability. Agriculture produces foodstuffs, sugar cane and cotton for export, and increased production of coca, from which cocaine is derived, has resulted in an illicit economy.

Bosnia & Herzegovina

Area 51,129 sq km (19,741 sq miles); *population* 3,500,000; *capital* Sarajevo; *other major cities* Banja Luka, Mostar, Tuzla; *form of government* Republic; *religions* Eastern Orthodox, Sunni Islam, RC; *currency* Dinar

Bosnia & Herzegovina, a republic of former Yugoslavia, was formally recognized as an independent state in March 1992. It is a very mountainous country and includes part of the Dinaric Alps, which are densely forested and deeply cut by rivers flowing northwards to join the Sava river. Half the country is forested, and timber is an important product of the northern areas. One quarter of the land is cultivated, and corn, wheat and flax are the principal products of the north. In the south, tobacco, cotton, fruits and grapes are the main products. Bosnia & Herzegovina has large deposits of lignite, iron ore and bauxite, but there is little industrialization. Despite the natural resources the economy has been devastated by civil war which began in 1991 following the secession of Croatia and Slovenia from the former Yugoslavia. Dispute over control of Bosnia and Herzegovina continued, leading to UN intervention in an attempt to devise a territorial plan acceptable to all factions. A peace agreement signed in late 1995 has resulted in the division of the country into two self governing provinces. The population of the state was significantly diminished when refugees from the civil war fled between 1992 and 1993.

Botswana

Area 581,730 sq km (224,606 sq miles); *population* 1,326,800; *capital* Gaborone; *other major cities* Francistown, Molepolole, Selibe-Pikwe; *form of government* Republic; *religions* Animism, Christian; *currency* Pula

Botswana is a landlocked republic in southern Africa which straddles the Tropic of Capricorn. Much of the west and south-west of the country forms part of the Kalahari Desert. In the north the land is marshy around the Okavango Delta, which is home for a wide variety of wildlife. With the exception of the desert area, most of the country has a subtropical climate. In winter, days are warm and nights cold while summer is hot with sporadic rainfall. The people are mainly farmers and cattle rearing is the main activity. After independence in 1966 the exploitation of minerals started. Diamonds became an important revenue earner and the copper from the nickel/copper complex at Selebi-Pikwe was also exported. Mineral resources in the north-east are now being investigated and the exploitation of these resources has facilitated a high rate of economic growth withihn the country. About 17% of the land is set aside for wildlife preservation in National Parks, Game Reserves, Game Sanctuaries and controlled hunting areas.

Brazil

Area 8,511,965 sq km (3,285,488 sq miles); *population* 156,500,000; *capital* Brasília; *other major cities* Belo Horizonte, Porto Alegre, Recife, Rio de Janeiro, Salvador, São Paulo; *form of government* Federal Republic; *religion* RC; *currency* Cruzeiro

Brazil is a huge South American country bounded to the north, south and east by the Atlantic ocean. It is the fifth largest country in the world and covers nearly half of South America. The climate is mainly tropical, but altitude, distance from the sea and prevailing winds cause many variations. In the Amazonia area it is constantly warm and humid, but in the tropical areas winters are dry and summers wet. Droughts may occur in the north-east, where it is hot and arid. About 14% of the population is employed in agriculture and the main products exported are coffee, soya beans and cocoa. Brazil is rich in minerals and is the only source of high grade quartz crystal in commercial quantities. It is also a major producer of chrome ore and it is now developing what is thought to be the richest iron ore deposits in the world.

Brunei

Area 5,765 sq km (2,226 sq miles); *population* 276,000; *capital* Bandar Seri Begawan; *other major cities* Kuala Belait, Seria; *form of government* Monarchy (Sultanate); *religion* Sunni Islam; *currency* Brunei dollar

Brunei is a sultanate located on the north-west coast of Borneo in South-East Asia. It is bounded on all sides by the Sarawak territory of Malaysia, which splits the sultanate into two separate parts. Broad tidal swamplands cover the coastal plains and inland Brunei is hilly and covered with tropical forest. The climate is tropical marine, hot and moist, with cool nights. Rainfall is heavy (2500 mm/98 inches) at the coast but even heavier (5000 mm/197 inches) inland. The main crops grown are rice, vegetables and fruit, but economically the country depends on its oil industry, which employs 7% of the working population. Oil production began in the 1920s and now oil and natural gas account for almost all exports. Other minor products are rubber, pepper, sawn timber, gravel and animal hides.

Bulgaria

Area 110,912 sq km (42,823 sq miles); *population* 8,473,000; *capital* Sofia (Sofiya); *other major cities* Burgas, Plovdiv, Ruse, Varna; *form of government* Republic; *religion* Eastern Orthodox; *currency* Lev

Bulgaria is a south-east European republic located on the east Balkan peninsula and has a coast on the Black Sea. It is bounded to the north by Romania, west by Serbia and The Former Yugoslav Republic of Macedonia and south by Greece and Turkey. The centre of Bulgaria is crossed from west to east by the Balkan Mountains. The south of the country has a Mediterranean climate with hot dry summers and mild winters. Further north the temperatures become more extreme and rainfall is higher in summer. Traditionally Bulgaria is an agricultural country and a revolution in farming during the 1950s has led to great increases in output. This was due to the collectivization of farms and the use of more machinery, fertilizers and irrigation. Each agricultural region now has its own specialized type of farming. Increased mechanization led to more of the workforce being available to work in mines and industry. However, following the break up of the former Soviet Union, with whom Bulgaria had particularly close trade links, the country has suffered very high rates of inflation and unemployment in the early 90s. The tourist trade has flourished though, with over 10,000,000 people visiting the Black Sea resorts annually.

Burkina Faso (Burkina)

Area 274,200 sq km (105,869 sq miles); *population* 9,780,000; *capital* Ouagadougou; *form of government* Republic; *religions* Animist, Sunni Islam; *currency* Franc CFA

Burkina Faso, a landlocked state in West Africa, lies on the fringe of the Sahara, to the north. The country is made up of vast monotonous plains and low hills which rise to 700 m (2297 ft) in the south-west. Precipitation is generally low, the heaviest rain falling in the south-west, while the rest of the country is semi-desert. In the last two decades the country has been stricken by drought. The dusty gray plains in the north and west have infertile soils which have been further impoverished by overgrazing and overcultivation. About 90% of the people live by farming, and food crops include sorghum, beans and maize. Some cotton, livestock and oil seeds are exported. There is a great poverty and shortage of work and many of the younger population go to Ghana and Côte d'Ivoire for employment. The only main industries are textiles and metal products.

Burundi

Area 27,834 sq km (10,747 sq miles); *population* 5,958,000; *capital* Bujumbura; *form of government* Republic; *religion* RC; *currency* Burundi franc

Burundi is a small densely populated country in central east Africa, bounded by Rwanda to the north, Tanzania to the east and south, and Zaïre to the west. It has a mountainous terrain, with much of the country above 1500 m (4921 ft). The climate is equatorial but modified by altitude. The savanna in the east is several degrees hotter than the plateau and there are two wet seasons. The soils are not rich but there is enough rain to grow crops in most areas. The main food crops are bananas, sweet potatoes, peas, lentils and beans. Cassava is grown near the shores of Lake Tanganyika. The main cash crop is coffee, accounting for 90% of Burundi's export earnings. There is a little commercial fishing on Lake Tanganyika, otherwise industry is very basic. Since 1994 Burundi has been afflicted by ethnic conflict between the majority Hutu and minority Tutsi. Between 1994 and 1995 it is estimated that 150,000 were killed as a result of ethnic violence and the political situation remains highly volatile.

Cambodia

Area 181,035 sq km (69,898 sq miles); *population* 9,280,000; *capital* Phnom-Penh; *other major cities* Battambang, Kampong Cham,; *form of government* People's Republic; *religion* Buddhism; *currency* Riel

Cambodia is a South-East Asian state bounded by Thailand, Laos and Vietnam and its southern coast lies on the Gulf of Thailand. The heart of the country is saucer-shaped, and gently rolling alluvial plains are drained by the Mekong river. The Dangrek Mountains form the frontier with Thailand in the north-west. In general Cambodia has a tropical Monsoon climate and about half of the land is tropical forest. During the rainy season the Mekong swells and backs into the Tonle Sap (Great Lake), increasing its size threefold. Almost 162,000 hectares of land are flooded by this seasonal rise of the Mekong and this area is left with rich silt when the river recedes. Crop production depends entirely on the rainfall and floods but production was badly disrupted during the civil war and yields still remain low. Despite the gradual rebuilding of the infrastructure in the early 1990s, Cambodia remains one of the world's poorest nations.

Cameroon

Area 475,442 sq km (183,568 sq miles); *population* 12,800,000; *capital* Yaoundé; Other major city : Douala; *form of government* Republic; *religions* Animism, RC, Sunni Islam; *currency* Franc CFA

Cameroon is a triangular-shaped country of diverse landscapes in west central Africa. It stretches from Lake Chad at its apex to the northern borders of Equatorial Guinea, Gabon and the Congo in the south. The landscape ranges from low-lying lands, through the semi-desert Sahel, to dramatic mountain peaks and then to the grassy savanna, rolling uplands, steaming tropical forests and hardwood plantations. Further south are the volcanoes, including Mount Cameroon, and the palm beaches at Kribi and Limbe. The climate is equatorial with high temperatures and plentiful rain. The majority of the population lives in the south where they grow maize and vegetables. In the drier north where drought and hunger are well known, life is harder. Bananas, coffee and cocoa are the major exports although oil, gas and aluminum are becoming increasingly important.

Canada

Area 9 ,970,610 sq km (3,849,674 sq miles); *population* 28,150,000; *capital* Ottawa; *other major cities* Toronto, Montréal, Vancouver, Québec City; *form of government* Federal Parliamentary State; *religions* RC, United Church of Canada, Anglicanism; *currency* Canadian dollar

Canada is the second largest country in the world, and the largest in North America. Canada is a land of great climatic and geographical extremes. It lies to the north of the USA and has Pacific, Atlantic and Arctic coasts. The Rocky Mountains and Coast Mountains run down the west side, and the highest point, Mount Logan (5951 m/ 19,524 ft), is in the Yukon. Climates range from polar conditions in the north, to cool temperate in the south with considerable differences from west to east. More than 80% of its farmland is in the prairies that stretch from Alberta to Manitoba. Wheat and grain crops cover three-quarters of the arable land. Canada is rich in forest reserves which cover more than half the total land area. The most valuable mineral deposits (oil, gas, coal and iron ore) are found in Alberta. Most industry in Canada is associated with processing its natural resources.

Cape Verde

Area 4033 sq km (1575 sq miles); *population* 370,000; *capital* Praia; *form of government* Republic; *religion* RC; *currency* Cape Verde escudo

Cape Verde, one of the world's smallest nations, is situated in the Atlantic Ocean, about 640 km (400 miles) north-west of Senegal. It consists of 10 islands and 5 islets. The islands are divided into the Windward group and the Leeward group. Over 50% of the population live on São Tiago on which is Praia, the capital. The climate is arid with a cool dry season from December to June and warm dry conditions for the rest of the year. Rainfall is sparse and the islands suffer from periods of severe drought. Agriculture is mostly confined to irrigated inland valleys and the chief crops are coconuts, sugar cane, potatoes and cassava. Bananas and some coffee are grown for export. Fishing for tuna and lobsters is an important industry but in general the economy is shaky and Cape Verde relies heavily on foreign aid.

Central African Republic

Area 622,984 sq km (240,535 sq miles); *population* 3,173,000; *capital* Bangui; *form of government* Republic; *religions* Animism, RC; *currency* Franc CFA

Central African Republic is a landlocked country in central Africa bordered by Chad in the north, Cameroon in the west, Sudan in the east and the Congo and Zaïre in the south. The terrain consists of a 610–915-m (2000–3000-ft) high undulating plateau with dense tropical forest in the south and a semi-desert area in the east. The climate is tropical with little variation in temperature throughout the year. The wet months are May, June, October and November. Most of the population live in the west and in the hot, humid south and south-west. Over 86% of the working population are subsistence farmers and the main crops grown are cassava, groundnuts, bananas, plantains, millet and maize. Livestock rearing is small-scale because of the prevalence of the tsetse fly. Gems and industrial diamonds are mined and vast deposits of uranium have been discovered.

Chad

Area 1,284,000 sq km (495,750 sq miles); *population* 6,100,000; *capital* N'Djamena; *other major cities* Sarh, Moundou; *form of government* Republic; *religions* Sunni Islam, Animism; *currency* Franc CFA

Chad, a landlocked country in the centre of northern Africa, extends from the edge of the equatorial forests in the south to the middle of the Sahara Desert in the north. It lies more than 1600 km (944 miles) from the nearest coast. The climate is tropical with adequate rainfall in the south but the north experiences semi-desert conditions. In the far north of the country the Tibesti Mountains rise from the desert sand more than 3000 m (9843 ft). The southern part of Chad is the most densely populated and its relatively well-watered savanna has always been the country's most arable region. Recently, however, even here the rains have failed. Normally this area is farmed for cotton (the main cash crop), millet, sorghum, groundnuts, rice and vegetables. Fishing is carried out in the rivers and in Lake Chad. Cotton ginning is the principal industry. Chad remains one of the poorest countries in the world, a result of drought and the civil war, which lasted from 1960 to 1988. Some unrest ontinues in the country.

Chile

Area 756,945 sq km (292,258 sq miles); *population* 13,813,000; *capital* Santiago; *other major cities* Arica, Talcahuano, Viña del Mar; *form of government* Republic; *religion* RC; *currency* Chilean peso

Chile lies like a backbone down the Pacific coast of the South American continent. Its Pacific coastline is 4200 km (2610 miles) long. Because of its enormous range in latitude it has almost every kind of climate from desert conditions to icy wastes. The north, in which lies the Atacama Desert, is extremely arid. The climate of the central region is Mediterranean and that of the south cool temperate. 60% of the population live in the central valley where the climate is similar to southern California. The land here is fertile and the principal crops grown are wheat, sugar beet, maize and potatoes. It is also in the central valley that the vast copper mine of El Teniente is located. This is one of the largest copper mines in the world and accounts for Chile's most important source of foreign exchange.

China

Area 9,571,300 sq km (3,695,500 sq miles); *population* 1,200,000,000; *capital* Beijing (Peking); *Other major cities*: Chengdu, Guangzhou, Shanghai, Tianjin, Wuhan; *Form of government*: People's Republic; *religions* Buddhism, Confucianism, Taoism; *currency* Yuan

China, the third largest country in the world, covers a large area of East Asia. In western China most of the terrain is very inhospitable—in the north-west there are deserts which extend into Mongolia and the Russian Federation, and much of the south-west consists of the ice-capped peaks of Tibet. The south-east has a green and well watered landscape comprising terraced hillsides and paddy fields. Most of China has a temperate climate but in such a large country wide ranges of latitude and altitudes produce local variations. China is an agricultural country, and intensive cultivation and horticulture is necessary to feed its population of over one billion. Since the death of Mao in 1976, and under the leadership of Deng Xiao Ping, China has experienced a huge modernization of agriculture and industry due to the supply of expertize, capital and technology from Japan and the West. The country has been opened up to tourists and to a degree has adopted the philosophy of free enterprise, resulting in a dramatic improvement in living standards for a significant proportion of the population. However, the change towards a market economy has created internal political problems within the last decade. Pro-democracy demonstrations in 1989 resulted in the Tianmen Square massacre, which was condemned throughout the world, and raised questions regarding China's human rights approach. Deng

Xiao Ping had been a *de facto* leader since announcing his retirement in 1989, but his influence on the country was profound until his death in February 1997.

Colombia

Area 1,141,748 sq km (439,735 sq miles); *population* 34,900,000; *capital* Bogotá; *other major cities* Barranquilla, Cali, Cartagena, Medellin; *form of government* Republic; *religion* RC; *currency* Peso

Colombia is situated in the north of South America and most of the country lies between the equator and 10° north. The Andes, which split into three ranges (the Cordilleras) in Colombia, run north along the west coast and gradually disappear toward the Caribbean Sea. Half of Colombia lies east of the Andes and much of this region is covered in tropical grassland. Toward the Amazon Basin the vegetation changes to tropical forest. The climates in Colombia include equatorial and tropical according to altitude. Very little of the country is under cultivation although much of the soil is fertile. The range of climates result in an extraordinary variety of crops of which coffee is the most important. Colombia is rich in minerals and produces about half of the world's emeralds. It is South America's leading producer of coal, and oil has recently been discovered.

Comoros

Area 1862 sq km (719 sq miles) excluding Mayotte; *population* 510,000; *capital* Moroni; *form of government* Federal Islamic Republic; *religion* Sunni Islam; *currency* Comorian franc

The Comoros consist of three volcanic islands in the Indian Ocean between mainland Africa and Madagascar. Physically four islands make up the group but the island of Mayotte remained a French dependency when the three western islands became a federal Islamic republic in 1975. The islands are mostly forested and the tropical climate is affected by Indian monsoon winds from the north. There is a wet season from November to April. Only small areas of the islands are cultivated and most of this land belongs to foreign plantation owners. The chief product was formerly sugar cane, but now vanilla, copra, maize, cloves and essential oils are the most important products. The forests provide timber for building and there is a small fishing industry.

Congo

Area 342,000 sq km (132,046 sq miles); *population* 2,700,000; *capital* Brazzaville; Other major city : Pointe-Noire; *form of government* Republic; *religion* RC; *currency* Franc CFA

Formerly a French colony, the Republic of the Congo is situated in west central Africa where it straddles the equator. The climate is equatorial, with a moderate rainfall and a small range of temperature. The Bateke Plateau has a long dry season but the Congo Basin is more humid and rainfall approaches 2500 mm (98 inches) each year. About 62% of the total land area is covered with equatorial forest from which timbers such as okoume and sapele are produced. Valuable hardwoods such as mahogany are exported. Cash crops such as coffee and cocoa are mainly grown on large plantations but food crops are grown on small farms usually worked by the women. A manufacturing industry is now growing and oil discovered offshore accounts for much of the Congo's revenues.

Congo, Democratic Republic of (Zaïre)

Area 2,344,860 km (905,350 miles); *population* 44,504,000; *capital* Kinshasa; *other major cities* Lubumbashi, Mbuji-Mayi, Kananga,; *form of government* Republic; *religion* RC, Protestantism, Animism; *currency* Zaïre

Situated in west central Africa, The Democratic Republic of Congo is a vast country with a short coastline of only 40 km (25 miles) on the Atlantic Ocean. Rain forests, which cover about 55% of the country, contain valuable hardwoods such as mahogany and ebony. The country is drained by the river Zaïre and its main tributaries. Mountain ranges and plateaux surround the Zaïre Basin, and in the east the Ruwenzori Mountains overlook the lakes in the Great Rift Valley. In the central region the climate is hot and wet all year but elsewhere there are well-marked wet and dry seasons. Agriculture employs 75% of the population yet less than 3% of the country can be cultivated. Grazing land is limited by the infestation of the tsetse fly. Cassava is the main subsistence crop, and coffee, tea, cocoa, rubber and palms are grown for export. Minerals, mainly copper, cobalt, zinc and diamonds, account for 60% of exports.

Costa Rica

Area 51,100 sq km (19,730 sq miles); *population* 3,323,000; *capital* San José; Other major city : Límon; *form of government* Republic; *religion* RC; *currency* Colon

With the Pacific Ocean to the south and west and the Caribbean Sea to the east, Costa Rica is sandwiched between the central American countries of Nicaragua and Panama. Much of the country consists of volcanic mountain chains which run north-west to south-east. The climate is tropical with a small temperature range and abundant rain. The dry season is from December to April. The most populated area is the Valle Central which was first settled by the Spanish in the 16th century. The upland areas have rich volcanic soils which are good for coffee growing and the slopes provide lush pastures for cattle. Coffee and bananas are grown commercially and are the major agricultural exports. Costa Rica's mountainous terrain provides hydro electric power, which makes it almost self-sufficient in electricity, and attractive scenery for its growing tourist industry.

Côte d'Ivoire

Area 322,463 sq km (124,503 sq miles); *population* 13,316,000; *capital* Yamoussoukro; *other major cities* Abidjan, Bouaké, Daloa; *form of government* Republic; *religions* Animism, Sunni Islam, RC; *currency* CFA Franc

A former French colony in west Africa, Côte d'Ivoire is located on the Gulf of Guinea with Ghana to the east and Liberia to the west. The south-west coast has rocky cliffs but further east there are coastal plains which are the country's most prosperous region. The climate is tropical and affected by distance from the sea. The coastal area has two wet seasons but in the north, there is only the one. Côte d'Ivoire is basically an agricultural country which produces cocoa, coffee, rubber, bananas and pineapples. It is the world's largest producer of cocoa and the fourth largest producer of coffee. These two crops bring in half the country's export revenue. Since independence industrialization has developed rapidly, particularly food processing, textiles and sawmills.

Croatia (Hrvatska)

Area 56,538 sq km (21,824 sq miles); *population* 4850,500; *capital* Zagreb; *other major cities* Rijeka, Split; *form of government* Republic; *religions* RC, Eastern Orthodox; *currency* Kuna

Croatia, a republic of former Yugoslavia, made a unilateral declaration of independence on June 25, 1991. Sovereignty was not formally recognized by the international community until early in 1992. Located in south-east Europe, it is bounded to the west by the Adriatic Sea, to the north by Slovenia and Romania, and to the south by Bosnia & Herzegovina. Western Croatia lies in the Dinaric Alps. The eastern region, drained by the rivers Sava and Drava, is low-lying and agricultural. The chief farming region is the Pannonian Plain. Over one third of the country is forested and timber is a major export. Deposits of coal, bauxite, copper, oil and iron ore are substantial, and most of the republic's industry is based on the processing of these. In Istria in the north-west and on the Dalmatian coast tourism was a major industry until the Croatia became embroiled in the Serbo-Croat war prior to its secession in 1992. Following the formal recognition of Croatia's independence by the international community, the fighting abruptly ceased, however, the tourism industry continued to suffer from the effects of the on-going hostilities in other parts of the former Yugoslavia.

Cuba

Area 110,861 sq km (42,803 sq miles); *population* 10,905,000; *capital* Havana (La Habana); *other major cities* Camaguey, Holguin, Santiago de Cuba; *form of government* Socialist Republic; *religion* RC; *currency* Cuban peso

Cuba is the largest and most westerly of the Greater Antilles group of islands in the West Indies. It is strategically positioned at the entrance to the Gulf of Mexico and lies about 140 km (87 miles) south of the tip of Florida. Cuba is as big as all other Caribbean islands put together and is home to a third of the whole West Indian population. The climate is warm and generally rainy and hurricanes are liable to occur between June and November. The island consists mainly of extensive plains and the soil is fertile. The most important agricultural product is sugar and its by-products, and the processing of these is the most important industry. Most of Cuba's trade was with other communist countries, particularly the former USSR, and the country's economy has suffered as a result of a US trade embargo.

Cyprus

Area 9251 sq km (3572 sq miles); *population* 740,000; *capital* Nicosia; *other major cities* Limassol, Larnaca; *form of government* Republic; *religions* Greek Orthodox, Sunni Islam; *currency* Cyprus pound

Cyprus is an island which lies in the eastern Mediterranean about 85 km (53 miles) south of Turkey. It has a long thin panhandle and is divided from west to east by two parallel ranges of mountains which are separated by a wide central plain open to the sea at either end. The highest point is Mount Olympus (1951 m/6401 ft) in the south-west. The climate is Mediterranean with very hot dry summers and warm damp winters. This contributes towards the great variety of crops grown e.g. early potatoes, vegetables, cereals, tobacco, olives, bananas, and grapes. The grapes are used for the strong wines and sherries for which Cyprus is famous. Fishing is a significant industry, but above all the island depends on visitors and it is the tourist industry which has led to a recovery in the economy since 1974.

Czech Republic, The

Area 78,864 sq km (30,449 sq miles); *population* 10,325,700; *capital* Prague (Praha); *other major cities* Brno, Ostrava, Plzen; *form of government* Republic; *religions* RC, Protestantism; *currency* Koruna

The Czech Republic was newly constituted on January 1,1993, with the dissolution of the 74-year-old federal republic of Czechoslovakia. It is landlocked at the heart of central Europe, bounded by Slovakia, Germany, Poland and Austria. Natural boundaries are formed by the Sudeten Mountains in the north, the Erzgebirge, or Ore Mountains, to the north-west, and the Bohemian Forest in the south-west. The climate is humid continental with warm summers and cold winters. Most rain falls in summer and thunderstorms are frequent. Agriculture, although accounting for only a small percentage of the national income, is highly developed and efficient. Major crops are sugar beet, wheat and potatoes. Over a third of the labour force is employed in industry, the most important being iron and steel, coal, machinery, cement and paper. Recently investment has gone into electronic factories and research establishments.

Denmark

Area 43,077 sq km (16,632 sq miles); *population* 5,215,710 (excluding the Faeroe Islands); *capital* Copenhagen (København); *other major cities* Ålborg, Århus, Odense; *form of government* Constitutional Monarchy; *religion* Lutheranism; *currency* Danish krone

Denmark is a small European state lying between the North Sea and the entrance to the Baltic. It consists of a western peninsula and an eastern archipelago of 406 islands only 89 of which are populated. The country is very low lying and the proximity of the sea combined with the effect of the Gulf Stream result in warm sunny summers and cold cloudy winters. The scenery is very flat and monotonous but the soils are good and a wide variety of crops can be grown. It is an agricultural country and three-quarters of the land is cultivated mostly by the rotation of grass, barley, oats and sugar beet. Animal husbandry is however the most important activity, its produce including the famous bacon and butter. Despite Denmark's limited range of raw materials it produces a wide range of manufactured goods and is famous for its imaginative design of furniture, silverware and porcelain.

Djibouti

Area 23,200 sq km (8958 sq miles); *population* 520,000; *capital* Djibouti (*population* 340,700); *form of government* Republic; *religion* Sunni Islam; *currency* Djibouti franc

Djibouti is situated in north-east Africa and is bounded almost entirely by Ethiopia except in the south-east where it shares a border with Somalia and in the north-west where it shares a border with Eritrea. Its coastline is on the Gulf of Aden. The land which is mainly basalt plains has some mountains rising to over 1500 m (4922 ft). The climate is hot, among the world's hottest, and extremely dry. Only a tenth of the land can be farmed even for grazing so it has great difficulty supporting its modest population. The native population are mostly nomadic, moving from oasis to oasis or across the border to Ethiopia in search of grazing land. Most foodstuffs for the urban population in Djibouti city are imported. Cattle, hides and skins are the main exports.

Dominica

Area 751 sq km (290 sq miles); *population* 871,200; *capital* Roseau; Form of govt : Republic; *religion* RC; *currency* Franc

Discovered by Columbus, Dominica is the most northerly of the Windward Islands in the West Indies. It is situated between the islands of Martinique and Guadeloupe. The island is very rugged and with the exception of 225 sq km (87 sq miles) of flat land, it consists of three inactive volcanoes, the highest of which is 1447 m (4747 ft). The climate is tropical and even on the leeward coast it rains two days out of three. The wettest season is from June to October when hurricanes often occur. The steep slopes are difficult to farm but agriculture provides almost all Dominica's exports. Bananas are the main agricultural export but copra, citrus fruits, cocoa, bay leaves and vanilla are also revenue earners. Industry is mostly based on the processing of the agricultural products.

Dominican Republic

Area 48,734 sq km (18,816 sq miles); *population* 7,680,000; *capital* Santo Domingo; Other major city : Santiago de los Caballeros; *form of government* Republic; *currency* Dominican peso
The Dominican Republic forms the eastern portion of the island of Hispaniola in the West Indies. It covers two-thirds of the island, the smaller portion consisting of Haiti. The west of the country is made up of four almost parallel mountain ranges and between the two most northerly is the fertile Cibao valley. The south-east is made up of fertile plains. Although well endowed with fertile land, only about 30% is cultivated. Sugar is the main crop and mainstay of the country's economy. It is grown mainly on plantations in the south-east plains. Other crops grown are coffee, cocoa and tobacco. Some mining of gold, silver, platinum, nickel and aluminium is carried out but the main industries are food processing and making consumer goods. The island has fine beaches and the tourism industry is now very important to the economy.

Ecuador

Area 283,561 sq km (109,484 sq miles); *population* 10,981,000; *capital* Quito; *other major cities* Guayaquil, Cuenca; *form of government* Republic; *religion* RC; *currency* Sucre
Ecuador is an Andean country situated in the north-west of the South American continent. It is bounded to the north by Colombia and to the east and south by Peru. The country contains over thirty active volcanos. Running down the middle of Ecuador are two ranges of the Andes which are divided by a central plateau. The coastal area consists of plains and the eastern area is made up of tropical jungles. The climate varies from equatorial through warm temperate to mountain conditions according to altitude. It is in the coastal plains that plantations of bananas, cocoa, coffee and sugar cane are found. In contrast to this the highland areas are adapted to grazing, dairying and cereal growing. The fishing industry is important on the Pacific Coast and processed fish is one of the main exports. Oil is produced in the eastern region and crude oil is Ecuador's most important export.

Egypt

Area 1,001,449 sq km (386,662 sq miles); *population* 58,980,000; *capital* Cairo (El Qahira); *other major cities* Alexandria, El Gîza, Port Said; *form of government* Republic; *religions* Sunni Islam, Christianity; *currency* Egyptian pound
Egypt is situated in north-east Africa, acting as the doorway between Africa and Asia. Its outstanding physical feature is the river Nile, the valley and delta of which cover about 35,580 sq km (13,737 sq miles). The climate is mainly dry but there are winter rains along the Mediterranean coast. The temperatures are comfortable in winter but summer temperatures are extremely high particularly in the south. The rich soils deposited by floodwaters along the Nile can support a large population and the delta is one of the world's most fertile agricultural regions. 96% of the population live in the delta and Nile valley where the main crops are rice, cotton, sugar cane, maize, tomatoes and wheat. The main industries are food processing and textiles. The economy has been boosted by the discovery of oil and although not in large quantities it is enough to supply Egypt's needs and leave surplus for export. The Suez Canal shipping and tourism connected with the ancient sites are also important revenue earners.

El Salvador

Area 21,041 sq km (8124 sq miles); *population* 5,743,000; *capital* San Salvador; *other major cities* Santa Ana, San Miguel; *form of government* Republic; *religion* RC; *currency* Colón

El Salvador is the smallest and most densely populated state in Central America. It is bounded north and east by Honduras and has a Pacific coast to the south. Two volcanic ranges run from east to west across the country. The Lempa river cuts the southern ranges in the centre of the country and opens as a large sandy delta to the Pacific Ocean. Although fairly near to the equator, the climate tends to be warm rather than hot and the highlands have a cooler temperate climate. The country is predominantly agricultural and 32% of the land is used for crops such as coffee, cotton, maize, beans, rice and sorghum, and a slightly smaller area is used for grazing cattle, pigs, sheep and goats. A few industries such as food processing, textiles and chemicals are found in the major towns.

Equatorial Guinea

Area 28,051 sq km (10,830 sq miles); *population* 440,000; *capital* Malabo; Other major city : Bata; *form of government* Republic; *religion* RC; *currency* Franc CFA

Equatorial Guinea lies about 200 km (124 miles) north of the Equator on the hot humid coast of West Africa. The country consists of a square-shaped mainland area (Mbini) with its few small offshore islets, and the islands of Bioko and Pagalu. The climate is tropical and the wet season in Bioko and Pegalu lasts from December to February. Bioko is a very fertile volcanic island and it is here the capital Malabo is sited beside a volcanic crater flooded by the sea. It is also the centre of the country's cocoa production. The country now relies heavily on foreign aid. There is, however, much potential for a tourist industry.

Eritrea

Area 93,679 sq km (36,170 sq miles); *population* 3,850,000; *capital* Asmara; *other major cities* Mitsiwa, Keren; *form of government* In transition; *religion* Sunni Islam, Christianity; *currency* Ethiopian birr

Eritrea, formerly an autonomous province of Ethiopia, gained independence in May 1993 shortly after a landslide vote in favor of sovereignty. Bounded by Djibouti, Sudan and Ethiopia, Eritrea has acquired Ethiopia's entire coastline along the Red Sea. Eritrea's climate is hot and dry along its desert coast but is colder and wetter in its central highland regions. Most of the population depend on subsistence farming. Future revenues may come from developing fishing, tourism and oil industries. Eritrea's natural resources include gold, potash, zinc, copper, salt, fish and probably oil.

Estonia

Area 45,100 sq km (17,413 sq miles); *population* 1,530,000; *capital* Tallinn; *other major cities* Tartu, Narva; *form of government* Republic; *religion* Eastern Orthodox, Lutheranism; *currency* Rouble

Estonia lies to the north-west of the Russian Federation and is bounded to the north by the Gulf of Finland, to the west by the Baltic Sea and to the south by Latvia. It is the smallest of the three previous Soviet Baltic Republics. Agriculture and dairy farming are the chief occupations and there are nearly three hundred agricultural collectives and state farms. The main products are grain, potatoes, vegetables, meat, milk and eggs. Livestock includes cattle, sheep, goats and pigs. Almost 22% of Estonia is forested and this provides material for sawmills, furniture, match and pulp industries. The country has rich, high quality shale deposits and phosphorous has been found near Tallinn. Peat deposits are substantial and supply some of the electric power stations.

Ethiopia

Area 1,221,900 sq km (471,778 sq miles); *population* 55,500,000; *capital* Addis Ababa (Adis Abeba); *other major cities* Dire Dawa, Nazret; *form of government* In transition; *religion* Ethiopian Orthodox, Sunni Islam; *currency* Ethiopian birr

Ethiopia is a landlocked, east African country with borders on Sudan, Kenya, Somalia, Djibouti and Eritrea. Most of the country consists of highlands which drop sharply toward Sudan in the west. Because of the wide range of latitudes, Ethiopia has many climatic variations between the high temperate plateau and the hot humid lowlands. The country is very vulnerable to drought but in some areas thunderstorms can erode soil from the slopes reducing the area available for crop planting. Coffee is the main source of rural income and teff is the main food grain. The droughts in 1989-90 have brought much famine. Employment outside agriculture is confined to a small manufacturing sector in Addis Ababa. The country is wrecked with environmental, economic and political problems that culminated in May 1993 when one of Ethiopia's provinces, Eritrea, became independent.

Fiji

Area 18,274 sq km (7056 sq miles); *population* 773,000; *capital* Suva; *form of government* Republic; *religion* Christianity, Hinduism; *currency* Fiji dollar

Fiji is one of the largest nations in the western Pacific and consists of some 320 islands and atolls, but only 150 are inhabited. It is situated around the 180° International Date Line and lies about 17° south of the Equator. Fiji has high rainfall, high temperatures and plenty of sunshine all year round. The two main islands, Viti Levu and Vanua Levu, are extinct volcanoes and most of the islands in the group are fringed with coral reefs. The south-east of the islands have tropical rain forests but a lot of timber has been felled and soil erosion is a growing problem. The main cash crop is sugar cane although copra, ginger and fish are also exported. Tourism is now a major industry.

Finland

Area 338,000 sq km (130,500 sq miles); *population* 5,125,000; *capital* Helsinki (Helsingfors); *other major cities* Turku, Tampere; *form of government* Republic; *religion* Lutheranism; *currency* Markka

Finland lies at the eastern limit of western Europe with the Russian Federation to the east and the Gulf of Bothnia to the west. Most of the country is lowlying except for the north which rises to over 1000 m (3281 ft) in Lappland. It is covered with extensive forests and thousands of lakes. The climate has great extremes between summer and winter. Winter is very severe and lasts about six months. Even in the south snow covers the ground for three months in winter. Summers are short but quite warm with light rain throughout the country. Finland is largely self-sufficient in food and produces great surpluses of dairy produce. Most crops are grown in the south-west. In the north reindeer are herded and forests yield great quantities of timber for export. Major industries are timber products, wood pulp and paper, machinery and shipbuilding, which has developed due to the country's great need for an efficient fleet of ice breakers.

France

Area 547,026 sq km (211,208 sq miles); *population* 58,285,000; *capital* Paris; *other major cities* Bordeaux, Lyon, Marseille, Toulouse; *form of government* Republic; *religion* RC; *currency* Franc

France is the largest country in western Europe and has a coastline on the English Channel, the Mediterranean Sea and on the Atlantic Ocean. The lowest parts of the country are the great basins of the north and south-west from which it rises to the Massif Central and the higher Alps, Jura and Pyrénées. Climate ranges from moderate maritime in the north-west to Mediteranneаn in the south. Farming is possible in all parts of France. The western shores are ideal for rearing livestock, while the Paris Basin is good arable land. It is in the south-west around Bordeaux that the vineyards produce some of the world's best wines. The main industrial area of France is in the north and east, and the main industries are iron and steel, engineering, chemicals, textiles and electrical goods.

Gabon

Area 267,667 sq km (103,346 sq miles); *population* 1,316,000; *capital* Libreville; Other major city : Port Gentile; *form of government* Republic; *religion* RC, Animism; *currency* Franc CFA

Gabon is a small country in west-central Africa which straddles the Equator. It has a low narrow coastal plain and the rest of the country comprises a low plateau. Three quarters of Gabon is covered with dense tropical forest. The climate is hot, humid and typically equatorial with little seasonal variation. Until the 1960s timber was virtually Gabon's only resource and then oil was discovered. By the mid-1980s it was Africa's sixth largest oil producer and other minerals such as manganese, uranium and iron ore were being exploited. Much of the earnings from these resources were squandered and most of the Gabonese people remain subsistence farmers. The country has great tourist potential but because of the dense hardwood forests transport links with the interior are very difficult.

Gambia

Area 11,295 sq km (4361 sq miles); *population* 1,144,000; *capital* Banjul; *form of government* Republic; *religion* Sunni Islam; *currency* Dalasi

Gambia, the smallest country in Africa, pokes like a crooked finger into Senegal. The country is divided along its entire length by the river Gambia which can only be crossed at two main ferry crossings. Gambia has two very different seasons. In the dry season there is little rainfall, then the south-west monsoon sets in with spectacular storms producing heavy rain for four months. Most Gambians live in villages with a few animals, and grow enough millet and sorghum to feed themselves. Groundnuts are the main and only export crop of any significance. The river provides a thriving local fishing industry and the white sandy beaches on the coast are becoming increasingly popular with foreign tourists.

Georgia

Area 69,773 sq km (26,911 sq miles); *population* 5,493,000; *capital* Tbilisi; *other major cities* Kutaisi, Rustavi, Batumi; *form of government* Republic; *religion* Russian Orthodox; *currency* Rouble

Georgia is a republic in the south-west of the former USSR occupying the central and western parts of the Caucasus. It shares borders with Turkey, Armenia, Azerbaijan and the Russian Federation. It is bounded to the west by the Black Sea. Almost 40% of the country is covered with forests. Agriculture, which is the main occupation of the population, includes tea cultivation and fruit growing, especially citrus fruits and viticulture. The republic is rich in minerals, especially manganese. Industries include coal, timber, machinery, chemicals, silk, food processing and furniture. Georgia declared itself independent in 1991.

Germany

Area 365,755 sq km (137,738 sq miles); *population* 81,075,000; *capital* Berlin, Bonn (Seat of government); *other major cities* Cologne, Frankfurt, Hamburg, Leipzig, Munich, Stuttgart; *form of government* Republic; *religions* Lutheranism, RC; *currency* Deutsche Mark

Germany is a large country in northern central Europe which comprises the former East and West German republics, re-united in 1990. In the north is the North German Plain which merges with the North Rhinelands in the west. Further south, a plateau which stretches across the country from east to west, is divided by the river Rhine. In the south-west the Black Forest separates the Rhine Valley from the fertile valleys and scarplands of Swabia. The Bohemian Uplands and Erz Mountains mark the border with the Czech Republic. Generally the country has warm summers and cold winters. Agricultural products include wheat, rye, barley, oats, potatoes and sugar beet. The main industrial and most densely populated areas are in the Rhur Valley. Principal industries are mechanical and electrical engineering. Chemical and textile industries are found in the cities along the Rhine and motor vehicle industry in the large provincial cities. The country depends heavily on imports.

Ghana

Area 238,537 sq km (92,100 sq miles); *population* 17,460,000; *capital* Accra; *other major cities* Kumasi, Tamale, Sekondi-Takoradi; *form of government* Republic; *religion* Protestant, Animism, RC; *currency* Cedi

Ghana is located on the southern coast of West Africa between Côte d'Ivoire and Togo. In 1957, as the former British Gold Coast, it became the first black African state to achieve independence from European colonial rule. It has palm-fringed beaches of white sand along the Gulf of Guinea and where the great river Volta meets the sea there are peaceful blue lagoons. The climate on the coast is equatorial and towards the north there are steamy tropical evergreen forests which give way in the far north to tropical savanna. The landscape becomes harsh and barren near the border with Burkina Faso. Most Ghanaians are village dwellers whose homes are made of locally available materials. The south of the country has been most exposed to European influence and it is here that cocoa, rubber, palm oil and coffee are grown. Ghana has important mineral resources such as manganese and bauxite. Most of Ghana's towns are in the south but rapid growth has turned many of them into unplanned sprawls.

Greece

Area 131,944 sq km (50,944 sq miles); *population* 10,500,000; *capital* Athens (Athinai); *other major cities* Patras, Piraeus, Thessaloníki; *form of government* Republic; *religion* Greek Orthodox; *currency* Drachma

The Greek peninsula is the most south-easterly extension of Europe. The Pindus Mountains divide Greece from the Albanian border in the north to the Gulf of Corinth in the south. About 70% of the land is hilly with harsh mountain climates and poor soils. The Greek islands and coastal regions have a typical Mediterranean climate with mild rainy winters and hot dry summers. Winter in the northern mountains is severe with deep snow and heavy precipitation. Agriculture is the chief activity and large scale farming is concentrated on the east coasts. The main industries are small processing plants for tobacco, food and leather. Fishing is an important activity around the 2000 islands which lie off the mainland. Tourism is also a major industry.

Greenland

Area: 2,175,600 sq km (840,000 sq miles); *Population*: 59,000; *Capital*: Gothåb (Nuuk); *Form of government*: Self-governing part of the Danish realm; *Religion*: Lutheranism; *Currency*: Danish krone

Greenland, a huge island to the north-east of North America, most of which lies within the Arctic Circle. A province of Denmark, the island was granted home rule in 1979. The economy is heavily reliant on fishing and most of the population is Eskimo.

Grenada

Area 344 sq km (133 sq miles); *population* 95,000; *capital* St Georges; *form of government* Constitutional Monarchy; *religion* RC, Anglicanism, Methodism; *currency* East Caribbean dollar

Grenada is the most southerly of the Windward Island chain in the Caribbean. Its territory includes the southern Grenadine Islands to the north. The main island consists of the remains of extinct volcanoes and has an attractive wooded landscape. In the dry season its typical climate is very pleasant with warm days and cool nights but in the wet season it is hot day and night. Agriculture is the islands main industry and the chief crops grown for export are cocoa, nutmegs, bananas and mace. Apart from the processing of its crops Grenada has little manufacturing industry although tourism is an important source of foreign revenue. It is a popular port of call for cruise ships.

Guatemala

Area 108,889 sq km (42,042 sq miles); *population* 10,624,000; *capital* Guatemala City; *other major cities* Puerto Barrios, Quezaltenango; *form of government* Republic; *religion* RC; *currency* Quetzal

Guatemala is situated between the Pacific Ocean and the Caribbean Sea where North America meets Central America. It is a mountainous country with a ridge of volcanoes running parallel to the Pacific coast. It has a tropical climate with little or no variation in temperature and a distinctive wet season. The Pacific slopes of the mountains are exceptionally well watered and fertile and it is here that most of the population are settled. Coffee growing on the lower slopes dominates the economy. A small strip on the coast produces sugar, cotton and bananas. Industry is mainly restricted to the processing of the agricultural products. Guatemala is politically a very unstable country and civil conflict has practically destroyed tourism.

Guiana (French) *or* Guyane

Area 91,000 sq km (35,135 sq miles); *population* 154,000; *capital* Cayenne; *form of government* French overseas department; *religion* RC; *currency* Franc

Guiana is situated on the north-east coast of South America and is still an overseas department of France. It is bounded to the south and east by Brazil and to the west by Suriname. The climate is tropical with heavy rainfall. Guiana's economy relies almost completely on subsidies from France. It has little to export apart from shrimps and the small area of land which is cultivated produces rice, manioc and sugar cane. Recently the French have tried to develop the tourist industry and exploit the extensive reserves of hardwood in the jungle interior.

Guinea

Area 245,857 sq km (94,925 sq miles); *population* 7,200,000; *capital* Conakry; *other major cities* Kankan, Labé; *form of government* Republic; *religion* Sunni Islam; *currency* Guinea franc

Guinea, formerly a French West African territory, is located on the coast at the 'bulge' in Africa. It is a lush green beautiful country about the same size as the United Kingdom. It has a tropical climate with constant heat and a high rainfall near the coast. Guinea has great agricultural potential and many of the coastal swamps and forested plains have been cleared for the cultivation of rice, cassava, yams, maize and vegetables. Further inland on the plateau of Futa Jalon dwarf cattle are raised and in the valleys bananas and pineapples are grown. Coffee and kola nuts are important cash crops grown in the Guinea highlands to the south-west. Minerals such as bauxite, iron ore and diamonds are mined but development is hampered by lack of transport.

Guinea-Bissau

Area 36,125 sq km (13,948 sq miles); *population* 1,050,000; *capital* Bissau; *form of government* Republic; *religion* Animism, Sunni Islam; *currency* Peso

Formerly a Portuguese territory, Guinea-Bissau is located south of Senegal on the Atlantic coast of West Africa. It is a country of stunning scenery and rises from a deeply indented and island-fringed coastline to a low inland plateau. The adjacent Bijagos archipelago forms part of its territory. The climate is tropical with abundant rain from June to November but hot dry conditions for the rest of the year. Years of Portuguese rule and civil war have left Guinea-Bissau impoverished, and it is one of the poorest West African states. The country's main aim is to become self-sufficient in food, and the main crops grown are groundnuts, sugar cane, plantains, coconuts and rice. Fishing is an important export industry.

Guyana

Area 214,969 sq km (83,000 sq miles); *population* 830,000; *capital* Georgetown; Other major city : New Amsterdam; *form of government* Cooperative Republic; *religion* Hinduism, Protestantism, RC; *currency* Guyana dollar

Guyana, the only English-speaking country in South America, is situated on the north-east coast of the continent on the Atlantic Ocean. The country is intersected by many rivers and the coastal area comprises tidal marshes and mangrove swamps. It is on this coastal area that rice is grown and vast plantations produce sugar. The jungle in the south-west has potential for the production of minerals, hardwood and hydroelectric power, but 90% of the population live in the coastal area where the climate is moderated by sea breezes. The country is deeply divided politically and nothing has been done to improve productivity with the result that today the country is in an economic crisis.

Haiti

Area 27,750 sq km (10,714 sq miles); *population* 7,180,000; *capital* Port-au-Prince; *other major cities* Les Cayes, Gonaïves, Jérémie; *form of government* Republic; *religion* RC, Voodooism; *currency* Gourde

Haiti occupies the western third of the large island of Hispaniola in the Caribbean. It is a mountainous country, the highest point reaching 2680 m (8793 ft) at La Selle. The mountain ranges are separated by deep valleys and plains. The climate is tropical but semi-arid conditions can occur in the lee of the central mountains. Hurricanes and severe thunderstorms are a common occurrence. Only a third of the country is arable, yet agriculture is the chief occupation. Many farmers grow only enough to feed their own families, and the export crops—coffee, sugar and sisal—are grown on large estates. Severe soil erosion caused by extensive forest clearance has resulted in a decline in crop yields. Haiti is the poorest country in the Americas and has experienced many uprisings and attempted coups.

Honduras

Area 112,088 sq km (43,277 sq miles); *population* 5,940,000; *capital* Tegucigalpa; *form of government* Republic; *religion* RC; *currency* Lempira

Honduras is a fan-shaped country in Central America which spreads out toward the Caribbean Sea at the Gulf of Honduras. Four fifths of the country is covered in mountains which are indented with river valleys running toward the very short Pacific coast. There is little change in temperatures throughout the year and rainfall is heavy, especially on the Caribbean coast where temperatures are also higher than inland. The country is sparsely populated and although agricultural, only about 25% of the land is cultivated. Honduras was once the world's leading banana exporter and although that fruit is still its main export, agriculture is now more diverse. Grains, coffee and sugar are important crops, and these are grown mainly on the coastal plains of the Pacific and Caribbean. The forests are not effectively exploited and industry is small-scale.

Hong Kong

Area 1074 sq km (416 sq miles); *population* 6,000,000; *form of government* Colony under Chinese administration; *religion* Buddhism, Taoism, Christianity; *currency* Hong Kong dollar

Hong Kong was a British crown colony from 1842 until July 1, 1997 when it was returned to China as a Special Administrative Region. It is located in the South China Sea and consists of Hong Kong Island (once a barren rock), the peninsula of Kowloon and about 1000 sq km (386 sq miles) of adjacent land known as the New Territories. Hong Kong is situated at the mouth of the Pearl River about 130 km (81 miles) south-east of Guangzhou (Canton). The climate is warm subtropical with cool dry winters and hot humid summers. Hong Kong has no natural resources, even its water comes from reservoirs across the Chinese border. Its main assets are its magnificent natural harbor and its position close to the main trading routes of the Pacific. Hong Kong's economy is based on free enterprise and trade, an industrious work force and an efficient and aggressive commercial system. Hong Kong's main industry is textiles and clothing which accounts for 38% of its domestic exports.

Hungary

Area 93,032 sq km (35,920 sq miles); *population* 10,546,000; *capital* Budapest; *other major cities* Debrecen, Miskolc, Pécs, Szeged; *form of government* Republic; *religion* RC, Calvinism, Lutheranism; *currency* Forint

Landlocked in the heartland of Europe, Hungary is dominated by the great plain to the east of the river Danube which runs north-south across the country. In the west lies the largest lake in Central Europe, Lake Balaton. Winters are severe, but the summers are warm and although wet in the west, summer droughts often occur in the east. Hungary experienced a modest boom in its economy in the 1970s and 1980s. The government invested money in improving agriculture by mechanizing farms, using fertilizers and bringing new land under cultivation. Yields of cereals for breadmaking and rice have since soared and large areas between the Danube and Tisza rivers are now used to grow vegetables. Industries have been carefully developed where adequate natural resources exist. New industries like electrical and electronic equipment are now being promoted and tourism is fast developing around Lake Balaton.

Iceland

Area 103,000 sq km (39,768 sq miles); *population* 266,790; *capital* Reykjavík; *form of government* Republic; *religion* Lutheranism; *currency* Icelandic króna

Iceland is a large island situated in a tectonically unstable part of the North Atlantic Ocean, just south of the Arctic Circle. The island has over 100 volcanoes, at least one of which erupts every five years. One ninth of the country is covered with ice and snowfields and there are about seven hundred hot springs which are an important source of central heating. The climate is cool temperate but because of the effect of the North Atlantic Drift it is mild for its latitude. The south-west corner is the most densely populated area as the coast here is generally free from ice. Only 1% of the land is cultivated mostly for fodder and root crops to feed sheep and cattle. The island's economy is based on its sea fishing industry which accounts for 70% of exports. Wool sweaters and sheepskin coats are also exported.

India

Area 3,287,590 sq km (1,269,346 sq miles); *population* 897,560,000; *capital* New Delhi; *other major cities* Bangalore, Bombay, Calcutta,; Delhi, Hyderabad, Madras; *form of government* Federal Republic, Secular Democracy; *religion* Hinduism, Islam, Sikkism, Christianity, Jainism, Buddhism; *currency* Rupee

India is a vast country in South Asia which is dominated in the extreme north by the world's youngest and highest mountains, the Himalayas. At the foot of the Himalayas, a huge plain, drained by the Indus and Ganges rivers, is one of the most fertile areas in the world and the most densely populated part of India. Further south the ancient Deccan plateau extends to the southern tip of the country. India generally has four seasons, the cool, the hot, the rainy and the dry. Rainfall varies from 100 mm (3.94 inches) in the north-west desert to 10,000 mm (394 inches) in Assam. About 70% of the population depend on agriculture for their living and the lower slopes of the Himalayas represent one of the world's best tea growing areas. Rice, sugarcane and wheat are grown in the Ganges plain. India is self-sufficient in all of its major food crops.

Indonesia

Area 1,904,570 sq km (735,358 sq miles); *population* 189,907,000; *capital* Jakarta; *other major cities* Badung, Medan, Semarang, Surabaya; *form of government* Republic; *religion* Sunni Islam, Christianity, Hinduism; *currency* Rupiah

Indonesia is made up of 13,667 islands which are scattered across the Indian and Pacific Oceans in a huge crescent. Its largest landmass is the province of Kalimantan which is part of the island of Borneo. Sumatra is the largest individual island. Java, however, is the dominant and most densely populated island. The climate is generally tropical monsoon and temperatures are high all year round. The country has one hundred volcanoes, and earthquakes are frequent in the southern islands. Over-population is a big problem especially in Java, where its fertile rust coloured soil is in danger of becoming exhausted. Rice, maize and cassava are the main crops grown. Indonesia has the largest reserves of tin in the world and is one of the world's leading rubber producers. Indonesia's resources are not as yet fully developed but there is great potential for economic development.

Iran

Area 1,648,000 sq km (636,296 sq miles); *population* 66,000,000; *capital* Tehran; *other major cities* Esfahan, Mashhad, Tabriz; Government : Islamic Republic; *religion* Shia Islam; *currency* Rial

Iran lies across The Gulf from the Arabian peninsula and stretches from the Caspiar Sea to the Arabian Sea. It is a land dominated by mountains in the north and west, with a huge expanse of desert in its centre. The climate is hot and dry, although more temperate conditions are found on the shores of the Caspian Sea. In winter, terrible dust storms sweep the deserts and almost no life can survive. Most of the populatior live in the north and west, where Tehran is situated. The only good agricultural lanc is on the Caspian coastal plains, where rice is grown. About 5% of the population are nomadic herdsmen who wander in the mountains. Most of Iran's oil is in the south-west, and other valuable minerals include coal, iron ore, copper and lead. Precious stones are found in the north-east. Main exports are petrochemicals, carpets anc rugs, textiles, raw cotton and leather goods.

Iraq

Area 434,924 sq km (167,935 sq miles); *population* 19,951,000; *capital* Baghdad; *other major cities* Al-Basrah, Al Mawsil; *form of government* Republic; *religion* Shia Islam, Sunni Islam; *currency* Iraqi dinar

Iraq is located in south-west Asia, wedged between The Gulf and Syria. It is almos landlocked except for its outlet to The Gulf at Shatt al Arab. Its two great rivers, the Tigris and the Euphrates, flow from the north-west into The Gulf at this point. The climate is arid with very hot summers and cold winters. The high mountains on the border with Turkey are snow covered for six months of the year, and desert in the south-west covers nearly half the country. The only fertile land in Iraq is in the basins of the Tigris and Euphrates where wheat, barley, rice, tobacco and cotton are grown The world's largest production of dates also comes from this area. Iraq profited fron the great oil boom of the 1970s, but during the war with Iran oil terminals in The Gul were destroyed and the Trans-Syrian Pipeline closed. Iraq is now wholly reliant or the pipeline from Kirkuk to the Mediterranean.

Ireland, Republic of

Area 70,284 sq km (27,137 sq miles); *population* 3,621,000; *capital* Dublin (Baile Atha Cliath); *other major cities* Cork, Galway, Limerick, Waterford; *form of government* Republic; *religion* RC *currency* Punt = 100 pighne

Ireland is one of Europe's most westerly countries, situated in the Atlantic Ocean anc separated from Great Britain by the Irish Sea. It has an equable climate, with milc south-west winds which makes temperatures uniform over most of the country. The Republic extends over four fifths of the island of Ireland and the west and south-wes is mountainous, with the highest peak reaching 1041 m (3416 ft) at Carrauntoohil The central plain is largely limestone covered in boulder clay which provides gooc farmland and pasture. The rural population tend to migrate to the cities, mainl Dublin, which is the main industrial centre and the focus of radio, television publishing and communications. Lack of energy resources and remoteness fron major markets has slowed industrial development, although the economy has improved in recent years.

Israel

Area 20,770 sq km (8019 sq miles); *population* 5,451,000; *capital* Jerusalem; *other major cities* Tel Aviv-Jaffa, Haifa; *form of government* Republic; *religion* Judaism, Sunni Islam, Christianity; *currency* Shekel

Israel occupies a long narrow stretch of land in the south-east of the Mediterranear Its eastern boundary is formed by the Great Rift Valley, through which the river Jorda flows to the Dead Sea. The south of the country is made up of a triangular wedge of the Negev Desert which ends at the Gulf of Aqaba. The climate in summer is hot and dry, in winter it is mild with some rain. The south of the country is very arid and barren. Most of the population live on the coastal plain bordering the Mediterranean where Tel Aviv-Jaffa is the main commercial city. Israel's agriculture is based on collective settlements known as Kibbutz. The country is virtually self-sufficient in foodstuffs and a major exporter of its produce. Jaffa oranges are famous throughout Europe. A wide range of products is processed or finished in the country, and main exports include finished diamonds, textiles, fruit, vegetables, chemicals, machinery and fertilizers.

Italy

Area 301,225 sq km (116,304 sq miles); *population* 57,181,000; *capital* Rome (Roma); *other major cities* Milan, Naples, Turin, Genoa, Palermo, Florence; *form of government* Republic; *religion* RC; *currency* Lira

Italy is a republic in southern Europe, which comprises a large peninsula and the two main islands of Sicily and Sardinia. The Alps form a natural boundary with its northern and western European neighbours, and the Adriatic Sea to the east separates it from the countries of former Yugoslavia. The Apennine Mountains form the backbone of Italy and extend the full length of the peninsula. Between the Alps and the Apennines lies the Po valley, a great fertile lowland. Sicily and Sardinia are largely mountainous. Much of Italy is geologically unstable and it has four active volcanoes, including Etna and Vesuvius. Italy enjoys warm dry summers and mild winters. The north is the main industrial centre and agriculture is well mechanized. In the south farms are small and traditional. Industries in the north include motor vehicles, textiles, clothing, leather goods, glass and ceramics. Tourism is an important source of foreign currency.

Jamaica

Area 10,990 sq km (4243 sq miles); *population* 2,513,000; *capital* Kingston; *other major cities* Montego Bay, Spanish Town; *form of government* Constitutional Monarchy; *religion* Anglicanism, RC, other Protestantism; *currency* Jamaican dollar

Jamaica is an island state in the Caribbean Sea about 150 km (93 miles) south of Cuba. The centre of the island comprises a limestone plateau and this is surrounded by narrow coastal flatlands and palm fringed beaches. The highest mountains, the Blue Mountains, are in the east of the island. The climate is tropical with high temperatures at the coast, with slightly cooler and less humid conditions in the highlands. The island lies right in the middle of the hurricane zone. The traditional crops grown are sugar cane, bananas, peppers, ginger, cocoa and coffee, and new crops such as winter vegetables fruit and honey are being developed for export. Despite this the decline in the principal export products, bauxite and alumina, has resulted in near economic stagnation. Tourism is a particularly important industry, as is the illegal trade in cannabis.

Japan

Area 377,708 sq km (145,834 sq miles); *population* 124,764,200; *capital* Tokyo; *other major cities* Osaka, Nagoya, Sapporo, Kobe, Kyoto, Yokohama; *form of government* Constitutional Monarchy; *religion* Shintoism, Buddhism, Christianity; *currency* Yen

Japan is located on the eastern margin of Asia and consists of four major islands, Honshu, Hokkaido, Kyushu and Shikoku, and many small islands. It is separated from the mainland of Asia by the Sea of Japan. The country is made up of six chains of steep serrated mountains, which contain about 60 active volcanoes. Earthquakes are frequent and widespread and often accompanied by giant waves (tsunami) Summers are warm and humid and winters mild, except on Hokkaido which is covered in snow in winter. Japan's agriculture is highly advanced with extensive use made of fertilizers and miniature machinery for the small fields. Fishing is important Japan is the second largest industrial economy in the world. It is very dependent on imported raw materials, and its success is based on manufacturing industry, which employs about one third of the workforce.

Jordan

Area 97,740 sq km (37,737 sq miles); *population* 4,095,000; *capital* Amman; *other major cities* Irbid, Zarga; *form of government* Constitutional Monarchy; *religion* Sunni Islam; *currency* Jordan dinar

Jordan, almost landlocked except for a short coastline on the Gulf of Aqaba, is bounded by Saudi Arabia, Syria, Iraq and Israel. Almost 80% of the country is desert and the rest comprises the East Bank Uplands and Jordan Valley. In general summers are hot and dry and winters cool and wet, with variations related to altitude The east has a desert climate. Only one fifth of the country is fertile enough to be farmed but the country is self-sufficient in potatoes, onions and poultry meat. The agricultural system is intensive and efficient. Amman is the main industrial centre of the country and the industries include phosphates, petroleum products, cement iron and fertilizers. The rich Arab states such as Saudi Arabia give Jordan substantial economic aid.

Kazakhstan

Area 2,717,300 sq km (1,050,000 sq miles); *population* 17,185,000; *capital* Alma-Ata; Other major city : Karaganda; *form of government* Republic; *religion* Sunni Islam; *currency* Rouble

Kazakhstan, the second largest republic of the former USSR, extends approximately 3000 km (1864 miles) from the coast of the Caspian Sea to the north-west corner of Mongolia. The west of the country is low-lying, the east hilly, and in the south-east mountainous areas include parts of the Tian Shan and Altai ranges. The climate is continental and very dry with great extremes of temperature. Much of the country is semi-desert. Crops can only be grown in the wetter north-west regions or on land irrigated by the Syrdar'ya river. Extensive pastoral farming is carried out in most of the country, and cattle, sheep and goats are the main livestock reared. The country is rich in minerals, particularly copper, lead, zinc, coal, tungsten, iron ore, oil and gas. Kazakhstan declared itself independent in 1991.

Kenya

Area 580,367 sq km (224,080 sq miles); *population* 28,113,080,000; *capital* Nairobi; *other major cities* Mombasa, Kisumu; *form of government* Republic; *religions* RC, Protestantism, other Christianity, Animism; *currency* Kenya shilling

Located in east Africa, Kenya straddles the Equator and extends from Lake Victoria in the south-west, to the Indian Ocean in the south-east. Highlands run north to south through central Kenya and are divided by the steep-sided Great Rift Valley. The coastal lowlands have a hot humid climate but in the highlands it is cooler and rainfall heavier. In the east it is very arid. The south-western region is well watered with huge areas of fertile soil and this accounts for the bulk of the population and almost all its economic production. The main crops grown for domestic consumption are wheat and maize. Tea, coffee, sisal, sugar cane and cotton are grown for export. Oil refining

:t Mombasa is the country's largest single industry, and other industry includes food processing and textiles. Tourism is an important source of foreign revenue.

Kiribati

area 726 sq km (280 sq miles); *population* 77,000; *capital* Tarawa; *form of government*: Republic; *religions* RC, Protestantism; *currency* Aus. dollar

Kiribati comprises three groups of coral atolls and one isolated volcanic island spread over a large expanse of the central Pacific. The group includes Banaba Island, the Phoenix Islands and some of the Line Islands. The climate is maritime equatorial with a high rainfall. Most islanders are involved in subsistence agriculture. The principal tree is the coconut which grows well on all the islands. Palm and breadfruit trees are also found. Soil is negligible and the only vegetable which can be grown is calladium. Tuna fishing is an important industry and Kiribati had granted licences to the former USSR to fish its waters. Phosphate sources have now been exhausted and the country is heavily dependent on overseas aid.

Korea, Democratic People's Republic of

area 120,538 sq km (46,540 sq miles); *population* 23,472,000; *capital* P'yongyang; *other major cities* Chongjin, Nampo; *form of government* Socialist Republic; *religions* Chondoism, Buddhism; *currency* N. Korean won

The Democratic People's Republic of Korea (formerly North Korea) occupies just over half of the Korean peninsula in east Asia. The Yala and Tumen rivers form its northern border with China and the Russian Federation. Its southern border with South Korea is just north of the 38th parallel. It is a mountainous country, three quarters of which is forested highland or scrubland. The climate is warm temperate, although winters can be cold in the north. Most rain falls during the summer. Nearly 90% of its arable land is farmed by cooperatives employing over 40% of the labour force and rice is the main crop grown. North Korea is quite well endowed with fuel and minerals. Deposits of coal and hydro-electric power generate electricity, and substantial deposits of iron ore are found near P'yongyang and Musan. 60% of the labour force are employed in industry, the most important of which are metallurgical, building, cement and chemicals.

Korea, Republic of

area 98,484 sq km (38,025 sq miles); *population* 44,563,000; *capital* Seoul (Soul); *other major cities* Pusan, Taegu, Inch'on; *form of government* Republic; *religions* Buddhism, Christianity; *currency* South Korean won

The Republic of Korea (formerly South Korea) occupies the southern half of the Korean peninsula and stretches about 400 km (249 miles), from the Korea Strait to the demilitarized zone bordering North Korea. It is predominantly mountainous with the highest ranges running north to south along the east coast. The west is lowland which is extremely densely populated. The extreme south has a humid warm temperate climate while farther north it is more continental. Most rain falls in summer. Cultivated land represents only 23% of the country's total area and the main crop is rice. The country has few natural resources but has a flourishing manufacturing industry and is the world's leading supplier of ships and footwear. Other important industries are electronic equipment, electrical goods, steel, petrochemicals, motor vehicles and toys. Its people enjoy a reasonably high standard of living brought about by hard work and determination.

Kuwait

Area 18,049 sq km (6969 sq miles); *population* 1,575,980; *capital* Kuwait city (Al Kuwayt); Government : Constitutional Monarchy; *religion* Sunni Islam, Shia Islam; *currency* Kuwait dinar

Kuwait is a tiny Arab state on The Gulf, comprising the city of Kuwait at the southerr entrance of Kuwait Bay, a small undulating desert between Iraq and Saudi Arabia an nine small offshore islands. It has a dry desert climate, cool in winter but very hot an humid in summer. There is little agriculture due to lack of water; major crops produce are melons, tomatoes, onions and dates. Shrimp fishing is becoming an importan industry. Large reserves of petroleum and natural gas are the mainstay of the economy It has about 950 oil wells, however 600 were fired during the Iraqi occupation in 199 and are unlikely to resume production for several years. Apart from oil, industr includes boat building, food production, petrochemicals, gases and construction.

Kyrgyzstan

Area 198,501 sq km (76,642 sq miles); *population* 4,500,000; *capital* Bishkek; (formerly Frunze); Government : Republic; *religion* Sunni Islam; *currency* Rouble

Kyrgyzstan, a central Asian republic of the former USSR, independent since 1991 It is located on the border with north-west China. Much of the country is occupie by the Tian Shan Mountains which rise to spectacular peaks. The highest is Pi Pobedy 7439 m (24,406 ft), lying on the border with China. In the north-east of th country is Issyk-Kul', a large lake heated by volcanic action, so it never freezes. Mos of the country is semi-arid or desert, but climate is greatly influenced by altitude. Soils are badly leached except in the valleys, where some grains are grown. Grazing o sheep, horses and cattle is extensive. Industries include non-ferrous metallurgy machine building, coal mining, tobacco, food processing, textiles and gold mining hydroelectricity and the raising of silkworms.

Laos

Area 236,800 sq km (91,428 sq miles); *population* 4,605,000; *capital* Vientiane; *form of government* People's Republic; *religion* Buddhism; *currency* Kip

Laos is a landlocked country in South-East Asia which is ruggedly mountainous apart from the Mekong river plains along its border with Thailand. The Annan mountains, which reach 2500 m (8203 ft), form a natural border with Vietnam. It ha a tropical monsoon climate with high temperatures throughout the year and heav rains in summer. Laos is one of the poorest countries in the world and it development has been retarded by war, drought and floods. The principal crop i rice, grown on small peasant plots. There is some export of timber, coffee an electricity. All manufactured goods must be imported. The capital and largest city Vientiane, is the country's main trade outlet via Thailand.

Latvia

Area 63,700 sq km (24,595 sq miles); *population* 2,558,000; *capital* Riga; *other major cities* Liepaja Daugavpils, Jurmala; *form of government* Republic; *religion* Lutheranism; *currency* Lats

Latvia is a Baltic state that regained its independence in 1991 with the break-up c the former Soviet Union. It is located in north-east Europe on the Baltic Sea and sandwiched between Estonia and Lithuania. It has cool summers, wet summers an long, cold winters. Latvians traditionally lived by forestry, fishing and livestoc rearing. The chief agricultural occupations are cattle and dairy farming and the ma crops grown are oats, barley, rye, potatoes and flax. Latvia's population is now 70 ırban and agriculture is no longer the mainstay of the economy. Cities such as Riga, ıe capital, Daugavpils, Ventspils and Liepaja now produce high quality textiles, ıachinery, electrical appliances, paper, chemicals, furniture and foodstuffs. Latvia as extensive deposits of peat which is used to manufacture briquettes. It also has eposits of gypsum and in the coastal areas amber is frequently found.

.ebanon

ırea 10,400 sq km (4015 sq miles); *population* 2,970,000; *capital* Beirut (Beyrouth); Other nportant cities : Tripoli, Zahle; *form of government* Republic; *religions* Shia Islam, Sunni Islam, hristianity; *currency* Lebanese pound

ebanon is a mountainous country in the eastern Mediterranean. A narrow coastal lain runs parallel to its 240-km (149-mile) Mediterranean coast and gradually rises ɔ the spectacular Lebanon Mountains, which are snow covered in winter. The Anti ebanon Mountains form the border with Syria, and between the two ranges lies the eqa'a Valley. The climate is Mediterranean with short warm winters and long hot nd rainless summers. Rainfall can be torrential in winter and snow falls on high round. Lebanon is an agricultural country, the main regions of production being the eqa'a Valley and the coastal plain. Main products include olives, grapes, citrus uits, apples, cotton, tobacco and sugar beet. Industry is small scale and manufacıres include, cement, fertilizers and jewellery. There are oil refineries at Tripoli and idon.

.esotho

rea 30,355 sq km (11,720 sq miles); *population* 1,943,000; *capital* Maseru; *form of overnment* Constitutional monarchy; *religions* RC, other Christianity; *currency* Loti

esotho is a small landlocked kingdom entirely surrounded by the Republic of South frica. Snow-capped mountains and treeless uplands, cut by spectacular gorges, over two thirds of the country. The climate is pleasant with variable rainfall. Winters re generally dry with heavy frosts in lowland areas and frequent snow in the highlands. ue to the mountainous terrain, only one eighth of the land can be cultivated and the ıain crop is maize. Yields are low due to soil erosion on the steep slopes and overrazing by herds of sheep and cattle. Wool, mohair and diamonds are exported but ıost foreign exchange comes from money sent home by Lesotho workers in South frica. Tourism is beginning to flourish, the main attraction to South Africans being ıe casinos in the capital Maseru, as gambling is prohibited in their own country.

.iberia

rea 111,369 sq km (43,000 sq miles); *population* 2,644,000; *capital* Monrovia; *form of overnment* Republic; *religion* Animism, Sunni Islam, Christianity; *currency* Liberian dollar

beria is located in West Africa and has a 560-km (348-mile) coast stretching from ierra Leone to Côte d'Ivoire. It is the only African country never to be ruled by a ɔreign power. It has a treacherous coast with rocky cliffs and lagoons enclosed by and bars. Inland the land rises to a densely forested plateau dissected by deep, arrow valleys. Farther inland still, there are beautiful waterfalls and the Nimba ountains rise to over 1700 m (5577 ft). Agriculture employs three quarters of the ıbour force and produces cassava and rice as subsistence crops and rubber, coffee nd cocoa for export. The Nimba Mountains are rich in iron ore, which accounts for 0% of export earnings. There is potential for tourism to develop. Forest and animal eserves are magnificent and beaches and lagoons are beautiful but so far the facilities re average.

Libya

Area 1,759,540 sq km (679,358 sq miles); *population* 4,280,000; *capital* Tripoli (Tarabulus); *other major cities* Benghazi, Misurata; *form of government* Socialist People's Republic; *religior* Sunni Islam; *currency* Libyan dinar

Libya is a large north African country which stretches from the south coast of th Mediterranean to, and in some parts beyond, the Tropic of Cancer. The Saha Desert covers much of the country extending right to the Mediterranean coast at th Gulf of Sirte. The only green areas are the scrublands found in the north-west ar the forested hills near Benghazi. The coastal area has mild wet winters and hot d summers but the interior has had some of the highest recorded temperatures anywhere in the world. Only 14% of the people work on the land, the main agricultur region being in the north-west near Tripoli. Many sheep, goats and cattle are reare and there is an export trade in skins, hides and hairs. Libya is one of the world largest producers of oil and natural gas. Other industries include food processin textiles, cement and handicrafts.

Liechtenstein

Area 160 sq km (62 sq miles); *population* 30,000; *capital* Vaduz; *form of government* Constitutional Monarchy; *religion* RC; *currency* Swiss franc

The principality of Liechtenstein is a tiny central European state situated on the ea bank of the River Rhine, bounded by Austria to the east and Switzerland to the wes In the east of the principality the Alps rise to 2599 m (8527 ft) at Grauspitze. Th climate is mild alpine. Once an agricultural country, Liechtenstein has rapidly move into industry in the last thirty years, with a variety of light industries such as textile high quality metal goods, precision instruments, pharmaceuticals and ceramics. It a popular location for the headquarters of foreign companies, in order that they ca benefit from the lenient tax laws. Tourism also thrives, beautiful scenery and goo skiing being the main attractions.

Lithuania

Area 65,200 sq km (25,174 sq miles); *population* 3,724000; *capital* Vilnius; *other major cities* Kaunas, Klaipeda, Siauliai; *form of government* Republic; *religion* RC; *currency* Rouble

Lithuania lies to the north-west of the Russian Federation and Belarus and bounded to the north by Latvia and west by Poland. It is the largest of the three form Soviet Baltic Republics. Before 1940 Lithuania was a mainly agricultural country b has since been considerably industrialized. Most of the land is lowland covered forest and swamp, and the main products are rye, barley, sugar beet, flax, meat, m and potatoes. Industry includes heavy engineering, shipbuilding and building mat rials. Oil production has started from a small field at Kretinga in the west of t country, 16 km (10 miles) north of Klaipeda. Amber is found along the Baltic coa and used by Lithuanian craftsmen for making jewellery.

Luxembourg

Area 2586 sq km (998 sq miles); *population* 406,500; *capital* Luxembourg (pop. 75,800); *form government* Constitutional Monarchy; *religion* RC; *currency* Luxembourg franc

The Grand Duchy of Luxembourg is a small independent country bounded Belgium on the west, France on the south and Germany on the east. In the north the Duchy a wooded plateau, the Oesling, rises to 550 m/1804 ft and in the sou a lowland area of valleys and ridges is known as the Gutland. Northern winters a cold and raw with snow covering the ground for almost a month, but in the south winters are mild and summers cool. In the south the land is fertile and crops grown include maize, roots, tubers and potatoes. Dairy farming is also important. It is in the south, also, that beds of iron ore are found and these form the basis of the country's iron and steel industry. In the east Luxembourg is bordered by the Moselle river in whose valley wines are produced.

Macedonia, The Former Yugoslav Republic of

Area 25,713 sq km (9929 sq miles); *population* 2,173, 000; *capital* Skopje; *other major cities* Tetova, Prilep; *form of government* Republic; *religion* Eastern Orthodox, Muslim; *currency* Dinar

The Former Yugoslav Republic of Macedonia, under the name of Macedonia, declared its independence from Yugoslavia in 1991. However Greece, angered at the use of 'Macedonia'—also the name of the neighbouring Greek province—imposed a trade embargo and convinced the UN to refuse to recognize the nation's independence. In 1993, Macedonia was admitted to the UN after changing its official name to The Former Yugoslav Republic of Macedonia. In 1995 an agreement was reached with Greece whereby both countries would respect the territory, sovereignty and independence of the other, with Macedonia agreeing to adopt a new flag. A landlocked country, Macedonia shares its borders with Albania, Bulgaria, Greece and Yugoslavia. Its terrain is mountainous, covered with deep valleys and has three large lakes. Its climate consists of hot, dry summers and relatively cold winters. It is the poorest of the six former Yugoslav republics but sustains itself through agriculture and the coal industries. Some of its natural resources include chromium, lead, zinc, nickel, iron ore and timber.

Madagascar

Area 587,041 sq km (226,657 sq miles); *population* 15,206,000; *capital* Antananarivo; *other major cities* Fianarantsoa, Mahajanga, Toamasina; *form of government* Republic; *religions* Animism, RC, Protestantism; *currency* Malagasy franc

Madagascar is an island state situated off the south-east coast of Africa, separated from the mainland by the Mozambique Channel. Madagascar is the fourth largest island in the world and the centre of it is made up of high savanna-covered plateaux. In the east, forested mountains fall steeply to the coast and in the south-west, the land falls gradually through dry grassland and scrub. The staple food crop is rice and 80% of the population grow enough to feed themselves. Cassava is also grown but some 58% of the land is pasture and there are more cattle than people. The main export earners are coffee, vanilla, cloves and sugar. There is some mining for chromite and an oil refinery at Toamasina on the east coast. Upon independence in 1960, Madagascar became known as the Malagasy Republic, but was changed back by referendum in 1975.

Malawi

Area 118,484 sq km (45,747 sq miles); *population* 9,800,000; *capital* Lilongwe; *other major cities* Blantyre, Mzuzu, Zomba; *form of government* Republic; *religions* Animism, RC, Presbyterianism; *currency* Kwacha

Malawi lies along the southern and western shores of the third largest lake in Africa, Lake Malawi. To the south of the lake the Shire river flows through a valley, overlooked by wooded, towering mountains. The tropical climate has a dry season from May to October and a wet season for the remaining months. Agriculture is the predominant occupation and many Malawians live on their own crops. Plantation farming is used for export crops. Tea is grown on the terraced hillsides in the sout and tobacco on the central plateau, with sugar and maize also important crops Malawi has bauxite and coal deposits but due to the inaccessibility of their locations mining is limited. Hydroelectricity is now being used for the manufacturing industr but imports of manufactured goods remain high, and the country remains one of th poorest in the world. Malawi was formerly the British colony of Nyasaland, a nam meaning 'Land of the Lake', which was given to it by the 19th-century explorer, Davi Livingstone.

Malaysia

Area 330,434 sq km (127,580 sq miles); *population* 20,174,000; *capital* Kuala Lumpur; *other major cities* Ipoh, George Town, Johor Baharu; *form of government* Federal Constitutional Monarchy; *religion* Islam; *currency* Ringgit

The Federation of Malaysia lies in the South China Sea in south-east Asia, an comprises peninsular Malaysia on the Malay Peninsula and the states of Sabah an Sarawak on the island of Borneo. Malaysia is affected by the monsoon climate. Th north-east monsoon brings rain to the east coast of peninsular Malaysia in winte and the south-west monsoon brings rain to the west coast in summer. Throughou the country the climate is generally tropical and temperatures are uniformly hc throughout the year. Peninsular Malaysia has always had thriving rubber-growin and tin dredging industries and now oil palm growing is also important on the eas coast. Sabah and Sarawak have grown rich by exploiting their natural resources, th forests. There is also some offshore oil and around the capital, Kuala Lumpur, ne industries such as electronics are expanding.

Maldives

Area 298 sq km (115 sq miles); *population* 254,000; *capital* Malé; *form of government* Republic *religion* Sunni Islam; *currency* Rufiyaa

The Republic of Maldives lies 640 km (398 miles) south-west of Sri Lanka in the India Ocean and comprises 1200 low-lying coral islands grouped into 12 atolls. Rough 202 of the islands are inhabited, and the highest point is only 1.5 m (5 ft) above sea leve The climate is hot and humid and affected by monsoons from May to August. Th islands are covered with coconut palms, and some millet, cassava, yams and tropic fruit are grown. Rice, the staple diet of its islanders, is imported. Fishing is a important occupation and the chief export is now canned or frozen tuna. Tourism now developing fast and has taken over fishing as the major foreign currency earne

Mali

Area 1,240,192 sq km (478,838 sq miles); *population* 10,700,000; *capital* Bamako; *other major cities* Segou, Mopti; *form of government* Republic; *religions* Sunni Islam, Animism; *currency* Franc CFA

Mali is a landlocked state in West Africa. The country mainly comprises vast an monotonous plains and plateaux. It rises to 1155 m (3790 ft) in the Adrar des Ifora range in the north-east. The Sahara in the north of the country is encroachin southwards. Mali is one of the poorest countries in the world. In the south there some rain and plains are covered by grassy savanna and a few scattered trees. Th river Niger runs through the south of the country and small steamboats use it fo shipping between Koulikoro and Gao. Only a fifth of the land can be cultivated. Ric cassava and millet are grown for domestic consumption and cotton for expor Droughts in the 1970s resulted in thousands of cattle dying, crop failure, famine an disease killing many of the population. Iron ore and bauxite have been discovered but have yet to be exploited.

Malta

Area 316 sq km (122 sq miles); *population* 367,000; *capital* Valletta; *form of government* Republic; *religion* RC; *currency* Maltese pound

Malta, a small republic in the middle of the Mediterranean, lies just south of the island of Sicily. It comprises three islands, Malta, Gozo and Comino, which are made up of low limestone plateaux with little surface water. The climate is Mediterranean with hot, dry sunny summers and little rain. Winters are cooler and wetter. Malta is virtually self-sufficient in agricultural products and exports potatoes, vegetables, wine and cut flowers. The British military base on Malta was once the mainstay of the economy but after the British withdrew in the late 1970s, the naval dockyard was converted for commercial shipbuilding and repairs, which is now one of the leading industries. Tourism has also boomed and the island has become popular with people who wish to retire to a suunier climate.

Marshall Islands

Area 181 sq km/70 sq miles; *population* 55,000; *capital* Dalag-Uliga-Darrit (on Majuro atoll); *form of government* Republic in free association with the USA; *religion* Protestant; *currency* US dollar

Formerly part of the US administered UN territory, this self-governing republic, independent since 1991, comprises a scatter of some 1250 coral atolls and 34 main islands, arranged in two parallel chains, Ratak and Ralik, located in eastern Micronesia in the western Pacific Ocean, and lying to the north-west of Kiribati. The climate is tropical maritime, with little variation in temperature, and rainfall that is heaviest from July to October. The republic remains in free association with the USA and the economy is almost totally dependent on US-related payments for use of the islands as bases. Attempts are being made to diversify the economy before US aid runs out in 2001. The main export is copra.

Mauritania

Area 1,025,520 sq km (395,953 sq miles); *population* 2,268,000; *capital* Nouakchott; *form of government* Republic; *religion* Sunni Islam; *currency* Ouguiya

Mauritania, a country nearly twice the size of France, is located on the west coast of Africa. About 47% of the country is desert, the Sahara covering much of the north. The only settlements found in this area are around oases, where a little millet, dates and vegetables can be grown. The main agricultural regions are in the Senegal river valley in the south. The rest of the country is made up of the drought-stricken Sahel grasslands. The majority of the people are traditionally nomadic herdsmen, but the severe droughts since the 1970s have killed about 70% of the nation's animals, and the population has settled along the Senegal river. As a result, vast shanty towns have sprung up around all the towns. Deposits of iron ore and copper provide the country's main exports, and development of these and the fishing industry on the coast form the only hope for a brighter future.

Mauritius

Area 2040 sq km (788 sq miles); *population* 1,112,669; *capital* Port Louis; *form of government* Republic; *religions* Hinduism, RC, Sunni Islam; *currency* Mauritius rupee

Mauritius is a beautiful island with tropical beaches which lies about 20° south in the Indian Ocean, 800 km (497 miles) east of Madagascar. The islands of Rodrigues and

Agalega are part of Mauritius. Mauritius is a volcanic island with many crater surrounded by lava flows. The central plateau rises to over 800 m (2625 ft), the drops sharply to the south and west coasts. The climate is hot and humid, and south westerly winds bring heavy rain in the uplands. The island has well-watered fertile soi ideal for the sugar plantations that cover 45% of the island. Although the export c sugar still dominates the economy, diversification is being encouraged. The clothin and electronic equipment industries are becoming increasingly important an tourism is now the third largest source of foreign exchange.

Mexico

Area 1,958,201 sq km (756,061 sq miles); *population* 93,342,000; *capital* México City; *other major cities* Guadalajara, Monterrey, Puebla de Zaragoza; *form of government* Federal Republic; *religion* RC; *currency* Mexican peso

Mexico, the most southerly country in North America, has its longest border with th USA. to the north, a long coast on the Pacific Ocean and a smaller coast in the wes of the Gulf of Mexico. It is a land of volcanic mountain ranges and high plateaux. Th highest peak is Citlaltepetl, 5699 m (18,697 ft), which is permanently snow cappec Coastal lowlands are found in the west and east. Its wide range of latitude and relie produce a variety of climates. In the north there are arid and semi arid conditions whil in the south there is a humid tropical climate. 30% of the labour force are involve in agriculture growing maize, wheat, kidney beans and rice for subsistence an coffee, cotton, fruit and vegetables for export. Mexico is the world's largest produce of silver and has large reserves of oil and natural gas. Developing industries ar petrochemicals, textiles, motor vehicles and food processing.

Micronesia, Federated States of

Area 701 sq km (271 sq miles); *population* 125,000; *capital* Palikir; *form of government*Republic; *religion* Christianity; *currency* US dollar

The Federated States of Micronesia, formerly part of the US administered UN Trus Territory of the Pacific, known as the Caroline Islands, this self-governing republi became independent in 1991. It comprises an archipelago of over 600 islands, mos of which are uninhabited and are located in the western Pacidic Ocean 1600kr (1000 miles) north of Papua New Guinea. The climate is tropical maritime, with hig temperatures and rainfall all year round, but a pronounced precipitation pea between July and October. Micronesia is still closely linked to the USA, with a heav reliance on aid. Attempts are being made to diversify the economy whose export are mainly fishing and copra.

Moldova (Moldavia)

Area 33,700 sq km (13,000 sq miles); *population* 4,434,000; *capital* Chisinau; *other major citie* Tiraspol, Bendery; *form of government* Republic; *religion* Russian Orthodox; *currency* Rouble

Moldova was a Soviet socialist republic from 1940 until 1991 when it became independ ent of the former USSR. It is bounded to the west by Romania and to the north, eas and south by Ukraine. The republic consists of a hilly plain that rises to 429 m (140 ft) in the centre. Its main rivers are the Prut in the west and the Dniester in the nort and east. Moldova's soils are fertile, and crops grown include wheat, corn, barle tobacco, sugar beet, soybeans and sunflowers. There are also extensive fruit orchard vineyards and walnut groves. Beekeeping and silkworm breeding are widesprea throughout the country. Food processing is the main industry. Other industrie include metal working, engineering and the manufacture of electrical equipment.

Monaco

Area 1.95 sq km/(0.75 sq miles); *population* 32,000; *capital* Monaco-Ville; *form of government* Constitutional Monarchy; *religion* RC; *currency* Franc

Monaco is a tiny principality on the Mediterranean. It is surrounded landwards by the Alpes Maritimes department of France. It comprises a rocky peninsula and a narrow stretch of coast. It has mild moist winters and hot dry summers. The old town of Monaco-Ville is situated on a rocky promontory and houses the royal palace and the cathedral. The Monte Carlo district has its world-famous casino and La Condamine has thriving businesses, shops, banks and attractive residential areas. Fontvieille is an area reclaimed from the sea where now marinas and light industry are located. Light industry includes chemicals, plastics, electronics, engineering and paper but it is tourism that is the main revenue earner.

Mongolia

Area 1,566,500 sq km (604,826 sq miles); *population* 2,363,000; *capital* Ulan Bator (Ulaanbaatar); *other major cities* Darhan, Erdenet; Form of govt : Republic; *religion* Buddhist, Shamanist, Muslim; *currency* Tugrik

Mongolia is a landlocked country in north-east Asia which is bounded to the north by the Russian Federation and by China to the south, west and east. Most of Mongolia is mountainous and over 1500 m (4922 ft) above sea level. In the north-west are the Hangayn Mountains and the Altai, rising to 4362 m (14,312 ft). In the south there are grass-covered steppes and desert wastes of the Gobi. The climate is very extreme and dry. For six months the temperatures are below freezing and the summers are mild. Mongolia has had a nomadic pastoral economy for centuries and cereals, including fodder crops, are grown on a large scale on state farms. Industry is small scale and dominated by food processing. The collapse of trade with the former Soviet Union has created severe economic problems and Mongolia is increasingly looking to Japan and China for trade and economic assistance.

Morocco

Area 446,550 sq km (172,413 sq miles); *population* 26,857,000; *capital* Rabat; *other major cities* Casablanca, Fez, Marrakech; *form of government* Constitutional Monarchy; *religion* Sunni Islam; *currency* Dirham

Morocco, in north-west Africa, is strategically placed at the western entrance to the Mediterranean Sea. It is a land of contrasts with high rugged mountains, the arid Sahara and the green Atlantic and Mediterranean coasts. The country is split from south-west to north-east by the Atlas mountains. The north has a pleasant Mediterranean climate with hot dry summers and mild moist winters. Farther south winters are warmer and summers even hotter. Snow often falls in winter on the Atlas mountains. Morocco is mainly a farming country, wheat, barley and maize are the main food crops and it is one of the world's chief exporters of citrus fruit. Morocco's main wealth comes from phosphates, reserves of which are the largest in the world. The economy is very mixed. Morocco is self sufficient in textiles, it has car assembly plants, soap and cement factories and a large sea fishing industry. Tourism is a major source of revenue.

Mozambique

Area 801,590 sq km (309,494 sq miles); *population* 17,800,000; *capital* Maputo; *other major cities* Beira, Nampula; *form of government* Republic; *religions* Animism, RC, Sunni Islam; *currency* Metical

Mozambique is a republic located in south-east Africa. A coastal plain covers most of the southern and central territory, giving way to the western highlands and north to a plateau including the Nyasa Highlands. The Zambezi river separates the high plateaux in the north from the lowlands in the south. The country has a humid tropical climate with highest temperatures and rainfall in the north. Normally conditions are reasonably good for agriculture but a drought in the early 1980s, followed a few years later by severe flooding, resulted in famine and more than 100,000 deaths. A lot of industry was abandoned when the Portuguese left the country and, due to lack of expertise, was not taken over by the local people. There is little incentive to produce surplus produce for cash and food rationing has now been introduced. This also has led to a black market which now accounts for a sizable part of the economy.

Myanmar

Area 676,552 sq km (261,218 sq miles); *population* 44,613,000; *capital* Yangon (formerly Rangoon); *other major cities* Mandalay, Moulmein, Pegu; *form of government* Republic; *religion* Buddhism; *currency* Kyat

The Union of Myanmar (formerly Burma) is the second largest country in South-East Asia. The heartland of the country is the valley of the Irrawaddy. The north and west of the country are mountainous and in the east the Shan Plateau runs along the border with Thailand. The climate is equatorial at the coast, changing to tropical monsoon over most of the interior. The Irrawaddy river flows into the Andaman Sea, forming a huge delta area which is ideal land for rice cultivation. Rice is the country's staple food and accounts for half the country's export earnings. Myanmar is rich in timber and minerals but because of poor communications, lack of development and unrest among the ethnic groups, the resources have not been fully exploited.

Namibia

Area 824,292 sq km (318,259 sq miles); *population* 1,610,000; *capital* Windhoek; *form of government* Republic; *religions* Lutheranism, RC, other Christianity; *currency* Rand

Namibia is situated on the Atlantic coast of south-west Africa. There are three main regions in the country. Running down the entire Atlantic coastline is the Namib Desert, east of which is the Central Plateau of mountains, rugged outcrops, sandy valleys and poor grasslands. East again and north is the Kalahari Desert. Namibia has a poor rainfall, the highest falling at Windhoek, the capital. Even here it only amounts to 200–250 mm (8–10 inches) per year. It is essentially a stock-rearing country with sheep and goats raised in the south and cattle in the central and northern areas. Diamonds are mined just north of the River Orange, and the largest open groove uranium mine in the world is located near Swakopmund. One of Africa's richest fishing grounds lies off the coast of Namibia, and mackerel, tuna and pilchards are an important export.

Nauru

Area 21 sq km (8 sq miles); *population* 12,000; *capital* Yaren; *form of government* Republic; *religions* Protestantism, RC; *currency* Australian dollar

Nauru is the world's smallest republic. It is an island situated just 40 km (25 miles) south of the Equator and is halfway between Australia and Hawaii. It is an oval-shaped coral island only 20 km (12 miles) in diameter and is surrounded by a reef. The centre of the island comprises a plateau which rises to 60 m (197 ft) above sea level. The climate is tropical with a high and irregular rainfall. The country is rich, due entirely to the deposits of high quality phosphate rock in the central plateau. This is sold for fertilizer to Australia, New Zealand, Japan and South Korea. Phosphate deposits are likely to be exhausted by 2010 but the government is investing overseas.

Nepal

Area 140,800 sq km (54,362 sq miles); *population* 21,953,000; *capital* Kathmandu; *form of government* Constitutional Monarchy; *religion* Hinduism, Buddhism; *currency* Nepalese rupee

Nepal is a long narrow rectangular country, landlocked between China and India on the flanks of the eastern Himalayas. Its northern border runs along the mountain tops. In this border area is Everest (8848 m /29,028 ft), the highest mountain in the world. The climate is subtropical in the south, and all regions are affected by the monsoon. Nepal is one of the world's poorest and least developed countries, with most of the population trying to survive as peasant farmers. It has no significant minerals, however with Indian and Chinese aid roads have been built from the north and south to Kathmandu. The construction of hydroelectric power schemes is now underway.

Netherlands, The

Area 37,330 sq km (15,770 sq miles); *population* 15,495,000; *capital* Amsterdam; Seat of government : The Hague (Den Haag, 's-Gravenhage); *other major cities* Eindhoven, Rotterdam; *form of government* Constitutional Monarchy; *religions* RC, Dutch reformed, Calvinism; *currency* Guilder

The Netherlands, situated in north-west Europe, is bounded to the north and west by the North Sea. Over one-quarter of the Netherlands is below sea level and the Dutch have tackled some huge reclamation schemes to add some land area to the country. One such scheme is the IJsselmeer, where four large areas (polders) reclaimed have added an extra 1650 sq km (637 sq miles) for cultivation and an overspill town for Amsterdam. The Netherlands has mild winters and cool summers. Agriculture and horticulture are highly mechanized, and the most notable feature is the sea of glass under which salad vegetables, fruit and flowers are grown. Manufacturing industries include chemicals, machinery, petroleum, refining, metallurgy and electrical engineering. The main port of the Netherlands, Rotterdam, is the largest in the world.

New Zealand

Area 270,986 sq km (104,629 sq miles); *population* 3,567,000; *capital* Wellington; *other major cities* Auckland, Christchurch, Dunedin, Hamilton; *form of government* Constitutional Monarchy; *religions* Anglicanism, RC, Presbyterianism; *currency* New Zealand dollar

New Zealand lies south-east of Australia in the South Pacific. It comprises two large islands, North Island and South Island, Stewart Island and the Chatham Islands. New Zealand enjoys very mild winters with regular rainfall and no extremes of heat or cold. North Island is hilly with isolated mountains and active volcanoes. On South Island the Southern Alps run north to south, and the highest point is Mount Cook (3753 m/ 12,313 ft). The Canterbury Plains lie to the east of the mountains. Two-thirds of New Zealand is suitable for agriculture and grazing, meat, wool and dairy goods being the main products. Forestry supports the pulp and paper industry and a considerable source of hydroelectric power produces cheap electricity for the manufacturing industry which now accounts for 30% of New Zealand's exports.

Nicaragua

Area 130,000 sq km (50,193 sq miles); *population* 4,544,000; *capital* Managua; *form of government* Republic; *religion* RC; *currency* Córdoba

Nicaragua lies between the Pacific Ocean and the Caribbean Sea, on the isthmus of Central America, and is sandwiched between Honduras to the north and Costa Rica to the south. The east coast contains forested lowland and is the wettest part of the island. Behind this is a range of volcanic mountains and the west coast is a belt of savanna lowland running parallel to the Pacific coast. The western region, which contains the two huge lakes, Nicaragua and Managua, is where most of the population live. The whole country is subject to devastating earthquakes. Nicaragua is primarily an agricultural country and 65% of the labour force work on the land. The main export crops are coffee, cotton and sugar cane. All local industry is agriculture-related.

Niger

Area 1,267,000 sq km (489,189 sq miles); *population* 9,149,000; *capital* Niamey; Form of govt : Republic; *religion* Sunni Islam; *currency* Franc CFA

Niger is a landlocked republic in west Africa, just south of the Tropic of Cancer. Over half of the country is covered by the encroaching Sahara Desert in the north, and the south lies in the drought-stricken Sahel. In the extreme south-west corner, the river Niger flows through the country, and in the extreme south-east lies Lake Chad, but the rest of the country is very short of water. The people in the south-west fish and farm their own food, growing rice and vegetables on land flooded by the river. Farther from the river, crops have failed as a result of successive droughts since 1968. In the north, where the population are traditionally herdsmen, drought has wiped out whole clans. Uranium mined in the Aïr mountains is Niger's main export.

Nigeria

Area 923,768 sq km (356,667 sq miles); *population* 108,448,000; *capital* Abuja (New Federal *Capital*) Lagos (*Capital* until 1992); *other major cities* Ibadan, Kano, Ogbomsho; *form of government* Federal republic; *religions* Sunni Islam, Christianity; *currency* Naira

Nigeria is a large and populous country in west Africa, and from the Gulf of Guinea it extends north to the border with Niger. It has a variable landscape, from the swampy coastal areas and tropical forest belts of the interior, to the mountains and savanna of the north. The two main rivers are the Niger and the Benue, and just north of their confluence lies the Jos Plateau. The climate is hot and humid and rainfall, heavy at the coast, gradually decreases inland. The dry far north is affected by the Harmattan, a hot dry wind blowing from the Sahara. The main agricultural products are cocoa, rubber, groundnuts and cotton. However, only cocoa is of any significance for export. The country depends on revenue from petroleum exports but fluctuations in the world oil market have left Nigeria with economic problems.

Norway

Area 323,895 sq km (125,056 sq miles); *population* 4,361,000; *capital* Oslo; *other major cities* Bergen, Trondheim, Stavanger; *form of government* Constitutional Monarchy; *religion* Lutheranism; *currency* Norwegian krone

Norway occupies the western half of the Scandinavian peninsula in northern Europe, and is surrounded to the north, west and south by water. It shares most of its eastern border with Sweden. It is a country of spectacular scenery of fjords, cliffs, rugged uplands and forested valleys. Two-thirds of the country is over 600 m/1969 ft and it has some of the deepest fjords in the world. The climate is temperate as a result of the warming effect of the Gulf Stream. Summers are mild and although the winters are long and cold, the waters off the west coast remain ice-free. Agriculture is chiefly concerned with dairying and fodder crops. Fishing is an important industry and the large reserves of forest provide timber for export. Industry is now dominated by petrochemicals based on the reserves of Norwegian oil in the North Sea.

Oman

Area 212,457 sq km (82,030 sq miles); *population* 2,252,000; *capital* Muscat (Musqat); *form of government* Monarchy (sultanate); *religion* Ibadi Islam, Sunni Islam; *currency* Rial Omani

Oman situated in the south-east of the Arabian peninsula, Oman is a small country in two parts. It comprises a small mountainous area, overlooking the Strait of Hormuz, which controls the entrance to The Gulf, and the main part of the country, consisting of barren hills rising sharply behind a narrow coastal plain. Inland the hills extend into the unexplored Rub' al Khali (The Empty Quarter) in Saudi Arabia. Oman has a desert climate with exceptionally hot and humid conditions from April to October. As a result of the extremely arid environment, less than 1% of the country is cultivated, the main produce being dates. The economy is almost entirely dependent on oil, providing 90% of its exports. Over 15% of the resident population is made up by foreign workers. Oman has some deposits of copper and there is a smelter at Sohar.

Pakistan

Area 796,095 sq km (307,372 sq miles); *population* 143,595,000; *capital* Islamabad; *other major cities* Faisalabad, Hyderabad, Karachi, Lahore; *form of government* Federal Islamic Republic; *religion* Sunni Islam, Shia Islam; *currency* Pakistan rupee

Pakistan lies just north of the Tropic of Cancer and has as its southern border the Arabian Sea. The valley of the Indus river splits the country into a highland region in the west, and a lowland region in the east. A weak form of tropical monsoon climate occurs over most of the country and conditions in the north and west are arid. Temperatures are high everywhere in summer but winters are cold in the mountains. Most agriculture is subsistence, with wheat and rice as the main crops. Cotton is the main cash crop, but the cultivated area is restricted because of waterlogging and saline soils. Pakistan's wide range of mineral resources have not been extensively developed and industry concentrates on food processing, textiles and consumer goods.

Panama

Area 77,082 sq km (29,761 sq miles); *population* 2,629,000; *capital* Panama City; *other major cities* San Miguelito, Colón; *form of government* Republic; *religion* RC; *currency* Balboa

Panama is located at the narrowest point in Central America. Only 58 km (36 miles) separates the Caribbean Sea from the Pacific Ocean at Panama, and the Panama Canal which divides the country is the main routeway from the Caribbean and Atlantic to the Pacific. The climate is tropical with high temperatures throughout the year and only a short dry season from January to April. The country is heavily forested and very little is cultivated. Rice is the staple food. The economy is heavily dependent on the Canal and income from it is a major foreign currency earner. The country has great timber resources, and mahogany from these is an important export. Other exports are shrimps and bananas. In 1989 the country was briefly invaded by US military forces in order to depose the corrupt dictator, General Noriega.

Papua New Guinea

Area 462,840 sq km (178,703 sq miles); *population* 4,292,000; *capital* Port Moresby; *form of government* Constitutional Monarchy; *religion* Protestantism, RC; *currency* Kina

Papua New Guinea in the south-west Pacific, comprises the eastern half of the island of New Guinea, together with hundreds of islands of which New Britain, Bougainville and New Ireland are the largest. The country has a mountainous interior surrounded by broad swampy plains. The climate is tropical with high temperatures and heavy rainfall. Subsistence farming is the main economic activity although some coffee, cocoa and coconuts are grown for cash. Timber is cut for export and fishing and fish processing industries are developing. Minerals such as copper, gold, silver and oil form the mainstay of the economy. The country still receives valuable aid from Australia, which governed it before independence.

Paraguay

Area 406,752 sq km (157,047 sq miles); *population* 4,979,000; *capital* Asunción; Other major city : Ciudad Alfredo Stroessner; *form of government* Republic; *religion* RC; *currency* Guaraní

Paraguay, located in central South America, is a country without a coastline and is bordered by Bolivia, Brazil and Argentina. The climate is tropical with abundant rain and a short dry season. The River Paraguay splits the country into the Chaco, a flat semi-arid plain on the west, and a partly forested undulating plateau on the east. Almost 95% of the population live east of the river, where crops grown on the fertile plains include cassava, sugar cane, maize, cotton and soya beans. Immediately west of the river, on the low Chaco, are huge cattle ranches which provide meat for export. The world's largest hydro-electric dam has been built at Itaipú and cheap power from this has stimulated industry. Industry includes food processing, vegetable oil refining, textiles and cement.

Peru

Area 1,285,216 sq km (496,235 sq miles); *population* 25,588,000; *capital* Lima; *other major cities* Arequipa, Callao, Cuzco, Trujillo; Form of govrnment : Republic; *religion* RC; *currency* Sol

Peru is located just south of the Equator, on the Pacific coast of South America. The country has three distinct regions from west to east: the coast, the high sierra of the Andes, and the tropical jungle. The climate on the narrow coastal belt is mainly desert, while the Andes are wet, and east of the mountains is equatorial with tropical forests. Most large-scale agriculture is in the oases and fertile, irrigated river valleys that cut across the coastal desert. Sugar and cotton are the main exports. Sheep, llamas, vicuñas and alpacas are kept for wool. The fishing industry was once the largest in the world but recently the shoals have become depleted. Peru's main source of wealth is oil, but new discoveries are needed as present reserves are near exhaustion. In general, the economy has recently been damaged due to the declining value of exports, natural disasters and guerrilla warfare.

Philippines

Area 300,439 sq km (116,000 sq miles); *population* 67,167,000; *capital* Manila; *other major cities* Cebu, Davao, Quezon City; *form of government* Republic; *religions* Sunni Islam, RC, Animism; *currency* Philippine peso

The Philippines comprise a group of islands in the western Pacific which are scattered over a great area. There are four main groups, Luzon and Mindoro to the north, the Visayan Islands in the centre, Mindanao and the Sulu Archipelago in the south, and Palawan in the south-west. Manila, the capital, is on Luzon. Most of the island group is mountainous and earthquakes are common. The climate is humid with high temperatures and high rainfall. Typhoons are frequent. Rice and maize are the main subsistence crops and coconuts, sugarcane, pineapples and bananas are grown for export. Copper is a major export and there are deposits of gold, nickel and petroleum. Major industries include textiles, food processing, chemicals and electrical engineering.

Poland

Area 312,677 sq km (120,725 sq miles); *population* 38,587,000; *capital* Warsaw (Warszawa); *other major cities* Gdansk, Kraków, Lódz, Wroclow; *form of government* Republic; *religion* RC; *currency* Zloty

Poland is situated on the North European Plain. It borders Germany to the west, the Czech Republic and Slovakia to the south and Belarus and Ukraine to the east. Poland consists mainly of lowlands and the climate is continental, marked by long severe winters and short warm summers. Over one-quarter of the labour force is involved in, predominantly small-scale, agriculture. The main crops are potatoes, wheat, barley, sugar beet and fodder crops. The industrial sector of the economy is large scale. Poland has large deposits of coal and reserves of natural gas, copper and silver. Vast forests stretching inland from the coast supply the paper and furniture industries. Other industries include food processing, engineering and chemicals.

Portugal

Area 92,389 sq km (35,671 sq miles); *population* 10,600,000; *capital* Lisbon (Lisboa); *other major cities* Braga, Coimbra, Oporto, Setúbal; *form of government* Republic; *religion* RC; *currency* Escudo

Portugal, in the south-west corner of Europe, makes up about 15% of the Iberian peninsula. The most mountainous areas of Portugal lie to the north of the river Tagus. In the north-east are the steep sided mountains of Tras-os-Montes and to south of this the Douro valley, running from the Spanish border to Oporto, on the Atlantic coast. South of the Tagus river is the Alentajo, with its wheat fields and cork plantations, and this continues to the hinterland of the Algarve with its beautiful groves of almond, fig and olive trees. Agriculture employs one quarter of the labour force, and crops include wheat, maize, grapes and tomatoes. Manufacturing industry includes textiles and clothing, footwear, food processing and cork products. Tourism, particularly in the south, is the main foreign currency earner.

Puerto Rico

Area 8897 sq km (3435 sq miles); *population* 3,689,000; *capital* San Juan; *form of government* Self-governing Commonwealth (USA); Relgion : RC, Protestantism; *currency* US dollar

Puerto Rico is the most easterly of the Greater Antilles and lies in the Caribbean between the Dominican Republic and the US Virgin Islands. It is a self-governing commonwealth in association with the USA and includes the main island, Puerto Rico, the two small islands of Vieques and Culebra and a fringe of smaller uninhabited islands. The climate is tropical, modified slightly by cooling sea breezes. The main mountains on Puerto Rico are the Cordillera Central, which reach 1338 m (4390 ft) at the peak of Cerro de Punta. Dairy farming is the most important agricultural activity but the whole agricultural sector has been overtaken by industry in recent years. Tax relief and cheap labour encourages American businesses to be based in Puerto Rico. Products include textiles, clothing, electrical and electronic goods, plastics and chemicals. Tourism is another developing industry.

Qatar

Area 11,000 sq km (4247 sq miles); *population* 594,000; *capital* Doha (Ad Dawhah); *form of government* Monarchy; *religions* Wahhabi Sunni Islam; *currency* Qatari riyal

Qatar is a little emirate which lies halfway along the coast of The Gulf. It consists of a low barren peninsula and a few small islands. The climate is hot and uncomfortably humid in summer and the winters are mild with rain in the north. Most fresh water comes from natural springs and wells or from desalination plants. The herding of sheep, goats and some cattle is carried out and the country is famous for its high quality camels. The discovery and exploitation of oil has resulted in a high standard of living for the people of Qatar. The Dukhan oil field has an expected life of forty years and the reserves of natural gas are enormous. In order to diversify the economy, new industries such as iron and steel, cement, fertilizers, and petrochemical plants have been developed.

Romania

Area 237,500 sq km (91,699 sq miles); *Population* 22,863,000; *capital* Bucharest (Bucuresti); *other major cities* Brasov, Constanta, Timisoara; *form of government* Republic; *religions* Romanian Orthodox, RC; *currency* Leu

Apart from a small extension towards the Black Sea, Romania is almost a circular country. It is located in south-east Europe and bordered by Ukraine, Hungary, Serbia and Bulgaria. The Carpathian Mountains run through the north, east and centre of Romania and these are enclosed by a ring of rich agricultural plains which are flat in the south and west but hilly in the east. The core of Romania is Transylvania within the Carpathian arc. Romania has cold snowy winters and hot summers. Agriculture has been neglected in favor of industry but major crops include maize, sugar beet, wheat, potatoes and grapes for wine. There are now severe food shortages. Industry is state owned and includes mining, metallurgy, mechanical engineering and chemicals. Forests support timber and furniture making industries in the Carpathians.

Russian Federation, The

Area 17,075,400 sq km (6,592,800 sq miles); *population* 148,385,000; *capital* Moscow (Moskva); *other major cities* St Petersburg (formerly Leningrad), Nizhniy Novgorod, Novosibirsk; *form of government* Republic; *religions* Russian Orthodox, Sunni Islam, Shia Islam, RC; *currency* Rouble

The Russian Federation, which is the largest country in the world, extends from Eastern Europe through the Ural Mountains east to the Pacific Ocean. The Caucasus Range forms its boundary with Georgia and Azerbaijan, and it is here that the highest peak in Europe, Mt Elbrus, is located. In the east, Siberia is drained toward the Arctic Ocean by the great rivers Ob', Yenisey, Lena and their tributaries. Just to the south of the Central Siberian Plateau lies Lake Baikal, the world's deepest freshwater lake. The environment ranges from vast frozen wastes in the north to subtropical deserts in the south. Agriculture is organized into either state or collective farms, which mainly produce sugar beet, cotton, potatoes and vegetables. The country has extensive reserves of coal, oil, gas, iron ore and manganese. Major industries include iron and steel, cement, transport equipment, engineering, armaments, electronic equipment and chemicals. The Russian Federation declared itself independent in 1991.

Rwanda

Area 26,338 sq km (10,169 sq miles); *population* 7,899,000; *capital* Kigali; *form of government* Republic; *religions* RC, Animism; *currency* Rwanda franc

Rwanda is a small republic in the heart of central Africa which lies just 2° south of the Equator. It is a mountainous country with a central spine of highlands from which streams flow west to the Zaïre river and east to the Nile. Active volcanoes are found in the north where the land rises to about 4500 m (14,765 ft). The climate is highland tropical with temperatures decreasing with altitude. The soils are not fertile and subsistence agriculture dominates the economy. Staple food crops are sweet potatoes, cassava, dry beans, sorghum and potatoes. The main cash crops are coffee, tea and pyrethrum. There are major reserves of natural gas under Lake Kivu in the west, but these are largely unexploited. In 1994, half a million refugees fled to escape civil war in which an estimated 200,000 people were killed. In July 1994, victory in the civil war was claimed by the Tutsi-dominated rebel Rwandan Patriotic Front, who announced the formation of a coalition government, headed by Faustin Twagiramungu, a Hutu. Although the Rwandan Patriotic Front gave its assurance that there would be no reprisal against the defeated Hutus, and the refugees returned home, the situation remains volatile.

St Christopher (St Kitts) and Nevis

Area 262 sq km (101 sq miles); *population* 45,000; *capital* Basseterre; *form of government* Constitutional Monarchy; *religions* Anglicanism, Methodism; *currency* East Caribbean dollar

The islands of St Christopher (popularly known as St Kitts) and Nevis lie in the Leeward group in the eastern Caribbean. In 1983 it became a sovereign democratic federal state with Elizabeth II as head of state. St Kitts consists of three extinct volcanoes linked by a sandy isthmus to other volcanic remains in the south. Around most of the island sugar cane is grown on fertile soil covering the gentle slopes. Sugar is the chief export crop but market gardening and livestock are being expanded on the steeper slopes above the cane fields. Industry includes sugar processing, brewing, distilling and bottling. St Kitts has a major tourist development at Frigate Bay. Nevis, 3 km (2 miles) south, is an extinct volcano. Farming is declining and tourism is now the main source of income.

St Lucia

Area 622 sq km (240 sq miles); *population* 147,000; *capital* Castries; *Form of government*: Constitutional Monarchy; *religion* RC; *currency* East Caribbean dollar

St Lucia is one of the Windward Islands in the eastern Caribbean. It lies to the south of Martinique and to the north of St. Vincent. It was controlled alternately by the French and the British for some two hundred years before becoming fully independent in 1979. St Lucia is an island of extinct volcanoes and the highest peak is 950 m (3117 ft). In the west are the peaks of Pitons which rise directly from the sea to over 750 m (2461 ft). The climate is wet tropical with a dry season from January to April. The economy depends on the production of bananas and, to a lesser extent, coconuts. Production, however, is often affected by hurricanes, drought and disease. Tourism is becoming an important industry and Castries, the capital, is a popular calling point for cruise liners.

St Vincent and the Grenadines

Area 388 sq km (150 sq miles); *population* 112,000; *capital* Kingstown; *form of government* Constitutional Monarchy; *religions* Anglicanism, Methodism, RC; *currency* E. Caribbean dollar

St Vincent is an island of the Lesser Antilles, situated in the eastern Caribbean between St Lucia and Grenada. It is separated from Grenada by a chain of some 600 small islands known as the Grenadines, the northern islands of which form the other part of the country. The largest of these islands are Bequia, Mustique, Canouan, Mayreau and Union. The climate is tropical, with very heavy rain in the mountains. St Vincent Island is mountainous and a chain of volcanoes runs up the middle of the island. The volcano, Soufrière (1234 m/4049 ft), is active and it last erupted in 1979. Farming is the main occupation on the island. Bananas for the UK are the main export, and it is the world's leading producer of arrowroot starch. There is little manufacturing and the government is trying to promote tourism.

San Marino

Area 61 sq km (24 sq miles); *population* 26,000; *capital* San Marino; *form of government* Republic; *religion* RC; *currency* Lira

San Marino is a tiny landlocked state in central Italy, lying in the eastern foothills of the Apennines. It has wooded mountains and pasture land clustered around the limestone peaks of Monte Titano which rises to 739 m (2425 ft). San Marino has a mild Mediterranean climate. The majority of the population work on the land or in forestry. Wheat, barley, maize and vines are grown, and the main exports are wood machinery, chemicals, wine, textiles, tiles, varnishes and ceramics. Some 3.5 million tourists visit the country each year, and much of the country's revenue comes from the sale of stamps, postcards, souvenirs and duty-free liquor. Italian currency is in general use but San Marino issues its own coins.

São Tomé and Príncipe

Area 964 sq km (372 sq miles); *population* 133,000; *capital* São Tomé; *form of government* Republic; *religion* RC; *currency* Dobra

São Tomé and Príncipe are volcanic islands which lie off the west coast of Africa. São Tomé is covered in extinct volcanic cones, reaching 2024 m (6641 ft) at the highest peak. The coastal areas are hot and humid. Príncipe is a craggy island lying to the north-east of São Tomé. The climate is tropical with heavy rainfall from October to May. 70% of the workforce work on the land, mainly in state-owned cocoa plantations. Small manufacturing industries include food processing and timber products.

Saudi Arabia

Area 2,149,690 sq km (829,995 sq miles); *population* 18,395,000; *capital* Riyadh (Ar Riyah); *other major cities* Mecca, Jeddah, Medina, Ta'if; *form of government* Monarchy; *religions* Sunni Islam, Shia Islam; *currency* Rial

Saudi Arabia occupies over 70% of the Arabian Peninsula. Over 95% of the country is desert and the largest expanse of sand in the world, 'Rub'al-Khali' ('The Empty Quarter'), is found in the south-east of the country. In the west, a narrow, humid coastal plain along the Red Sea is backed by steep mountains. The climate is hot with very little rain and some areas have no precipitation for years. The government has spent a considerable amount on reclamation of the desert for agriculture, and the main products are dates, tomatoes, watermelons and wheat. The country's prosperity, however, is based almost entirely on the exploitation of its vast reserves of oil and natural gas. Industries include petroleum refining, petrochemicals and fertilizers. As a result of the Gulf War in 1990-91, 460km/285mi of the Saudi coastline has been polluted by oil threatening desalination plants and damaging the wildlife of saltmarshes, mangrove forest, and mudflats.

Senegal

Area 196,722 sq km (75,954 sq miles); *population* 8,308,000; *capital* Dakar; *other major cities* Kaolack, Thies, St Louis; *form of government* Republic; *religions* Sunni Islam, RC; *currency* Franc CFA

Senegal is a former French colony in West Africa which extends from the most western point in Africa, Cape Verde, to the border with Mali. Senegal is mostly low-lying and covered by savanna. The Fouta Djalon mountains in the south rise to 1515 m (4971 ft). The climate is tropical with a dry season from October to June. The most densely populated region is in the southwest. Almost 80% of the labour force work in agriculture, growing groundnuts and cotton for export and millet, maize, rice and sorghum as subsistence crops. Senegal has been badly affected by the drought that has afflicted the Sahel and relies on food imports and international aid.

Seychelles

Area 455 sq km (176 sq miles); *population* 75,000; *capital* Victoria; *form of government* Republic; *religion* RC; *currency* Seychelles rupee

The Seychelles are a group of volcanic islands which lie in the western Indian Ocean about 1200 km (746 miles) from the coast of East Africa. About forty of the islands are mountainous and consist of granite while just over fifty are coral islands. The climate is tropical maritime with heavy rain. About 90% of the people live on the island of Mahé which is the site of the capital, Victoria. The staple food is coconut, imported rice and fish. Tourism accounts for about 90% of the country's foreign exchange earnings and employs one-third of the labour force. The Seychelles were a one party socialist state until 1991, when a new constitution was introduced. The first free elections were held in 1993.

Sierra Leone

Area 71,740 sq km (27,699 sq miles); *population* 4,467,000; *capital* Freetown; *form of government* Republic; *religion* Animism, Sunni Islam, Christianity; *currency* Leone

Sierra Leone, on the Atlantic coast of West Africa, is bounded by Guinea to the north and east and by Liberia to the south-east. The coastal areas consist of wide swampy forested plains which rise to a mountainous plateau in the east. The highest parts of the mountains are just under 2000 m (6562 ft). The climate is tropical with a dry season from November to June. The main food of Sierra Leoneans is rice and this is grown in the swamplands at the coast. In the tropical forest areas, small plantations produce coffee, cocoa and oil palm. In the plateau much forest has been cleared for growing of groundnuts. Most of the country's revenue is from mining. Diamonds are panned from the rivers and there are deposits of iron ore, bauxite, rutile and some gold.

Singapore

Area 622 sq km (240 sq miles); *population* 2,990,000; *capital* Singapore; *form of government* Parliamentary Democracy; *religions* Buddhism, Sunni Islam, Christianity and Hinduism; *currency* Singapore dollar

Singapore, one of the world's smallest yet most successful countries, comprises 1 main island and 59 islets which are located at the foot of the Malay peninsula in South-East Asia. The main island of Singapore is very low-lying, and the climate is hot and wet throughout the year. Only 1.6% of the land area is used for agriculture and most food is imported. Singapore has the largest oil refining centre in Asia. The country has a flourishing manufacturing industry for which it relies heavily on imports.

Products traded in Singapore include machinery and appliances, petroleum, food and beverages, chemicals, transport equipment, paper products and printing, and clothes. The Jurong Industrial Estate on the south of the island has approximately 2,300 companies and employs nearly 141,000 workers. Tourism is an important source of foreign revenue.

Slovakia (Slovak Republic)

Area 49,032 sq km (18,931 sq miles); *population* 5,400,000; *capital* Bratislava; *other major city* Kovice; *form of government* Republic; *religion* RC; *currency* Koruna

Slovakia was constituted on January 1, 1993 as a new independent nation, following the dissolution of the 74-year old federal republic of Czechoslovakia. Landlocked in central Europe, its neighbours are the Czech Republic to the west, Poland to the north, Austria and Hungary to the south, and a short border with Ukraine in the east. The northern half of the republic is occupied by the Tatra Mountains which form the northern arm of the Carpathian Mountains. This region has vast forests and pastures used for intensive sheep grazing, and is rich in high-grade minerals. The southern part of Slovakia is a plain drained by the Danube and its tributaries. Farms, vineyards, orchards and pastures for stock form the basis of southern Slovakia's economy.

Slovenia

Area 20,251 sq km (7817 sq miles); *population* 2,000,000; *capital* Ljubljana; *other major cities* Maribor, Celje; *form of government* Republic; *religion* RC; *currency* Tolar

Slovenia is a republic which made a unilateral declaration of independence from former Yugoslavia on June 25, 1991. Sovereignty was not formally recognized by the European Community and the United Nations until early in 1992. It is bounded to the north by Austria, to the west by Italy, to the east by Hungary, and to the south by Croatia. Most of Slovenia is situated in the Karst Plateau and in the Julian Alps. Although farming and livestock raising are the chief occupations, Slovenia is very industrialized and urbanized. Iron, steel and aluminium are produced, and mineral resources include oil, coal and mercury. Tourism is an important industry. The Julian Alps are renowned for their scenery, and the Karst Plateau contains spectacular cave systems. The north-east of the republic is famous for its wine production.

Solomon Islands

Area 28,896 sq km (11,157 sq mi); *population* 378,000; *capital* Honiara; *form of government* Constitutional Monarchy; *religions* Anglicanism, RC, other Christianity; *currency* Solomon Is. dollar

The Solomon Islands lie in an area between 5° and 12° south of the Equator to the east of Papua New Guinea, in the Pacific Ocean. The nation consists of six large islands and innumerable smaller ones. The larger islands are mountainous and covered in forests with rivers prone to flooding. Guadal-canal is the main island and the site of the capital, Honiara. The climate is hot and wet and typhoons are frequent. The main food crops grown are coconut, cassava, sweet potatoes, yams, taros and bananas. The forests are worked commercially, and the fishing industry is developing with the help of the Japanese. Other industries include palm-oil milling, fish canning and freezing, saw milling, food, tobacco and soft drinks.

Somalia

Area 637,657 sq km (246,199 sq miles); *population* 9,180,000; *capital* Mogadishu; *other major cities* Hargeisa, Baidoa, Burao, Kismaayo; *form of government* Republic; *religion* Sunni Islam; *currency* Somali shilling

Somalia is shaped like a large number seven and lies on the horn of Africa's east coast. It is bounded north by the Gulf of Aden, south and east by the Indian Ocean, and its neighbours include Djibouti, Ethiopia, and Kenya. The country is arid and most of it is low plateaux with scrub vegetation. Its two main rivers, the Juba and Shebelle, are used to irrigate crops. Most of the population live in the mountains and river valleys and there are a few towns on the coast. Main exports are live animals, meat, hides and skins. A few large-scale banana plantations are found by the rivers. Years of drought have left Somalia heavily dependent on foreign aid, and many of the younger population are emigrating to oil-rich Arab states.

South Africa

Area 1,221,037 sq km (471,442 sq miles); *population* 44,000,000; *capital* Pretoria (Administrative), Cape Town (Legislative); *other major cities* Johannesburg, Durban, Port Elizabeth, Bloemfontein; *form of government* Republic; *religions* Dutch reformed, Independent African, other Christianity, Hinduism; *currency* Rand

South Africa is a republic that lies at the southern tip of the African continent and has a huge coastline on the Atlantic and Indian Oceans. The country occupies a huge saucer-shaped plateau, surrounding a belt of land which drops in steps to the sea. The rim of the saucer rises in the east, to 3482 m (11,424 ft), in the Drakensberg. In general the climate is healthy with plenty of sunshine and relatively low rainfall. This varies with latitude, distance from the sea, and altitude. Of the total land area 58% is used as natural pasture. The main crops grown are maize, sorghum, wheat, groundnuts and sugarcane. A drought-resistant variety of cotton is also now grown. It is South Africa's extraordinary mineral wealth which overshadows all its other natural resources. These include gold, coal, copper, iron ore, manganese and chrome ore, and diamonds. A system of apartheid existed in South Africa from 1948 until the early 1990s, effectively denying black South Africans civil rights and promoting racial segregation. During this time the country was subjected to international economic and political sanctions. In 1990 F. W. de Klerk, then president, lifted the ban on the outlawed African National Congress and released its leader, Nelson Mandela, who had been imprisoned since 1962. This heralded the dismantling of the apartheid regime and in the first multi-racial elections, held in 1994, the ANC triumphed, with Mandela voted in as the country's president. Since this time South Africa has once again become an active and recognized member of the international community.

Spain

Area 504,782 sq km (194,896 sq miles); *population* 39,664,000; *capital* Madrid; *other major cities* Barcelona, Seville, Zaragosa, Malaga, Bilbao; *form of government* Constitutional Monarchy; *religion* RC; *currency* Peseta

Spain is located in south-west Europe and occupies the greater part of the Iberian peninsula, which it shares with Portugal. It is a mountainous country, sealed off from the rest of Europe by the Pyrénées, which rise to over 3400 m (11,155 ft). Much of the country is a vast plateau, the Meseta Central, cut across by valleys and gorges. Its longest shoreline is the one that borders the Mediterranean Sea. Most of the country has a form of Mediterranean climate with mild moist winters and hot dry summers. Spain's principal agricultural products are cereals, vegetables and potatoes, and large areas are under vines for the wine industry. Industry represents 72% of the country's export value, and production includes textiles, paper, cement, steel and chemicals. Tourism is a major revenue earner, especially from the resorts on the east coast.

Sri Lanka

Area 65,610 sq km (25,332 sq miles); *population* 18,3597,000; *capital* Colombo; *other major cities* Dehiwela-Mt. Lavinia, Moratuwa, Jaffna; *form of government* Republic; *religions* Buddhism, Hinduism, Christianity, Sunni Islam; *currency* Sri Lankan rupee

Sri Lanka is a teardrop-shaped island in the Indian Ocean, lying south of the Indian peninsula from which it is separated by the Palk Strait. The climate is equatorial with a low annual temperature range but it is affected by both the north-east and south-west monsoons. Rainfall is heaviest in the south-west while the north and east are relatively dry. Agriculture engages 47% of the work force and the main crops are rice, tea, rubber and coconuts. Amongst the chief minerals mined and exported are precious and semiprecious stones. Graphite is also important. The main industries are food, beverages and tobacco, textiles, clothing and leather goods, chemicals and plastics. Attempts are being made to increase the revenue from tourism. Politically, Sri Lanka has been afflicted by ethnic divisions between the Sinhalese and Tamils. In the 1980s attempts by the Tamil extremists to establish an independent homeland bought the north-east of the country to the brink of civil war and the situation remains extremely volatile.

Sudan

Area 2,505,813 sq km (967,494 sq miles); *population* 29,980,000; *capital* Khartoum (El Khartum); *other major cities* Omdurman, Khartoum North, Port Sudan; *form of government* Republic; *religions* Sunni Islam, Animism, Christianity; *currency* Sudanese pound

Sudan is the largest country in Africa, lying just south of the Tropic of Cancer in north-east Africa. The country covers much of the upper Nile basin and in the north the river winds through the Nubian and Libyan deserts, forming a palm-fringed strip of habitable land. In 1994, the country was divided into 26 states, compared to the original nine. The climate is tropical and temperatures are high throughout the year. In winter, nights are very cold. Rainfall increases in amount from north to south, the northern areas being virtually desert. Sudan is an agricultural country, subsistence farming accounting for 80% of production. Cotton is farmed commercially and accounts for about two-thirds of Sudan's exports. Sudan is the world's greatest source of gum arabic used in medicines and inks. This is the only forest produce to be exported.

Suriname

Area 163,265 sq km (63,037 sq miles); *population* 421,000; *capital* Paramaribo; *form of government* Republic; *religions* Hinduism, RC, Sunni Islam; *currency* Surinam guilder

Suriname is a republic in north-east South America, bordered to the west by Guyana, to the east by Guiana, and to the south by Brazil. The country, formerly a Dutch colony, declared independence in 1975. Suriname comprises a swampy coastal plain, a forested central plateau, and southern mountains. The climate is tropical with heavy rainfall. Temperatures at Paramaribo average 26-27°C all year round. Rice and sugar are farmed on the coastal plains but the mining of bauxite is what the economy depends on. This makes up 80% of exports. Suriname has resources of oil and timber but these are so far underexploited. The country is politically very unstable and in need of financial aid to develop these resources.

Swaziland

Area 17,360 sq km (6716 sq miles); *population* 849,000; *capital* Mbabane; *other major cities* Big Bend, Manzini, Mhlume; *form of government* Monarchy; *religion* Christianity, Animism; *currency* emalangeni

Swaziland is a landlocked hilly enclave almost entirely within the borders of the Republic of South Africa. The mountains in the west of the country rise to almost 2000 m (6562 ft), then descend in steps of savanna toward hilly country in the east. The climate is subtropical moderated by altitude. The land between 400 m (1312 ft) and 850 m (2789 ft) is planted with orange groves and pineapple fields, while on the lower land sugar cane flourishes in irrigated areas. Asbestos is mined in the north-west of the country. Manufacturing includes fertilizers, textiles, leather and tableware. Swaziland attracts a lot of tourists from South Africa, mainly to its spas and casinos.

Sweden

Area 449,964 sq km (173,731 sq miles); *population* 8,893,000; *capital* Stockholm; *other major cities* Göteborg, Malmö, Uppsala, Orebro; *form of government* Constitutional Monarchy; *religion* Lutheranism; *currency* Krona

Sweden is a large country in northern Europe which makes up half of the Scandinavian peninsula. It stretches from the Baltic Sea north, to well within the Arctic Circle. The south is generally flat, the north mountainous, and along the coast there are 20,000 or more islands and islets. Summers are warm but short and winters are long and cold. In the north snow may lie for four to seven months. Dairy farming is the predominant agricultural activity. Only 7% of Sweden is cultivated, with the emphasis on fodder crops, grain and sugar beet. About 57% of the country is covered in forest, and the sawmill, wood pulp and paper industries are all of great importance. Sweden is one of the world's leading producers of iron ore, most of which is extracted from within the Arctic Circle. Other main industries are engineering and electrical goods, motor vehicles and furniture making.

Switzerland

Area 41,293 sq km (15,943 sq miles); *population* 7,268,000; *capital* Berne (Bern); *other major cities* Zürich, Basle, Geneva, Lausanne; *form of government* Federal republic; *religions* RC, Protestantism; *currency* Swiss franc

Switzerland is a landlocked country in central Europe, sharing its borders with France, Italy, Austria, Liechtenstein and Germany. The Alps occupy the southern half of the country, forming two main east-west chains divided by the rivers Rhine and Rhône. The climate is either continental or mountain type. Summers are generally warm and winters cold, and both are affected by altitude. Northern Switzerland is the industrial part of the country and where its most important cities are located. Basle is famous for its pharmaceuticals and Zürich for electrical engineering and machinery. It is also in this region that the famous cheeses, clocks, watches and chocolates are produced. Switzerland has huge earnings from international finance and tourism.

Syria

Area 185,180 sq km (71,498 sq miles); *population* 14,614,000; *capital* Damascus (Dimashq); *other major cities* Halab, Homs, Latakia, Hama; *form of government* Republic; *religion* Sunni Islam; *currency* Syrian pound

Syria is a country in south-west Asia which borders on the Mediterranean Sea in the west. Much of the country is mountainous behind the narrow fertile coastal plain. The eastern region is desert or semi-desert, a stony inhospitable land. The coast has a Mediterranean climate with hot dry summers and mild wet winters. About 50% of the workforce get their living from agriculture, sheep, goats and cattle are raised, and cotton, barley, wheat, tobacco, fruit and vegetables are grown. Reserves of oil are small compared to neighbouring Iraq but it has enough to make the country self-sufficient and provide three quarters of the nation's export earnings. Industries such as textiles, leather, chemicals and cement have developed rapidly in the last 20 years.

Taiwan

Area 36,179 sq km (13,969 sq miles); *population* 21,100,000; *capital* Taipei (T'ai-pei); *other major cities* Kaohsiung, Taichung, Tainan; *form of government* Republic; *religions* Taoism, Buddhism, Christianity; *currency* New Taiwan dollar

Taiwan is an island which straddles the Tropic of Cancer in East Asia. It lies about 160 km (99 miles) off the south-east coast of mainland China. It is predominantly mountainous in the interior, the tallest peak rising to 3997 m (13,114 ft) at Yu Shan. The climate is warm and humid for most of the year. Winters are mild and summers rainy. The soils are fertile, and a wide range of crops, including tea, rice, sugar cane and bananas, is grown. Taiwan is a major international trading nation with some of the most successful export-processing zones in the world, accommodating domestic and overseas companies. Exports include machinery, electronics, textiles, footwear, toys and sporting goods.

Tajikistan

Area 143,100 sq km (55,250 sq miles); *population* 6,102,000; *capital* Dushanbe; *Form of government*: Republic; *religion* Shia Islam; *currency* Rouble

Tajikistan, a republic of southern central former USSR, declared itself independent in 1991. It is situated near the Afghani and Chinese borders. The south is occupied by the Pamir mountain range, whose snow-capped peaks dominate the country. More than half the country lies over 3000 m (9843 ft). Most of the country is desert or semi-desert, and pastoral farming of cattle, sheep, horses and goats is important. Some yaks are kept in the higher regions. The lowland areas in the Fergana and Amudar'ya valleys are irrigated so that cotton, mulberry trees, fruit, wheat and vegetables can be grown. The Amudar'ya river is also used to produce hydro-electricity for industries such as cotton and silk processing. The republic is rich in deposits of coal, lead, zinc, oil and uranium, which are now being exploited.

Tanzania

Area 945,087 sq km (364,898 sq miles); *population* 29,710,000; *capital* Dodoma; *other major cities* Dar es Salaam, Zanzibar, Mwanza, Tanga; *form of government* Republic; *religions* Sunni Islam, RC, Anglicanism, Hinduism; *currency* Tanzanian shilling

Tanzania lies on the east coast of central Africa and comprises a large mainland area and the islands of Pemba and Zanzibar. The mainland consists mostly of plateaux broken by mountainous areas and the east African section of the Great Rift Valley. The climate is very varied and is controlled largely by altitude and distance from the sea. The coast is hot and humid, the central plateau drier, and the mountains semi-temperate. 80% of Tanzanians make a living from the land, but productivity is low and there is no surplus from the crops, mainly maize, that they grow. Cash crops include cotton and coffee. The islands are more successful agriculturally and have important coconut and clove plantations. Tanzania's mineral resources are limited and of low grade, and there are few manufacturing industries.

Thailand

Area 513,115 sq km (198,114 sq miles); *population* 58,432,00; *capital* Bangkok (Krung Thep); *other major cities* Chiengmai, Nakhon Ratchasima, Songkhla; *form of government* Constitutional Monarchy; *religions* Buddhism, Sunni Islam; *currency* Baht

Thailand, a country about the same size as France located in South-East Asia, is a tropical country of mountains and jungles, rain forests and green plains. Central Thailand is a densely populated, fertile plain and the mountainous Isthmus of Kra joins southern Thailand to Malaysia. Thailand has a subtropical climate with heavy monsoon rains from June to October, a cool season from October to March, and a hot season from March to June. The central plain of Thailand contains vast expanses of paddy fields which produce enough rice to rank Thailand as the world's leading exporter. The narrow southern peninsula is very wet, and it is here that rubber is produced. Thailand is the world's third largest exporter of rubber.

Togo

Area 56,785 sq km (21,925 sq miles); *population* 4,140,000; *capital* Lomé; *form of government* Republic; *religions* Animism, RC, Sunni Islam; *currency* Franc CFA; *Area* 750 sq km (290 sq miles); *population* 107,000; *capital* Nuku'alofa; *form of government* Constitutional Monarchy; *religions* Methodism, RC; *currency* Pa'anga

Togo is a tiny country with a narrow coastal plain on the Gulf of Guinea in West Africa. Grassy plains in the north and south are separated by the Togo Highlands, which run from south-west to north-east and rise to nearly 1000 m (3281 ft). High plateaux, mainly in the more southerly ranges, are heavily forested with teak, mahogany and bamboo. Over 80% of the population are involved in agriculture with yams and millet as the principal crops. Coffee, cocoa and cotton are grown for cash. Minerals, especially phosphates, are now the main export earners. Togo's exports are suffering from the recession in its major markets in Western Europe.

Tonga

Tonga is situated about 20° south of the Equator and just west of the International Date Line in the Pacific Ocean. It comprises over 170 islands and only about one-fifth of them are inhabited. It comprises a low limestone chain of islands in the east and a higher volcanic chain in the west. The climate is warm with heavy rainfall. The government owns all the land, and males can rent an allotment for growing food. Yams, cassava and taro are grown as subsistence crops, and fish from the sea supplements their diet. Bananas and coconuts are grown for export. The main industry is coconut processing.

Area 750 sq km (290 sq miles); *population* 107,000; *capital* Nuku'alofa; *form of government* Constitutional Monarchy; *religions* Methodism, RC; *currency* Pa'anga

Trinidad and Tobago

Area 5130 sq km (1981 sq miles); *population* 1,295,000; *capital* Port-of-Spain; *form of government* Republic; *religions* RC, Hinduism, Anglicanism, Sunni Islam; *currency* Trinidad and Tobago dollar

Trinidad and Tobago form the third largest British Commonwealth country in the West Indies and are situated off the Orinoco Delta in north-eastern Venezuela. The islands are the most southerly of the Lesser Antilles. Trinidad consists of a mountainous Northern Range in the north and undulating plains in the south. Tobago is more mountainous. The climate is tropical with little variation in temperatures throughout the year and a rainy season from June to December. Trinidad is one of the oldest oil-producing countries in the world. Output is small but provides 90% of Trinidad's exports. Sugar, coffee and cocoa are grown for export, but food now accounts for 10% of total imports. Tobago depends mainly on tourism for revenue.

Tunisia

Area 163,610 sq km (63,170 sq miles); *population* 8,906,000; *capital* Tunis; *other major cities* Sfax, Bizerta, Djerba; *form of government* Republic; *religion* Sunni Islam; *currency* Tunisian dinar

Tunisia is a North African country which lies on the south coast of the Mediterranean Sea. It's bounded by Algeria to the west and Libya to the south. Northern Tunisia consists of hills, plains and valleys. Inland mountains separate the coastal zone from the central plains before the land drops down to an area of salt pans and the Sahara Desert. Climate ranges from warm temperate in the north, to desert in the south. 40% of the population are engaged in agriculture, producing wheat, barley, olives, tomatoes, dates and citrus fruits. The mainstay of Tunisia's modern economy, however, is oil from the Sahara, phosphates, and tourism on the Mediterranean coast.

Turkey

Area 779,452 sq km (300,946 sq miles); *population* 61,303,000; *capital* Ankara; *other major cities* Istanbul, Izmir, Adana, Bursa; *form of government* Republic; *religion* Sunni Islam; *currency* Turkish lira

With land on the continents of Europe and Asia, Turkey forms a bridge between the two. It guards the sea passage between the Mediterranean and the Black Sea. Only 5% of its area, Thrace, is in Europe and the much larger area, known as Anatolia, is in Asia. European Turkey is fertile agricultural land with a Mediterranean climate. Asiatic Turkey is bordered to the north by the Pontine Mountains and to the south by the Taurus Mountains. The climate here ranges from Mediterranean to hot summers and bitterly cold winters in the central plains. Agriculture employs over half the workforce. Major crops are wheat, rice, tobacco and cotton. Manufacturing industry includes iron and steel, textiles, motor vehicles and Turkey's famous carpets. Hydroelectric power is supplied by the Tigris and Euphrates. Tourism is a fast-developing industry.

Turkmenistan

Area 488,100 sq km (186,400 sq miles); *population* 4,100,000; *capital* Ashkhabad; *form of government* Republic; *religion* Sunni Islam; *currency* Rouble

Turkmenistan, a central Asian republic of the former USSR, declared itself a republic in 1991. It lies to the east of the Caspian Sea and borders Iran and Afghanistan to the south. Much of the west and central areas of Turkmenistan are covered by the sandy Kara Kum Desert. The east is a plateau, which is bordered by the Amudar'ya river. The climate is extremely dry, and most of the population live in oasis settlements near the rivers. Agriculture is intensive around the settlements and consists of growing cereals, fruit, cotton and rearing Karakul sheep. There are rich mineral deposits, especially natural gas. Silk, oil and sulphur are also produced.

Tuvalu

Area 24 sq km (10 sq miles); *population* 10,000; *capital* Funafuti (or Fongafale); *form of government* Constitutional Monarchy; *religion* Protestantism; *currency* Australian dollar

Tuvalu is located just north of Fiji, in the South Pacific, and consists of nine coral atolls. The group was formerly known as the Ellice Islands, and the main island and capital is Funafuti. The climate is tropical with temperatures averaging 30°C and annual rainfall ranges from 3000–4000 mm (118–157 inches). Coconut palms are the main crop and fruit and vegetables are grown for local consumption. Sea fishing is extremely good and largely unexploited, although licenses have been granted to Japan, Taiwan and South Korea to fish the local waters. Most export revenue comes from the sale of elaborate postage stamps to philatelists.

Uganda

Area 235,880 sq km (91,073 sq miles); *population* 21,466,000; *capital* Kampala; *other major cities* Jinja, Masaka, Mbale; *Form of government*: Republic; *religions* RC, Protestantism, Animism, Sunni Islam; *currency* Uganda shilling

Uganda is a landlocked country in east central Africa. The Equator runs through the south of the country, and for the most part it is a richly fertile land, well watered, with a kindly climate. In the west are the Ruwenzori Mountains, which rise to over 5000 m (16,405 ft) and are snow-capped. The lowlands around Lake Victoria, once forested, have now mostly been cleared for cultivation. Agriculture employs over three quarters of the labour force, and the main crops grown for subsistence are plantains, cassava and sweet potatoes. Coffee is the main cash crop and accounts for 90% of the county's exports. Attempts are being made to expand the tea plantations in the west, to develop a copper mine and to introduce new industries to Kampala, the capital.

Ukraine

Area 603,700 sq km (233,100 sq miles); *population* 52,027,000; *capital* Kiev; *other major cities* Dnepropetrovsk, Donetsk, Kharkov, Odessa; *form of government* Republic; *religions* Russian Orthodox, RC; *currency* Rouble

Ukraine, formerly a Soviet socialist republic, declared itself independent of the former USSR in 1991. Its neighbours to the west are Poland, Slovakia, Hungary and Romania, and it is bounded to the south by the Black Sea. To the east lies the Russian Federation and to the north the republic of Belarus. Drained by the Dnepr, Dnestr, Southern Bug and Donets rivers, Ukraine consists largely of fertile steppes. The climate is continental, although this is greatly modified by the proximity of the Black Sea. The Ukrainian steppe is one of the chief wheat-producing regions of Europe. Other major crops include corn, sugar beet, flax, tobacco, soya, hops and potatoes. There are rich reserves of coal and raw materials for industry. The central and eastern regions form one of the world's densest industrial concentrations. Manufacturing industries include ferrous metallurgy, machine building, chemicals, food processing, gas and oil refining.

United Arab Emirates (UAE)

Area 83,600 sq km (32,278 sq miles); *population* 2,800,000; *capital* Abu Dhabi; *other major cities* Dubai, Sharjh, Ras al Khaymah; *Form of government*: Monarchy (emirates); *religion* Sunni Islam; *currency* Dirham

The United Arab Emirates is a federation of seven oil-rich sheikdoms located in The Gulf. As well as its main coast on the Gulf, the country has a short coast on the Gulf of Oman. The land is mainly flat sandy desert except to the north on the peninsula where the Hajar Mountains rise to 2081 m (6828 ft). The summers are hot and humid with temperatures reaching 49°C, but from October to May the weather is warm and sunny with pleasant, cool evenings. The only fertile areas are the emirate of Ras al Khaymah, the coastal plain of Al Fujayrah and the oases. Abu Dhabi and Dubai are the main industrial centres and, using their wealth from the oil industry, they are now diversifying industry by building aluminium smelters, cement factories and steel-rolling mills. Dubai is the richest state in the world.

United Kingdom (UK)

Area 244,880 sq km (94,548 sq miles); *population* 58,306,000; *capital* London; *other major cities* Birmingham, Manchester, Glasgow, Liverpool; *form of government* Constitutional Monarchy; *religion* Anglicanism, RC, Presbyterianism, Methodism; *currency* Pound sterling

Situated in north-west Europe, the United Kingdom of Great Britain and Northern Ireland, comprises the island of Great Britain and the north-east of Ireland, plus many smaller islands, especially off the west coast of Scotland. The south and east of Britain is low-lying, and the Pennines form a backbone running through northern England. Scotland has the largest area of upland, and Wales is a highland block. Northern Ireland has a few hilly areas. The climate is cool temperate with mild conditions and an even annual rainfall. The principal crops are wheat, barley, sugar beet, fodder crops and potatoes. Livestock includes cattle, sheep, pigs and poultry. Fishing is important off the east coast. The UK is primarily an industrial country, although the recent recession has left high unemployment and led to the decline of some of the older industries, such as coal, textiles and heavy engineering. A growing industry is electronics, much of it defence-related.

United States of America (USA)

Area 9,809,431 sq km (3,787,421 sq miles); *population* 263,563,000; *capital* Washington D.C.; *other major cities* New York, Chicago, Detroit, Houston, Los Angeles, Philadelphia, San Diego, San Francisco; *form of government* Federal Republic; *religion* Protestantism, RC, Judaism, Eastern Orthodox; *currency* US dollar

The United States of America stretches across central north America, from the Atlantic Ocean in the east to the Pacific Ocean in the west, and from Canada in the north to Mexico and the Gulf of Mexico in the south. It consists of fifty states, including outlying Alaska, north-west of Canada, and Hawaii in the Pacific Ocean. The climate varies a great deal in such a large country. In Alaska there are polar conditions, and in the Gulf coast and in Florida conditions may be subtropical. Although agricultural production is high, it employs only 1.5% of the population because primarily of its advanced technology. The USA is a world leader in oil production. The main industries are iron and steel, chemicals, motor vehicles, aircraft, telecommunications equipment, computers, electronics and textiles. The USA is the richest and most powerful nation in the world.

Uruguay

Area 177,414 sq km (68,500 sq miles); *population* 3,186,000; *capital* Montevideo; *form of government* Republic; *religions* RC, Protestantism; *currency* Uruguayan nuevo peso

Uruguay is one of the smallest countries in South America. It lies on the east coast of the continent, to the south of Brazil, and is bordered to the west by the Uruguay river, Rio de la Plata to the south, and the Atlantic Ocean to the east. The country consists of low plains and plateaux. In the south-east, hills rise to 500 m (1641 ft). About 90% of the land is suitable for agriculture but only 10% is cultivated, the remainder being used to graze vast herds of cattle and sheep. The cultivated land is made up of vineyards, rice fields and groves of olives and citrus fruits. Uruguay has only one major city in which half the population live. The country has no mineral resources, oil or gas, but has built hydroelectric power stations at Palmar and Salto Grande.

Uzbekistan

Area 447,400 sq km (172,741 sq miles); *population* 22,833,000; *capital* Tashkent; Other major city : Samarkand; *form of government* Republic; *religion* Sunni Islam; *currency* Rouble

Uzbekistan, a central Asian republic of the former USSR, declared itself independent in 1991. It lies between Kazakhstan and Turkmenistan and encompasses the southern half of the Aral Sea. The republic has many contrasting regions. The Tian Shan region is mountainous, the Fergana region is irrigated and fertile, the Kyzlkum Desert is rich in oil and gas, the lower Amudar'ya river region is irrigated and has oasis settlements, and the Usturt Plateau is a stony desert. Uzbekistan is one of the world's leading cotton producers, and Karakul lambs are reared for wool and meat. Its main industrial products are agricultural machinery, textiles and chemicals. It also has significant reserves of natural gas. Economic growth has been checked by concerns about political instability and much of the economy remains based on the centralized state-owned model.

Vanuatu

Area 12,189 sq km (4706 sq miles); *population* 167,000; *capital* Vila; *form of government* Republic; *religion* Protestantism, Animism; *currency* Vatu

Vanuatu, formerly known as the New Hebrides, is located in the western Pacific, south-east of the Solomon Islands and about 1750 km (1087 miles) east of Australia. About eighty islands make up the group. Some of the islands are mountainous and include active volcanoes. The largest islands are Espírtu Santo, Malekula and Efate, on which the capital Vila is sited. Vanuatu has a tropical climate which is moderated by the south-east trade winds from May to October. The majority of the labour force are engaged in subsistence farming, and the main exports include copra, fish and cocoa. Tourism is becoming an important industry.

Vatican City State

Area 0.44 sq km (0.17 sq miles); *population* 1000; *capital* Vatican City (Citta del Vaticano); *form of government* Papal Commission; *religion* RC; *currency* Vatican City lira

The Vatican City State lies in the heart of Rome on a low hill on the west bank of the river Tiber. It is the world's smallest independent state and headquarters of the Roman Catholic Church. It is a walled city made up of the Vatican Palace, the Papal Gardens, St Peter's Square and St Peter's Basilica. The state has its own police, newspaper, coinage, stamps and radio station. The radio station, 'Radio Vaticana,' broadcasts a service in thirty-four languages from transmitters within the Vatican City. Its main tourist attractions are the frescoes of the Sistine Chapel, painted by Michelangelo Buonarroti (1475–1564). The Pope exercises sovereignty and has absolute legislative, executive and judicial powers.

Venezuela

Area 912,050 sq km (352,143 sq miles); *population* 21,810,000; *capital* Caracas; *other major cities* Maracaibo, Valencia, Barquisimeto; *form of government* Federal Republic; *religion* RC; *currency* Bolívar

Venezuela forms the northernmost crest of South America. Its northern coast lies along the Caribbean Sea and it is bounded to the west by Columbia and to the south-east and south by Guyana and Brazil. In the north-west a spur of the Andes runs south-west to north-east. The river Orinoco cuts the country in two, and north of the river run the undulating plains known as the Llanos. South of the river are the Guiana Highlands. The climate ranges from warm temperate to tropical. Temperatures vary little throughout the year and rainfall is plentiful. In the Llanos area cattle are herded across the plains, and this region makes the country almost self-sufficient in meat. Sugar cane and coffee are grown for export but petroleum and gas account for 95% of export earnings. The oil fields lie in the north-west near Lake Maracaibo, where there are over 10,000 oil derricks.

Vietnam

Area 331,689 sq km (128,065 sq miles); *population* 74,580,000; *capital* Hanoi; *other major cities* Ho Chi Minh City, Haiphong; *form of government* Socialist Republic; *religion* Buddhism, Taoism, RC; *currency* Dong

Vietnam is a long narrow country in south-east Asia which runs down the coast of the South China Sea. It has a narrow central area which links broader plains centred on the Red and Mekong rivers. The narrow zone, now known as Mien Trung, is hilly and makes communications between north and south difficult. The climate is humid with tropical conditions in the south and subtropical in the north. The far north can be very cold when polar air blows over Asia. Agriculture employs over three quarters of the labour force. The main crop is rice but cassava, maize and sweet potatoes are also grown for domestic consumption. Rubber, tea and coffee are grown for export. Major industries are food processing, textiles, cement, cotton and silk manufacture. Vietnam, however, remains underdeveloped and is still recovering from the ravages of many wars this century.

Western Samoa

Area 2831 sq km (1093 sq miles); *population* 169,000; *capital* Apia; *form of government* Constitutional Monarchy; *religion* Protestantism; *currency* Tala

Western Samoa lies in the Polynesian sector of the Pacific Ocean, about 720 km (447 miles) north-east of Fiji. It consists of seven small islands and two larger volcanic islands, Savai'i and Upolu. Savai'i is largely covered with volcanic peaks and lava plateaux. Upolu is home to two-thirds of the population and the capital Apia. The climate is tropical with high temperatures and very heavy rainfall. The islands have been fought over by the Dutch, British, Germans and Americans, but they now have the lifestyle of traditional Polynesians. Subsistence agriculture is the main activity, and copra, cocoa and bananas are the main exports. Many tourists visit the grave of the Scottish writer Robert Louis Stevenson (1850–94) who died here and whose home is now the official home of the king.

Yemen

Area 527,970 sq km (203,849 sq miles); *population* 14,609,000; *capital* Sana'a, Commercial *capital* Aden; *form of government* Republic; *religion* Zaidism, Shia Islam, Sunni Islam; *currency* Riyal and dinar

Yemen is bounded by Saudi Arabia in the north, Oman in the east, the Gulf of Aden in the south, and the Red Sea in the west. The country was formed after the unification of the previous Yemen Arab Republic and the People's Democratic Republic of Yemen (South Yemen) in 1989. However, at this point there was no active integration of the two countries and politocally the country remained divided between north and south. In 1994 a civil war, which lasted three months, broke out between the former North and South Yemen. Most of the country comprises rugged mountains and trackless desert lands. The country is almost entirely dependent on agriculture even though a very small percentage is fertile. The main crops are coffee, cotton, millet, sorghum and fruit. Fishing is an important industry. Other industry is on a very small scale. There are textile factories, and plastic, rubber and aluminium goods, paints and matches are produced. Modernization of industry is slow because of lack of funds.

Yugoslavia

Area 102,172 sq km (39,449 sq miles); *population* 10,881,000; *capital* Belgrade (Beograd); *Other major cities* : Nis, Titograd; *form of government* Federal Republic; *religions* Eastern Orthodox; *currency* Dinar

Yugoslavia, which was created in 1918, became a single federal republic after World War II under the leadership of Marshal Tito (1892–1980). The six constituent republics were Serbia, Croatia, Slovenia, Bosnia & Herzegovina, Macedonia and Montenegro. Yugoslavia today refers only to Serbia and Montenegro, which operate as two equal republics under a federal authority. However, the situation remains particularly complex, with each republic operating its own legislature. The other republics, beginning with Slovenia and Croatia in 1991, have all declared their independence from Yugoslavia. The economy was devastated by the wars in Bosnia and Croatia, then by inflation to the degree that the financial infrastructure all but collapsed in late 1993. The economy has only just begun to take the first steps to recovery. It is largely agricultural, and produce includes wheat, maize, grpaes and citrus fruit. Exports include chemicals, machinery, textiles and clothing.

Zambia

Area 752,614 sq km (290,584 sq miles); *population* 9,500,000; *capital* Lusaka; *other major cities* Kitwe, Ndola, Mufulira; *form of government* Republic; *religion* Christianity, Animism; *currency* Kwacha

Zambia, situated in central Africa, is made up of high plateaux. Bordering it to the south is the Zambezi river, and in the south-west it borders on the Kalahari Desert. It has some other large rivers, including the Luangwa, and lakes, the largest of which is Lake Bangweulu. The climate is tropical, modified somewhat by altitude. The country has a wide range of wildlife, and there are large game parks on the Luangwa and Kafue rivers. Agriculture is underdeveloped and most foodstuffs have to be imported. Zambia's economy relies heavily on the mining of copper, lead, zinc and cobalt. The poor market prospects for copper, which will eventually be exhausted, make it imperative for Zambia to develop her vast agricultural potential.

Zimbabwe

Area 390,760 sq km (150,872 sq miles); *population* 11,453,000; *capital* Harare; *other major cities* Bulawayo, Mutare, Gweru; *form of government* Republic; *religion* Animism, Anglicanism, RC; *currency* Zimbabwe dollar;

Zimbabwe is a landlocked country in southern Africa. It is a country with spectacular physical features and is teeming with wildlife. It is bordered in the north by the Zambezi river, which flows over the mile-wide Victoria Falls before entering Lake Kariba. In the south, the River Limpopo marks its border with South Africa. Most of the country is over 300 m (984 ft) above sea level, and a great plateau between 1200 m (3937 ft) and 1500 m (4922 ft) occupies the central area. Massive granite outcrops, called *kopjes*, also dot the landscape. The climate is tropical in the lowlands and subtropical in the higher land. About 75% of the labour force are employed in agriculture. Tobacco, sugar cane, cotton, wheat and maize are exported and form the basis of processing industries. Tourism is a major growth industry.

Appendix to the Gazetteer

Principal Mountains of the World

Name (location)	Height (m)	Height (ft)
Everest (Asia)	8848	29,028
Godwin-Austen or K2 (Asia)	8611	28,250
Kangchenjunga (Asia)	8586	28,170
Makalu (Asia)	8463	27,766
Dhaulagiri (Asia)	8167	26,795
Nanga Parbat (Asia)	8125	26,657
Annapurna (Asia)	8091	26,545
Gosainthan (Asia)	8012	26,286
Nanda Devi (Asia)	7816	25,643
Kamet (Asia)	7756	25,446
Namcha Barwa (Asia)	7756	25,446
Gurla Mandhata (Asia)	7728	25,355
Kongur (Asia)	7720	25,325
Tirich Mir (Asia)	7691	25,230
Minya Kanka (Asia)	7556	24,790
Kula Kangri (Asia)	7555	24,784
Muztagh Ata (Asia)	7546	24,757
Kommunizma (Asia)	7495	24,590
Pobedy (Asia)	7439	24,406
Chomo Lhar (Asia)	7313	23,992
Lenina (Asia)	7134	23,405
Aconcagua (S Amer)	6960	22,834
Ojos del Salado (S Amer)	6908	22,664
Tupungato (S Amer)	6801	22,310
Huascarán (S Amer)	6769	22,205
Llullailaco (S Amer)	6723	22,057
Kailas (Asia)	6714	22,027
Tengri Khan (Asia)	6695	21,965
Sajama (S Amer)	6542	21,463
Chimborazo (S Amer)	6310	20,702
McKinley (N Amer)	6194	20,320
Logan (N Amer)	5951	19,524
Cotopaxi (S Amer)	5896	19,344
Kilimanjaro (Africa)	5895	19,340
Huila (S Amer)	5750	18,865
Citlaltepi (C Amer)	5699	18,697
Demavend (Asia)	5664	18,582
Elbrus (Asia)	5642	18,510
St Elias (N Amer)	5489	18,008
Popocatepetl (C Amer)	5452	17,887
Foraker (N Amer)	5304	17,400
Ixtaccihuati (C Amer)	5286	17,342
Dykh Tau (Europe)	5203	17,070
Kenya (Africa)	5200	17,058
Ararat (Asia)	5165	16,945
Vinson Massif (Antarctica)	5140	16,863
Kazbek (Europe)	5047	16,558
Jaya (Asia)	5030	16,502
Klyucheveyskava (Asia)	4750	15,584
Mont Blanc (Europe)	4808	15,774
Vancouver (N Amer)	4786	15,700
Trikora (Asia)	4750	15,584
Monte Rosa (Europe)	4634	15,203
Ras Dashen (Africa)	4620	15,158
Belukha (Asia)	4506	14,783
Markham (Antarctica)	4350	14,271
Meru (Africa)	4566	14,979
Karisimbi (Africa)	4508	14,787
Weisshorn (Europe)	4505	14,780
Matterhorn/Mont Cervin (Europe)	4477	14,690
Whitney (N Amer)	4418	14,495
Elbert (N Amer)	4399	14,431
Massive Mount (N Amer)	4397	14,424
Rainier or Tacoma (N Amer)	4392	14,410
Longs (N Amer)	4345	14,255
Elgon (Africa)	4321	14,176
Pikes Peak (N Amer)	4301	14,110
Finsteraarhorn (Europe)	4274	14,022

Principal Mountains of the World (contd)

Name (location)	*Height (m)*	*(ft)*	*Name (location)*	*Height (m)*	*(ft)*
Wrangell (N Amer)	4269	14,005	Assiniboine (N Amer)	3618	11,870
Mauna Kea (N Amer)	4205	13,796	Hood (N Amer)	3428	11,245
Gannet (N Amer)	4202	13,785	Pico de Aneto (Europe)	3404	11,168
Mauna Loa (N Amer)	4169	13,677	Etna (Europe)	3323	10,902
Jungfrau (Europe)	4158	13,642	St Helens (N Amer)	2950	9677
Kings (N Amer)	4124	13,528	Pulog (Asia)	2934	9626
Kinabalu (Asia)	4102	13,455	Tahat (Africa)	2918	9573
Cameroon (Africa)	4095	13,435	Shishaldin (N Amer)	2862	9387
Fridtjof Nansen (Antarctica)	4068	13,346	Roraima (S Amer)	2810	9219
Tacaná (C Amer)	4064	13,333	Ruapehu (Oceania)	2797	9175
Waddington (N Amer)	4042	13,262	Katherine (N Amer)	2637	8651
Yu Shan (Asia)	3997	13,113	Doi Inthanon (Asia)	2594	8510
Truchas (C Amer)	3994	13,102	Galdhöpiggen (Europe)	2469	8100
Wheeler (N Amer)	3981	13,058	Parnassus (Europe)	2457	8061
Robson (N Amer)	3954	12,972	Olympus (N Amer)	2425	7954
Granite (N Amer)	3902	12,799	Kosciusko (Oceania)	2230	7316
Borah (N Amer)	3858	12,655	Harney (N Amer)	2208	7242
Monte Viso (Europe)	3847	12,621	Mitchell (N Amer)	2038	6684
Kerinci (Asia)	3805	12,483	Clingmans Dome (N Amer)	2025	6642
Grossglockner (Europe)	3797	12,460	Washington (N Amer)	1917	6288
Erebus (Antarctica)	3794	12,447	Rogers (N Amer)	1807	5927
Fujiyama (Asia)	3776	12,388	Marcy (N Amer)	1629	5344
Cook (Oceania)	3753	12,313	Cirque (N Amer)	1573	5160
Adams (N Amer)	3752	12,307	Pelée (C Amer)	1463	4800
Teyde or Tenerife (Africa)	3718	12,198	Ben Nevis (Europe)	1344	4409
Mahameru (Asia)	3676	12,060	Vesuvius (Europe)	1281	4203

Principal Rivers of the World

Name (location)	Length (km)	Length (miles)
Nile (Africa)	6695	4160
Amazon (S Amer)	6516	4050
Yangtze (Asia)	6380	3965
Mississippi-Missouri (N Amer)	6019	3740
Ob-Irtysh (Asia)	5570	3460
Yenisel-Angara (Asia)	5553	3450
Hwang Ho (Asia)	5464	3395
Zaïre (Africa)	4667	2900
Mekong (Asia)	4426	2750
Amur (Asia)	4416	2744
Lena (Asia)	4400	2730
Mackenzie (N Amer)	4250	2640
Niger (Africa)	4032	2505
Paraná (S Amer)	4000	2485
Missouri (N Amer)	3969	2466
Mississippi (N Amer)	3779	2348
Murray-Darling (Oceania)	3750	2330
Volga (Europe)	3686	2290
Madeira (S Amer)	3203	1990
St. Lawrence (N Amer)	3203	1990
Yukon (N Amer)	3187	1980
Indus (Asia)	3180	1975
Syr Darya (Asia)	3079	1913
Darling (Oceania)	3057	1900
Salween (Asia)	3060	1901
Rio Grande (N Amer)	3034	1885
São Francisco (S Amer)	2897	1800
Danube (Europe)	2850	1770
Brahmaputra (Asia)	2840	1765
Euphrates (Asia)	2815	1750
Pará-Tocantins (S Amer)	2752	1710
Kolyma (Asia)	2600	1600
Ganges (Asia)	2525	1568
Arkansas (N Amer)	2350	1460
Colorado (N Amer)	2330	1450

Name (location)	Length (km)	Length (miles)
Xi Jiang (Asia)	2300	1437
Dnepr (Europe)	2285	1420
Negro (S Amer)	2254	1400
Aldan (Asia)	2242	1393
Irrawaddy (Asia)	2150	1335
Ohio (N Amer)	2102	1306
Orange (Africa)	2090	1299
Kama (Europe)	2028	1260
Xingú (S Amer)	2012	1250
Columbia (N Amer)	1950	1210
Juruá (S Amer)	1932	1200
Peace (N Amer)	1923	1195
Tigris (Asia)	1900	1180
Don (Europe)	1870	1165
Pechora (Europe)	1814	1127
Araguaya (S Amer)	1771	1100
Snake (N Amer)	1670	1038
Red (N Amer)	1639	1018
Churchill (N Amer)	1610	1000
Marañón (S Amer)	1610	1000
Pilcomayo (S Amer)	1610	1000
Ucayali (S Amer)	1610	1000
Uruguay (S Amer)	1610	1000
Magdalena (S Amer)	1529	950
Oka (Europe)	1481	920
Canadian (N Amer)	1459	906
Godavari (Asia)	1465	910
Parnaíba (S Amer)	1449	900
Dnestr (Europe)	1411	877
Brazos (N Amer)	1401	870
Fraser (N Amer)	1370	850
Salado (S Amer)	1368	850
Rhine (Europe)	1320	825
Narmada (Asia)	1288	800
Tobol (Asia)	1288	800

Principal Rivers of the World (contd)

Name (location)	Length (km)	(miles)	Name (location)	Length (km)	(miles)
Athabaska (N Amer)	1231	765	Loire (Europe)	1012	629
Pecos (N Amer)	1183	735	Tagus (Europe)	1007	626
Green (N Amer)	1175	730	Tisza (Europe)	997	619
Elbe (Europe)	1160	720	North Platte (N Amer)	995	618
Ottawa (N Amer)	1121	696	Ouachita (N Amer)	974	605
White (N Amer)	1111	690	Sava (Europe)	940	584
Cumberland (N Amer)	1106	687	Neman (Europe)	937	582
Vistula (Europe)	1090	677	Oder (Europe)	910	565
Yellowstone (N Amer)	1080	671	Cimarron (N Amer)	805	500
Donets (Europe)	1079	670	Gila (N Amer)	805	500
Tennessee (N Amer)	1050	652	Gambia (Africa)	483	300

Continents of the World

	Highest Point (m)	(ft)	Area (sq km)	(sq miles)
Asia	8848	29,028	43,608,000	16,833,000
Africa	5895	19,340	30,335,000	11,710,000
North & Central America	6194	20,320	25,349,000	9,785,000
South America	6960	22,834	17,611,000	6,798,000
Antarctica	5140	16,863	14,000,000	5,400,000
Europe	5642	18,510	10,498,000	4,052,000
Oceania	4205	13,796	8,900,000	3,400,000

Oceans of the World

	Maximum Depth (m)	(ft)	Area (sq km)	(sq miles)
Pacific	11,033	36,198	165,384,000	63,838,000
Atlantic	8381	27,496	82,217,000	31,736,000
Indian	8047	26,401	73,481,000	28,364,000
Arctic	5450	17,880	14,056,000	5,426,000

Principal Waterfalls of the World

Name (location)	Height (m)	Height (ft)
Angel (S Amer)	979	3212
Yosemite (N Amer)	740	2,425
Kukenaãm (S Amer)	610	2,000
Sutherland (Oceania)	581	1904
Wolloomombie (Oceania)	519	1700
Ribbon (N Amer)	492	1612
Upper Yosemite (N Amer)	436	1430
Gavarnie (Europe)	422	1384
Tugela (Africa)	412	1350
Takkakau (N Amer)	366	1200
Staubbach (Europe)	300	984
Trümmelbach (Europe)	290	950
Middle Cascade (N Amer)	278	910
Vettisfoss (Europe)	271	889
King Edward VIII (S Amer)	256	840
Gersoppa (Asia)	253	830
Skykjefos (Europe)	250	820
Kajeteur (S Amer)	226	741
Kalambo (Africa)	222	726
Maradalsfos (Europe)	199	650
Maletsunyane (Africa)	192	630
Bridalveil (N Amer)	189	620
Multnomah (N Amer)	189	620
Vöringfoss (Europe)	182	597
Nevada (N Amer)	181	594
Terni (Europe)	180	590
Skjeggedalsfoss (Europe)	160	525
Marina (S Amer)	153	500
Aughrabies (Africa)	147	480
Tequendama (S Amer)	131	427
Guaíra (S Amer)	114	374
Illilouette (N Amer)	113	370
Victoria (Africa)	108	355
Kegon-no-tali (Asia)	101	330
Lower Yosemite (N Amer)	98	320
Cauvery (Asia)	98	320
Vernal (N Amer)	97	317
Virginia (N Amer)	96	315
Lower Yellowstone (N Amer)	94	308
Churchill (N Amer)	92	302
Reichenbach (Europe)	91	300
Sluiskin (N Amer)	91	300
Lower Gastein (Europe)	86	280
Paulo Alfonso (S Amer)	84	275
Snoqualmie (N Amer)	82	268
Seven (N Amer)	81	266
Montmorency (N Amer)	77	251
Handegg (Europe)	76	250
Taughannock (N Amer)	66	215
Iguassú (S Amer)	64	210
Shoshone (N Amer)	64	210
Upper Gastein (Europe)	63	207
Comet (N Amer)	61	200
Narada (N Amer)	52	168
Niagara (N Amer)	51	167
Tower (N Amer)	41	132
Stora Sjöfallet (Europe)	40	131
Kabalega (Africa)	40	130
Upper Yellowstone (N Amer)	34	109

Cartography designed and produced by European Map
Graphics Ltd, Alberto House, Hogwood Lane,
Finchampstead, Berkshire, RG40 4RF.

This edition published 1997 by Parragon Publishing,
13 Whiteladies Road, Clifton, Bristol, BS8 1PB.

ISBN 0 75252 178 0

Printed and bound in the UK.